Intelligence Analysis

Intelligence Analysis: A Target-Centric Approach

Robert M. Clark

CQ PRESS

A Division of Congressional Quarterly Inc.
Washington, D.C.

CQ Press
1255 22nd Street, N.W., Suite 400
Washington, D.C. 20037

202-729-1900; toll-free, 1-866-4CQ-PRESS (1-866-427-7737)

www.cqpress.com

∞ The paper used in this publication exceeds the requirements of the American National Standard for Information Sciences—Permanence of Paper for Printed Library Materials, ANSI Z39.48-1992.

Composition by TechBooks, India

Cover design by Kimberly Glyder

Printed and bound in the United States of America

08   07   06   05   04   5   4   3   2   1

Library of Congress Catologing-in-Publication Data

Clark, Robert M.
   Intelligence analysis : a target-centric approach / Robert M. Clark.
     p. cm.
Includes bibliographical references and index.
   ISBN 1-56802-830-X (alk. paper)
   1.   Intelligence service—Methodology.   I. Title.
   JF1525.I6C553 2004
   327.12—dc21

                                                      2003009774

To the wonderful crew
who once worked at a little company
called STAC.
I miss you.

Contents

Part 2   Synthesis

Figures, Tables, and Boxes

Figures

Tables

Boxes

Preface

Intelligence is best done by a minimum number of men and women of the greatest possible ability.
R. V. Jones, assistant director of Britain's Royal Air Force
Intelligence Section during World War II

The terrorist attacks of September 11, 2001, focused our attention on an apparent failure of the U.S. intelligence community. The federal government is now considering major structural changes in the community's organization. Although the structure and function of the intelligence community could indeed use some reworking, it is unfortunate that the first response to a perceived intelligence failure always seems to focus on the structure or function of intelligence rather than on its basic processes. The U.S. intelligence community settled on its basic organizational structure and decisionmaking process in the 1940s and 1950s, patterning them after the dominant technology and business models of that era. It also followed the traditional hierarchical structure of the military, from which it borrowed many of its people and operational precepts.

Now, more than fifty years later, we work in a world radically changed by technology, in which a horizontal networked environment proves more effective, efficient, and logical. The U.S. intelligence community has been slow to adapt and has been described as having "fragmented, territorial, and risk-averse cultures."[1] To some extent, this fragmentation was part of the failure of September 11.

Most books on U.S. intelligence, whether critical or descriptive, focus on structure and function. But if the intelligence community is interested in real improvement, it must begin by rethinking *process*; then the form and structure of a new community will naturally follow. Thus the first objective of this book is to redefine the intelligence process—specifically the analytic process—to help make all parts of what is called the "intelligence cycle" run smoothly and effectively.

The intelligence process should accomplish three basic tasks. First, it should make it easy for customers to ask questions. Second, it should use the existing base of intelligence information to provide immediate responses to the customer. Third, it should manage the expeditious creation of new information to answer remaining questions. To do these things intelligence must be collaborative and predictive: collaborative to engage all participants while making it easy for customers to ask questions and get answers; predictive because intelligence customers need to know what will happen next.

What I call a target-centric intelligence process helps analysts and customers fulfill these three tasks by bringing together all participants in the production of sound intelligence. Though intelligence communities are organized hierarchically, the target-centric process outlines a collaborative approach for intelligence collectors, analysts, and consumers to operate cohesively against increasingly complex enemies. We cannot simply provide more intelligence to customers; they already have more information than they can process, and information overload encourages intelligence failures. The intelligence community has to provide intelligence that is relevant to customer needs—known as actionable intelligence. Collaboration enables such intelligence. The convergence of computers and multimedia communications allows intelligence producers and customers to interact more closely as they move from traditional hierarchies to networks—a process that is already beginning to emerge.

The second goal of this book is to clarify and refine the analysis process by drawing on existing prediction methodologies. These include the analytic tools used in organizational planning and problem solving, science and engineering, law, and economics. In many cases, these are tools and techniques that have endured despite dramatic changes in information technology over the past fifty years. All can be useful in making intelligence predictions, even in seemingly unrelated fields. In fact, a number of unifying concepts can be drawn from these disciplines and applied when creating scenarios of the future, assessing forces, and monitoring indicators. The book highlights these concepts in boxes called "Analysis Principles" and treats them as fundamental principles of intelligence analysis. These boxes should make the book a valuable reference even as the world continues to change.

The book begins by introducing the idea of a target-centric intelligence process and the central role that a target model plays in that process: *All* intelligence starts with a target model. The succeeding chapters follow the chronological approach that I have used to teach the process to both new and seasoned analysts over the past sixteen years. The analyst begins the intelligence process by synthesizing information that will go into the target model. Thus the book explains the information sources used in target model creation and then proceeds to the next step of defining the intelligence problem. The book then addresses the analysis phase. A discussion of how to use predictive intelligence methodologies follows before the book concludes with chapters on analysis. The appendix presents a case study on force analysis that illustrates the application of predictive methodologies.

This book is written primarily for the practicing intelligence analyst, though it will be of interest to all intelligence professionals, students, and customers of intelligence. Intelligence professionals can spend their entire careers on specialized topics such as behavioral analysis, and many books are devoted to topics covered only briefly here. This book, rather, is intended as a general guide, with references to lead the reader to in-depth studies and reports on specific techniques. But it also goes beyond that role in defining a better intelligence analysis process, putting specific analysis techniques in context, and showing how they interrelate within the process. The book offers insights that intelligence consumers and analysts alike need to become more proactive in the changing world of intelligence and to extract more useful intelligence.

Acknowledgments

R. V. Jones, whose quote leads off this preface, was a physicist on the staff of the Royal Aircraft Establishment in Farnborough, U.K., at the outbreak of World War II. He became the assistant director of intelligence of the Air Staff during the war and was responsible for assessing German developments in radio navigation aids, radar, guided missiles, and atomic energy. He is generally regarded as the father of scientific and technical intelligence, and insights from his numerous writings are found in these pages. In addition to R. V. Jones, many people throughout the U.S. and British intelligence communities and the business intelligence world have provided wisdom that I have incorporated; I cannot name them all, but I appreciate their help.

I am grateful to reviewers within and outside the U.S. intelligence community who have contributed their time to improving the text. In addition to several anonymous reviewers, I wish to thank Dr. Gary Goodrich and Mark Lowenthal. I also want to thank Charisse Kiino, Elise Frasier, and Molly Lohman at CQ Press for shaping the finished product and for teaching me so many things that I didn't know about writing a book. Finally, my special thanks to my bride, Abigail S. Clark, for her extensive work to improve the book, including rewriting major parts of it.

Robert M. Clark
Reston, Virginia

Note

1. Center for Strategic and International Studies, "Meeting the Challenges of Establishing a New Department of Homeland Security: A CSIS White Paper," Washington, D.C., n.d.

Introduction

The Intelligence Analyst

The greatest derangement of the mind is to believe in something because one wishes it to be so.

Louis Pasteur

We learn more from our failures than from our successes. In that spirit, this book starts with a summary of some major intelligence failures of the last century.

- *Operation Barbarossa, 1941.* Josef Stalin acted as his own intelligence analyst, and he proved to be a very poor one. He was unprepared for a war with Nazi Germany, so he ignored the mounting body of incoming intelligence that the Germans were preparing a surprise attack. German deserters who told the Russians about the pending attack were considered provocateurs and shot on Stalin's orders. When the attack, nicknamed Operation Barbarossa, came on June 22, 1941, Stalin's generals were surprised, their forward divisions trapped and destroyed.[1]

- *Singapore, 1942.* In one of the greatest military defeats that Britain ever suffered, 130,000 well-equipped British, Australian, and Indian troops surrendered to 35,000 weary and ill-equipped Japanese soldiers. On the way to the debacle, British intelligence failed in a series of poor analyses of their Japanese opponent, such as underestimating the capabilities of the Japanese Zero fighter and concluding that the Japanese would not use tanks in the jungle. (The Japanese tanks proved to be highly effective in driving the British out of Malaya and back to Singapore).[2]

- *Tet Offensive, 1968.* In 1968 the United States claimed to be winning the Vietnam War. Military intelligence, committed to supporting this claim, refused to accept the evidence of increasing North Vietnamese and Viet Cong strength. U.S. planners anticipated that the North Vietnamese, in attacking the United States, would repeat a pattern of attack that they had used against the French: surround

1

and defeat a major garrison. This preconception shaped the way that evidence indicating a very different type of attack was analyzed. The U.S. commanders therefore were surprised by a nationwide attack on January 30 and 31, 1968, during the Tet holiday. The attack was a military defeat but a political victory for North Vietnam. U.S. public reaction to the attack, fed by slanted press reporting, led to the withdrawal of U.S. forces.[3]

- *Yom Kippur, 1973*. Israel is regarded as having one of the world's best intelligence services. But in 1973 the intelligence leadership was closely tied to the Israeli cabinet, and often served both as policy advocate and information assessor. Furthermore, Israel's past military successes had led to a certain amount of hubris and belief in inherent Israeli superiority. Israeli leadership considered their overwhelming military advantage a deterrence to attack. Furthermore, the leadership assumed that Egypt needed to rebuild its air force and forge an alliance with Syria before attacking. Israeli intelligence was vulnerable to what became a successful Egyptian deception operation. In this atmosphere, the Israeli intelligence officer who correctly predicted the impending attack had his report suppressed by his superior, the chief intelligence officer of the Israeli Southern Command. The Israeli Defense Force therefore was caught by surprise when, *without* a rebuilt air force and having kept the agreement with Syria secret, the Egyptians launched an attack on Yom Kippur, October 6, 1973. The attack was ultimately repulsed, but only at a high cost in Israeli casualties.[4]

- *Falkland Islands, 1982*. An increasingly desperate Argentine regime wanted Great Britain to hand over the Falkland Islands, which Britain had occupied and colonized in 1837. Britain's approach was to conduct prolonged diplomatic negotiations without giving up the islands. There was abundant evidence of Argentine intent to invade, including reporting of an Argentine naval task force headed for the Falklands with a marine amphibious force. But the British Foreign and Commonwealth Office did not want to face the possibility of an Argentine attack because it would be costly to deter or repulse. Britain's Latin America Current Intelligence Group (dominated at the time by the Foreign and Commonwealth Office) accordingly concluded on March 30, 1982, that an invasion was not imminent. On April 2 Argentine marines landed and occupied the Falklands, provoking the British to assemble a naval task force and retake the islands.[5]

The common theme of these and many other intelligence failures is *not* the failure to collect intelligence. In each of these cases, the intelligence had been collected. The common theme, rather, is the failure to properly analyze the collected material. In some cases, as in Operation Barbarossa and the Falkland Islands, the intelligence customer did his own analysis without the proper analytical attitude. In all of the cases, intelligence analysts fell into one of the analytical traps such as bias and preconceptions that are discussed in this book.

What sort of intelligence analyst would avoid these failures? What qualities would he or she have? Perhaps one or two of every ten analysts in the business have that special combination of abilities needed to make the correct calls in intelligence problems like those above.

These top-tier analysts are calm, reasoned, logical, and unemotional, but have a passion for the truth and a determination to uncover it. They are inquisitive and skeptical. They ask such questions as "Why do you believe that?" "Is there an alternative explanation?" "Is that source credible?" They approach a problem from many perspectives, use the evidence to visualize what is happening, and put together a mental picture. They love research, writing, and presenting their results. Every day must hold a new challenge.

They are persuasive. They enjoy interacting with people and teaching others how the analytical game is played. They choose their words with care, and when they speak, customers listen and respect their opinions. They are highly regarded by their peers and can organize and work with a team on analyses. But they have the courage to stand alone in their judgments. They are good, and they know it. Their self-confidence, like that of the Israeli intelligence analyst who spotted the oncoming Yom Kippur attack, tends to perturb their superiors.

To some extent these qualities are innate, though they can be developed or improved with experience and training. It is the goal of this introduction to highlight these traits and to suggest ways that analysts may enhance them, for without them an analyst, no matter what tools he has at his disposal, cannot perform well. The chapters that follow will focus in detail on the specific techniques and tools an analyst must develop to earn recognition from the larger community as a credible analysis professional.

Two traits, the ability to maintain objectivity and to keep a broad perspective, are particularly crucial. Effective analysts seem to be born with an insatiable curiosity about a broad range of subjects. Since their earliest years, they have thrived on mastering challenges and solving complex problems (often to the annoyance of those around them). And they have an uncanny ability to see events through the eyes of a scientist who neatly extracts emotional considerations from any equation. Their most important problem-solving attribute is that of objectivity. In addition, effective analysts possess interpersonal skills and are able to learn synthesis/analysis techniques.

Objectivity

It may seem obvious that staying objective is a credible analyst's first commandment. She knows that a search for evidence to support preconceived notions has no place in intelligence. She knows that she cannot discard observations because they are contrary to what she expected. In fact, she knows that her goal is to function like the physical scientist. In the physical sciences, an astronomer is not emotionally affected when he finds that stars follow a certain development pattern. He does not think that this is good or bad; it simply is.

Unfortunately, an intelligence analyst is typically in a position more like that of a social scientist. Her thinking may be complicated by her inability to isolate her own emotional needs from the problem being studied. Put simply, she *cares* about the outcome. But if an analyst wishes to assess foreign events, for example, she must put aside her own opinions about war, poverty, racism, police brutality, and governmental corruption, to name a few tough ones. For instance, "political corruption" is a normal way of life in many areas of the world. It is neither good nor bad in an absolute sense; it is merely the accepted standard of conduct. An analyst who is given the task of assessing the international narcotics trade cannot begin with the view that the traffickers are opportunistic parasites. Instead, she must practice empathy, or the concept of putting herself in the shoes of the target. Empathy is a tool of objectivity as it allows the analyst to check her biases. The analyst must try to see things from the traffickers' perspective—they are a group of small businesspeople working to uphold the free enterprise system in the face of excessive government regulation. (As an aside, a well-rounded analyst who has read Machiavelli sometime in her past will know that it might be helpful to reread it, this time from the analyst's vantage point, since one of Machiavelli's major strengths was his ability to assess conduct rather than values.)

The objective approach becomes even more difficult to maintain and defend as answers to pressing intelligence questions become more politically relevant. The pressures to conform analysis to policy today are never as direct as those that Josef Stalin applied to his intelligence staff. Pressures today are much more subtle; intelligence that supports policy will be accepted and the analyst suitably rewarded, intelligence that contradicts policy will be ignored. Many of the major U.S. intelligence failures trace directly back to an objectivity dereliction motivated by political concerns like those the intelligence community faced in Vietnam in 1968. One of the longest-running resulting disputes concerned the Backfire bomber.

Throughout the 1960s U.S. Air Force intelligence had consistently predicted that the Soviets would develop a new heavy bomber capable of striking U.S. targets. In 1969 photos of a plant at Kazan revealed the existence of a new bomber, subsequently codenamed Backfire. Two alternative missions for Backfire became the center of controversy. Air force analysts took the position that Backfire could be used for intercontinental attack. CIA analysts argued that the aircraft's mission was peripheral attack, that is, attack of ground or naval targets near the Soviet mainland.

Over the next several years, national intelligence estimates shifted back and forth on the issue. The critical evaluation criterion was the aircraft's range.

A range of 5,500 miles or more would allow Backfire to strike U.S. targets from Soviet bases on one-way missions. A range of less than 5,000 miles would not allow such strikes, unless the Backfire received air-to-air refueling. The answer was important for the U.S. Department of Defense and particularly to the air force, because a Backfire threat to the United States would justify defense budgets to counter the threat. CIA analysts, who had no stake in defense funding, strongly opposed what they saw as an attempt to shape intelligence estimates to serve parochial air force interests.

The air force and the Defense Intelligence Agency (DIA) produced estimates from McDonnell Douglas engineers that showed the Backfire had a range between 4,500 and 6,000 miles. The CIA produced estimates from a different set of McDonnell Douglas engineers that showed a range of between 3,500 and 5,000 miles. Each side accused the other of slanting the evidence.

The issue of the range of the Backfire bomber became important because it became enmeshed in Strategic Arms Limitation Talks (SALT). A Soviet intercontinental bomber would have to be counted in the Soviet total of strategic weaponry. The Russians eventually agreed as part of the SALT II process to produce no more than thirty Backfires a year and not to equip them for in-flight refueling; the United States agreed not to count the Backfires as intercontinental bombers. In later years, evidence became clear that Backfire was in fact a somewhat overdesigned peripheral attack bomber, never intended for intercontinental attack missions.

This book spends considerable time discussing the vital importance of analysts' ability to objectively assess and understand their customers and their customers' business or field. In fact, most of the book centers upon the "target centric" approach to intelligence analysis, which demands a close working relationship among all stakeholders, including the customer, to gain the clearest conception of needs and the most effective results or products. It is crucial, in fact, that objectivity not stand for disengagement from customers. Many organizations, including the most illustrious, have suffered in the past from this disconnect. The CIA, in its early years, attempted to remain aloof from its intelligence customers to avoid losing objectivity in the national intelligence estimates process.[6] The disadvantages of this aloofness became apparent—analysis was not addressing the customer's current interests, and intelligence was becoming less useful to policymaking. During the 1970s CIA senior analysts began to expand contacts with policymakers. The results of this closer relationship, while mixed, have on the whole suggested that an analyst can work closely with a policymaker, thereby making intelligence analyses relevant without losing objectivity.

If the intelligence customer is in the business world, the challenge of keeping an objective attitude reaches new heights. In business intelligence, a different approach is often urged that goes one step beyond what government intelligence analysts do: that the analyst make a recommendation without specifically telling the decisionmaker what to do.[7] Intelligence professionals in government and military service would undoubtedly be amused at the suggestion that they should offer advice such as: "General, you should move your tank battalions to the positions I have indicated," or "Madam Secretary, it would be prudent if your ambassador in Botswana initiated a dialogue with the rebel alliance." Recommendations such as these are career enders for government intelligence officers, who typically have neither the policymaking or operations experience nor the current knowledge of operational factors needed to make such recommendations. Conversely, in many companies, the business intelligence analyst often has both the operations expertise and credibility to make operational recommendations. It remains a valid question as to whether the government intelligence officer should be more like the business intelligence analyst—qualified to make judgments on policy or operational issues. In either case, commitment to objectivity should be an analyst's priority.

Broad Perspective

Successful analysts have an inherent inquisitiveness and lifelong interest in learning about subjects and ideas that may seem to have little or no relevance to their current subject area. Relevant and wide-ranging reading on cultures, economies, military traditions, religious and political doctrines, philosophy, and the like give analysts a breadth of substantive competence that will serve them well throughout their careers.

Specifically, a long-term, historical perspective is essential in making predictions about a culture, a government, an industry, a system, or a technology. Each of these concerns, even technology, has a long history. With few exceptions, the policymakers or executives who control industries and organizations today earned their credentials ten to twenty years ago. Thus, the resulting organizations are bureaucracies shaped by the world view of the key individuals in control, who likely have held on to biases based on the lessons learned through earlier experience. An analyst cannot comprehend the present shape of the organization—public or private—or predict its likely evolution and organizational behavior without an understanding of what has happened within it during its history. And a historical perspective requires more knowledge than that of the last few decades. The study of organizations, management, and decisionmaking has gone on for decades, and some of the most pertinent observations on these subjects trace back to the thinking of Machiavelli, Sun Tzu, and Plato.

Interpersonal Skills

In addition to these intrinsic qualities, interpersonal skills (including the ability to express and present ideas clearly) are crucial to becoming an effective analyst. It is the premise of this book that collaboration is the only practical future for a relevant and successful intelligence community. Admittedly, analysts with who live by logic and the scientific method are not often described as "naturals" when it comes to soft skills. But practicing empathy, conflict resolution techniques, facilitation skills, and the art of knowing when and how to advocate versus when to follow and reflect, are crucial to analysis and the resulting product. These project management skills, along with some mastery over one's ego, can be learned (albeit sometimes through painful trial and error). Even the most logical and objective creature in popular television history, *Star Trek*'s Mr. Spock, was a consummate listener, dialoguer, and when appropriate, advocate.

Analyst as Team Player

Intelligence increasingly requires teamwork, and analysts should expect that nonintelligence actors will be part of the team. Given that many people have something at stake in how an intelligence question is answered, the process of getting to the answer, especially on complex intelligence problems, is fundamentally a *social* one. Most complex problems involve many stakeholders: Some, such as the analyst's managers, are involved in defining the problem that needs intelligence, while others, such as the customers, may add constraints to the solution. Teams working on related projects have a particularly large stake, because one team's answer is the next team's problem. For instance, an economic analyst's assessment that the economy of Egypt is headed for serious trouble would present a number of challenges to an analytical team assessing the political future of Egypt. No team leader is brilliant or experienced enough to go off and solve such problems alone. It is not even possible to assemble a team of brilliant people to go off and solve the problem, because the moment they go off they leave behind stakeholders whose input is essential. Again, a target-centric approach helps solve this by emphasizing the sharing of information and expertise among stakeholders. In this way the approach breaks down the long-held compartmental barriers that collectors, analysts, and customers have traditionally experienced in solving intelligence problems. Instead, all stakeholders contribute to the target model, which is an initial representation of the intelligence problem, and all participants have continued visibility and input into the target model.

Note that the process strictly adheres to the traditional scientific method: To observe some aspect of a particular phenomenon or event, create a tentative description (hypothesis) about what has been observed, and use the hypothesis to make predictions. Test the predictions by experiments or further observations, modifying the hypothesis based on the results. The fundamental difference is simply that any member of the team, a collector, an analyst, a customer, is no longer confined to using her expertise in just one area or at just one time during the process. Instead, synergistic discoveries and opportunities occur as pooled expertise and talents are brought to bear upon one relevant focus: the target model that is discussed in Chapter 2.

There are likely several thousands of books nowadays dedicated exclusively to the art of teamwork. If there is one key to successful team outcomes it would be efficient collaboration built on mutual trust—something that is very difficult to build and very easy to destroy in a large intelligence organization. By following the imperatives listed below, an analyst will consistently produce credible analysis reports of excellent quality, precisely because a coordinated team approach has been implemented.

- As part of an analyst's interpersonal skill set, she must be a strong team leader who can execute a team intelligence effort but also understands and is committed to the *inclusive* nature of complex problem solving. She must be capable of fostering active participation by the customer community, which will improve the quality of the synthesis and analysis of intelligence problems and support for the results. When customers are integrated into the study process, not only is their assistance invaluable, they will have confidence in, and use, the product.

- In managing this process, the analyst should encourage every possible form of communication: Welcome disagreement as a sign that the stakeholders are putting their cards on the table, and use meetings as occasions for learning and building shared mental models. Finally, the analyst should use technologies that support communication among the stakeholders and promote the value of capturing and sharing soft information, such as ideas, questions, problems, objections, opinions, assumptions, and constraints.

- The analyst should remember that she is managing an *opportunity-driven* process. She should look for opportunities for breakthroughs, synergies, connections, and allies. She drives for making decisions quickly, even before the team is ready, because she knows that decisions and partial solutions will flush out new contributions. This is equivalent to the concept of rapid prototyping in software development.

- Perhaps most important, the team leader must manage the scope of the problem. Determine which stakeholders to include in the process and how to include them. Choose which constraints to be ruled by, which to bend, and which to ignore. In this way, the analyst can make conscious and responsible choices about the scope of the problem.

If this teamwork approach works well, then the customer will normally accept and make use of the analysis results. But if not, the analyst must shift her interpersonal skills in the direction of advocacy and act as a spokesperson for the analytic conclusions.

Analyst as Advocate

While the proper analytic attitude is one of objectivity, once analysis is finished, political realities set in. The analyst must sell the product because he quickly encounters one of the fundamental principles of physics that is also a fundamental principle in intelligence: Every action produces an equal and opposite reaction. If his results are at all worthwhile, they will meet with skepticism or outright opposition.

Furthermore, if the customer is a U.S. government policymaker, the analyst typically must interact with lawyers, a relationship that is much different from what analysts are used to and one in which advocacy skills will be useful. Lawyers prefer to use intelligence experts as they would use scientific experts in a courtroom: receiving testimony on the facts and opinions, cross-examining, determining the key issues, and deciding. The existence of a controversy and of differing opinions is essential, in the lawyer's view, to establishing the truth. Lawyers are uncomfortable with a single expert opinion and with the intelligence compartmentation system. To them, the intelligence community's traditional compartmentation system for protecting sources and methods is suspect because it tends to conceal evidence and is therefore inconsistent with the goal of the discovery process in civil litigation.

Most intelligence analysts have difficulty being advocates because it goes against their objective nature. The advocacy process is an adversarial one, and the guidelines for conduct come from the legal profession where advocacy has been raised to a fine art and where the pitfalls of improper advocacy are well understood. R. V. Jones, assistant director of Britain's Royal Air Force Intelligence Section during World War II, quoted an Operations Research Society of America report when he said that "When an analyst participates in an adversary process he is, and should conduct himself as, and should expect to be treated as, an advocate. The rules for an adversary process are different from those of research. The former permit biased or slanted testimony and the latter are directed toward objective evaluation."[8] Jones noted his approval of the quotation, but reserved judgment as to whether the giving of "biased or slanted testimony" was compatible with honor in a scientist.[9]

The answer to this dilemma is the same one that Machiavelli gave to his Prince: The conduct that I am describing may not be proper or honorable, but it seems to work where proper and honorable conduct does not.[10] Jones himself, in the above example, went on to cite some examples of how he had slanted or strained the evidence when, in his judgment, it was the right thing to do.

Analyst as Communicator

If one is to be an effective project coordinator and advocate, one must learn the skills of effective communication, both in writing and speaking. There are procedures for conducting research and writing a report or presenting a briefing, some generally recognized across professions and some that are institution specific. It is the responsibility of the analyst to learn his particular intelligence organization's technical quality and style reviews and then pay strict attention to them. Also, an analyst must dually follow standards for finished intelligence publications and yet use terminology that the customer understands, addressing problems and issues that interest the customer. In general, analysts who develop this ability present results that:

- Are forward looking, with detailed predictions of the technical performance of future systems or of major trends in the subject area, and descriptions of the factors driving those trends.
- Contain clearly stated conclusions supported by in-depth research and technical reasoning.
- Include clear tutorials or explanations of complex technical subjects aimed at the expected customer.

Understanding of Synthesis and Analysis Techniques

An analyst must have a repertoire of techniques to apply in solving intelligence problems. These might include pattern synthesis/analysis, trend prediction, literature assessment, and statistical analysis. A number of these techniques are presented throughout the book in the form of synthesis/analysis principles. These synthesis and analysis techniques together form a problem-solving methodology that, when applied by an analyst having the qualities described in this Introduction, can help to avoid intelligence blunders.

The synthesis/analysis process that is discussed in Chapter 2 begins with the analyst assessing incoming information. A new analyst needs some way to fit this information into an analytic framework (the target model), and if possible to recover and organize all of the past analytical findings and discoveries that are relevant to the issue. Otherwise, the new analyst will spend far too much time getting access to raw data and reanalyzing material that his predecessors analyzed years ago; or worse still, using scarce collection assets to acquire data that is already available.

Summary

A few attributes are essential in a top-rate analyst. Having the proper investigative attitude is the starting point. That is, the analyst must be prepared to take an objective approach, relying on the scientific method. Ideally, the analyst should not care what the answer to an intelligence problem is when he begins an analytic effort. He should be prepared to observe and investigate the anomaly, the unexpected, the things that simply don't fit into the existing target model. But when the analysis is done, the analyst often must drop the objective attitude and act as an advocate. A good analyst at times has to become a salesperson and sell the analytic product to customers. To do this well, the analyst needs a well-developed ability to express ideas orally and in writing.

Because the synthesis/analysis process is increasingly a collaborative process, the analyst should be adept at teamwork. He should be familiar with the culture, processes, and problems of his team partners. Specifically, he should understand the information collectors and work closely with them to obtain intelligence and evaluate the collection process. He should also understand the intelligence customers' sensitivities and boundaries.

Finally, an analyst must understand the techniques and tools for synthesis and analysis. He must be able to call on an organized knowledge base from which to synthesize the target model. In both synthesis and analysis, he must draw on a historical perspective and apply substantive competence in the field. Both the perspective and the competence must exceed that of the intelligence customer if the analyst is to be respected and the product used.

Notes

1. Colonel John Hughes-Wilson, *Military Intelligence Blunders* (New York: Carroll and Graf, 1999), 38.
2. Ibid, 102.
3. Ibid, 165.
4. Ibid, 218.
5. Ibid, 260.
6. Harold P. Ford, *Estimative Intelligence* (Lanham, Md.: University Press of America, 1993), 107.
7. John H. Hovis, "CI at Avnet: A Bottom-Line Impact," *Competitive Intelligence Review,* 11 (third quarter 2000): 11.
8. "The Obligations of Scientists as Counsellors: Guidelines for the Practice of Operations Research," *Minerva* X (January 1972): 115.
9. R. V. Jones, "Temptations and Risks of the Scientific Adviser," *Minerva* X (July 1972): 441.
10. Niccolo Machiavelli, The Prince (New York: Bantam Classics, 1984).

1

The Intelligence Process

Future conflicts will be fought more by networks than by hierarchies, and whoever masters the network form will gain major advantages.

John Arquilla and David Ronfeldt, RAND

George Lucas's movie *Star Wars* describes the final stages of a human intelligence operation. The heroine, Princess Leia, gets the plans for the evil Galactic Empire's ultimate battle machine, the Death Star, from the robot R2-D2, who is functioning as a mobile dead drop.[1] Leia gives the plans to the rebel forces, whose scientific intelligence analyst briefs the rebel command on the plans, pinpoints the weak spot on the Death Star, and presents a brilliant analysis of the enemy defenses. Rebel fighter jockeys deliver proton torpedoes to the weak spot and destroy the Death Star. End of movie.

This *Star Wars* vignette accurately summarizes the intelligence process as it is popularly viewed. The people who collect intelligence information and execute the operations get the glory, the press, and the money. The intelligence analyst, working behind the scenes, gets the interesting problems to solve to make it all work.

Although the popular focus is on collection, most of the major failures in intelligence are due to inadequate or nonexistent analysis, and most of the rest are due to a failure to act on the analysis. The information is usually there, at least in hindsight. So, unfortunately, is a large volume of irrelevant material that has to be examined and discarded. All intelligence organizations today are saturated with incoming information. Furthermore, in large intelligence communities critical information about an intelligence issue may not be effectively shared because intelligence is organized around the flawed concept of an intelligence cycle. Before we explore this flawed concept we should define the term *intelligence*.

The Nature of Intelligence: Reducing Uncertainty in Conflict

Intelligence is about reducing uncertainty in conflict. Since conflict can consist of any competitive or opposing action resulting from the divergence of two or more parties' ideas or interests, conflict is not necessarily physical combat. If competition or negotiation exists, then two or more groups are in conflict. There can be many different levels of conflict, ranging from friendly competition to armed combat. Conflict, and the issue of whether another party is an opponent or an ally, is defined by context. As a rule, friends and allies don't conduct intelligence operations on one another. However, two or more parties can be allies in one conflict, opponents in another.[2] For example, France and the United States are usually military allies, but they are opponents in commercial affairs. Intelligence seeks not to resolve conflict per se, but to help one side better understand the causes of and participants in that conflict for the sake of that side's advantage.

Therefore, intelligence also is about reducing uncertainty by obtaining information that the opponent in a conflict wishes to deny you. This definition does not exclude use of openly available sources such as newspapers or the Internet, because competent analysis of such open sources frequently will reveal information that an opponent wishes to conceal. Indeed, intelligence in general can be thought of as the complex process of understanding meaning in available information. A typical goal of intelligence is to establish facts and then to develop precise, reliable, and valid inferences (hypotheses, estimations, conclusions, or predictions) for use in strategic decisionmaking or operational planning.

How, then, is intelligence any different from the market research that many companies conduct or from traditional research as it is carried out in laboratories, think tanks, and academia? After all, these types of research are also intended to reduce uncertainty. The answer is that most methods of intelligence and nonintelligence research are identical, with one important distinction. When accurate information is not available through traditional (and less expensive) means, then a wide range of specialized techniques and methods unique to the intelligence field are called into play. Academics are unlikely to have intercepted telephone communications at their disposal to use as a viable technique for collection and analysis. Nor must academics deal with concealment, denial, or deception.

Because intelligence is about conflict, it supports *operations* such as military planning and combat, diplomatic negotiations, trade negotiations and commerce policy, and law enforcement. The primary customer of intelligence is the person who will act on the information—the executive, the decisionmaker, the combat commander, or the law enforcement officer. Writers therefore describe intelligence as being *actionable* information. Not all actionable information is intelligence, however. A weather report is actionable, but it is not intelligence.

Furthermore, what distinguishes intelligence from plain news is this support for operations. The operations customer does (or should do) something about intelligence, whereas TV viewers normally do not do anything about the news. The same information can be both intelligence and news, of course: Food riots in Somalia can be both if the customer takes action on the information.

Finally, intelligence is always concerned with a *target*—the focus of the problem about which the operations people want answers. In the *Star Wars* example the target was the Death Star. The rebel intelligence effort clearly supported operations in locating its weak point.

Logic would dictate that the intelligence process should revolve around how to best approach the target. That is exactly what the remainder of this book is concerned with: the steps to solving an intelligence problem using a target-centric approach. This process is quite different from that depicted in most introductory texts and courses, but it is the new direction that intelligence is taking in practice. A brief review of the traditional intelligence cycle will illustrate why.

The Traditional Intelligence Cycle

Intelligence is traditionally described as following a series of steps called the *intelligence cycle*. Figure 1-1 illustrates this intelligence cycle in elementary form. Alternative views of the cycle will be discussed elsewhere in the book.

The cycle typically begins with a *requirements* or *needs* step, which equates to a definition of the intelligence problem. Usually this takes the form of a rather general question from an intelligence customer, such as: "How stable is the government of Ethiopia?"

Figure 1-1   The Traditional Intelligence Cycle

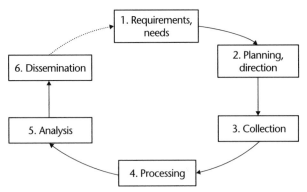

Note: The dotted line represents the transition from one cycle to the next, during which the customer reviews the analysis product and formulates new requirements and needs.

Then comes *planning,* or *direction*—determining how the other components of the cycle will address the problem. Collectors have to be tasked to gather missing bits of information. Analysts have to be assigned to do research and write a report on Ethiopian government stability.

The cycle then proceeds to *collection,* or gathering information. Ethiopian newspapers have to be acquired. Communications intelligence (*COMINT*) has to be focused on Ethiopian government communications. Human intelligence (*HUMINT*) operatives have to ask questions of sources with knowledge of Ethiopian internal affairs.

From there, the information has to be *processed.* Foreign language material must be translated. Encrypted signals must be decrypted. Film or digital signals must be translated into visible imagery. Responses from HUMINT sources must be validated and organized into a report format.

The newly collected and processed material has to be collated with historically relevant material to create intelligence in an *analysis* phase. An analyst has to create outcome scenarios of the current Ethiopian situation, generate profiles of Ethiopian leaders, and assess their responses to likely events.

The finished intelligence must be *disseminated* to the customer by a written report (usually sent electronically) or a briefing. Then comes a transition to new requirements or needs, and a new cycle begins.

Over the years the intelligence cycle has become somewhat of a theological concept: No one questions its validity. Yet when pressed, many intelligence officers admit that the intelligence process "really doesn't work like that." In other words, effective intelligence efforts are not cycles. Here are some reasons why.

The cycle defines an *antisocial* series of steps that constrains the flow of information. It separates collectors from processors from analysts and too often results in "throwing information over the wall" to become the next person's responsibility. Everyone neatly avoids responsibility for the quality of the final product. Because this compartmentalized process results in formalized and relatively inflexible requirements at each stage, it is more predictable and therefore more vulnerable to an opponent's countermeasures. In intelligence, as in most forms of conflict, if you can predict what your opponents will do, you can defeat them.

The cycle-defined view, when it considers the customer at all, tends to treat the customer in the abstract as a monolithic entity. The feedback loop inherent in a true cycle is absent; a gap exists between dissemination and needs. Customers, being outside the loop, cannot make their changing needs known. There are several reasons why the gap exists in government and the military.

In government, intelligence officers and policymakers often are almost totally ignorant of each other's business.[3] In the military the gap may be less severe—the importance of intelligence has been ingrained in the culture over a long time. But as in the civilian side of government, an organizational demarcation usually exists. Most commanders and their staffs have not had intelligence assignments, and intelligence officers usually have not had operations assignments. They tend to speak different jargon, and their definitions of what is important in an operation differ. Intelligence officers often know more about an opponent's capability than their own unit capability, and the commander too often has the inverse problem.

In large intelligence organizations, such as those of the U.S. government, the collection element shown in Figure 1-1 is typically well organized, well funded, and automated to handle high volumes of traffic. In contrast, the step where one moves from disseminated intelligence to new requirements is almost completely unfunded and requires extensive feedback from intelligence consumers. The system depends on a consumer voicing his needs. Military organizations have a formal system for doing so. Policymakers do not. The policymaker's input is largely informal, depending on feedback to the analyst and often passing through several intermediaries. And for the newest class of consumers of U.S. intelligence—law enforcement—the feedback is rudimentary. No entity has the clear responsibility to close the loop. Analysts and their managers, who normally have the closest ties to intelligence customers, usually determine customer needs. But this is too often a hit-or-miss proposition, because it depends on the inclination of analysts who are dealing with other pressing problems.

The traditional view of the intelligence cycle also is used because it fits a conventional paradigm for problem solving. It logically flows from the precept that the best way to work on an intelligence problem is to follow an orderly and linear process, working from the question (the problem) to the answer (the solution). One begins by understanding the question; the next step is to gather and analyze data. Analysis techniques are then applied to answer the question. This pattern of thinking is taught in problem-solving texts, and we use it almost instinctively. Conventional wisdom says that the more complex the problem, the more important it is to follow this orderly flow. The flaw of this linear problem-solving approach is that it obscures the real underlying cognitive process. The mind does not work linearly—it jumps around to different parts of the problem in the process of reaching a solution. In practice, intelligence officers might jump from analysis back to collection, then to requirements, to collection again, then back to analysis in what seems a very untidy process that in no way resembles a cycle.

U.S. intelligence analytic guru Sherman Kent noted that the problems with the intelligence cycle—the compartmentation of participants, the gap between dissemination and needs, and the attempt to linearize a nonlinear process—are worse in large organizations and in situations far removed from the heat of conflict.[4] As Keith Hall, former director of the National Reconnaissance Office, noted, "During crisis the seams go away and all the various players pull together to create end-to-end solutions . . . but we don't do that well in a noncrisis situation."[5]

In summary, the traditional cycle may adequately describe the structure and function of an intelligence community, but it does not describe the intelligence process. In the new world of information technology, the traditional cycle may be even less relevant. Informal networks (communities of interest) increasingly are forming to address the problems that Kent identified and enable a nonlinear intelligence process using secure Web technology.

The cycle is still with us, however, because it is a convenient rationale for organizing and managing an intelligence community like those in large governments and large military organizations. And it is in some respects a defensive measure; it makes it difficult to pinpoint responsibility for intelligence failures.

Fifty years ago, the automobile production "cycle" looked a lot like the traditional intelligence cycle. Marketing staff would come up with requirements for new cars. Designers would create a design and feed it to production. Production would retool the factory and produce the cars in a long assembly line. The cars came out at the end and went to a sales force that sold the cars to customers. And then marketing started on a new requirements set, beginning the cycle anew. No one had responsibility for the final result. Today automobile production is a team effort—with marketing, sales, design, and production staff sitting in the same room with consumer representatives, working together on a common target: the new automobile. This complex, interactive, collaborative, and social process results in the faster production of higher quality, more market-oriented products.

Although producing intelligence is a more complex undertaking than automobile manufacturing, the interactive approach works for both. This book defines an alternative approach, one that is gaining currency in intelligence communities, for a world where intelligence problems are becoming increasingly complex.

Intelligence as a Target-Centric Process

An alternative to the traditional cycle is to make all stakeholders (including customers) part of the intelligence process. Stakeholders in the intelligence community include collectors, processors, analysts, and the people who plan for and build systems to support them. Customers could include the president, the National Security Council staff, military command headquarters, diplomats, the Department of Homeland Security, local law enforcement, and the commanders of U.S. naval vessels, depending on the issue. To include these stakeholders in the intelligence process, the cycle must be redefined, not for convenience of implementation in a traditional organizational hierarchy, but so that it can take full advantage of evolving information technology and handle complex problems.

Figure 1-2 defines this *target-centric,* or objective-oriented, view of the intelligence process. The goal is to construct a shared picture of the target from which all participants can extract the elements they need to do their job and can contribute from their resources or knowledge to create a more accurate target picture. This is not a linear process, nor is it a cycle (though it contains many feedback loops, or cycles, within); it is a *network process,* a

Figure 1-2   A Target-Centric View of the Intelligence Process

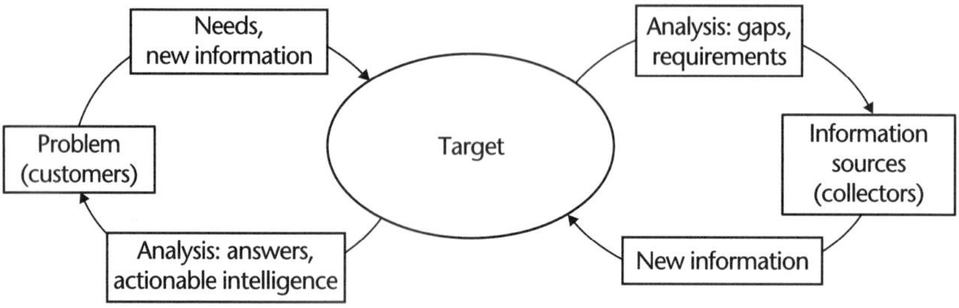

social process, with all participants focused on the objective. It has been accurately described within the U.S. intelligence community as a *network-centric collaboration process.*[6]

In Figure 1-2, the customers who have operational problems look at the current state of knowledge about the target (the current target picture) and identify information needs. Intelligence analysts, working with collectors who share the same target picture, translate the needs into knowledge gaps or information requirements for the collectors to address. As collectors obtain the needed information, it is incorporated into the shared target picture. From this picture, analysts extract actionable intelligence and provide it to the customers, who may in turn add their own insights to the shared target picture as well as add new information needs.

Let's bring some meaning to the process shown in Figure 1-2. The date is December 2, 1993. Colombian police Lieutenant Hugo Martinez watches the signal display on his computer screen and listens to his headphones as his police surveillance van moves through the streets of Medellín, Columbia. Electronic intelligence has traced the cell telephone calls of drug kingpin Pablo Escobar to this neighborhood. Hugo is trying to find the exact house where a desperate Escobar is talking to his son about getting the family out of Colombia.

The signal on the computer screen and in the headphones strengthens and peaks. The van stops next to a house, and Martinez looks up to see a fat man standing at a window, holding a cell phone. The man turns away, and the cell phone conversation abruptly ends. Martinez reports to his commander: "I've got him located. He's in this house." The commander snaps out orders for all units to converge and surround the building. Five police officers force their way in the front door and exchange gunshots with the occupants. Ten minutes later, the gunfire stops. On the building rooftop, Pablo Escobar lies dead.[7]

This example, a true story, was the end of an intense cooperative effort between U.S. and Colombian intelligence officers that had gone on for over a year. In this case, the intelligence effort had several customers—an operations team comprising the Colombian police, the U.S. Army support team in Colombia, and the Colombian and U.S. governments, each with different intelligence needs. The information sources included COMINT targeted on Escobar's cell phones and those of his associates, HUMINT from Escobar's associates, and financial information from other sources. The operations team focused on finding Escobar; the intelligence analysts who supported them had a more extensive target that included Escobar's family, his business associates, his bankers, and his agents in the Colombian government. Escobar would not have been caught if the intelligence search had focused solely on him and had ignored his network.

In the Escobar case, as in less time-critical operations, intelligence analysis is implicit and pervasive. But it is not all done by analysts. The customer and the providers of information also participate and will do so whether the analyst welcomes it or not. Both customers and providers possess valuable insights about the target, and both want their insights included in the final analytical product. However, someone has to make the process work—create and maintain the picture of the target, obtain customer needs and change them into requirements for new information, accept new information and incorporate it into the target picture, and then extract actionable intelligence and ensure that it gets to the customer. All of these are functions that analysts have always performed. Within the target-centric process, analysts still perform these functions, but collectors and customers have more visibility into the process and thus more opportunity to contribute to it. The analyst becomes more of a process manager and a conduit of information to the other participants.

This team-generated view of the target is intended to facilitate and encourage interaction among collectors, analysts, and operations personnel, all of whom may be geographically remote from each other, via an electronic web. Because the team view is more interactive, or social, it represents a better approach to handling complex problems. Because all participants share knowledge of the target, they are better able to identify gaps in knowledge and understand the important issues surrounding the target. The team-generated view brings the full resources of the team to bear on the target. During U.S. operations in Afghanistan in 2002, intelligence officers used screens similar to Internet chat rooms to share data in an interactive process that in no way resembled the traditional intelligence cycle.[8]

The process shown in Figure 1-2 is resilient. Because the participants work in a collaborative environment, there is no single point of failure, another member of the network could step in to act as facilitator, and the whole team accepts responsibility for the product.

The process is also able to satisfy a wide range of customers from a single knowledge base. There are usually many customers for intelligence about a given problem, and each customer has different needs. The military and foreign relations, financial, and foreign trade organizations all may need information about a specific country. Against a common target, all these needs will overlap, but each organization also will have unique needs.

The target-centric approach has more promise for complex problems and issues than the traditional cycle view. Though depicted as a cycle, the traditional process is in practice linear and sequential, whereas the target-centric approach is collaborative by design. Its nonlinear analytic process allows for participation by all stakeholders, so real insights into a problem can come from any knowledgeable source. Involving customers increases the likelihood that the resulting intelligence will be used. It also reminds the customers of (or introduces them to) the value of an analytical approach to problems that deal with complex issues. It has been asserted that in the United States, government has detached itself from the analytical process and relied too much on the intelligence community to do its analytical thinking.[9] Increasing exposure of policymakers to the analytical process could help reverse this trend.

The collaborative team concept also has the potential for addressing two important pressures that intelligence analysts face today:

- *The information glut.* Analysts are overloaded with incoming material from collectors. The team approach expands the analyst team to include knowledgeable people from the collector, processor, and customer groups, each of whom can take a chunk of the information glut and filter out the irrelevant material. Business organizations have been doing this for years, and they now rely heavily on Web-based means. Unfortunately, large intelligence communities such as that in the U.S. government have not succeeded in applying this remedy to the information glut. The barriers among collectors, processors, analysts, and customers still hold firm, and compartmentalization constrains collaboration.

- *The customer demand for more detail.* All intelligence customers are demanding increasingly more detail about the intelligence target. This should not be surprising given that targets are more complex, and the range of the customer's options to deal with opponents has become richer. If the operations target is a building (such as an embassy or a command and control center), for example, target intelligence may need to include the floor plan; number of levels; whether it has a basement; type of construction; roof characteristics; what type of heating, ventilation, and air conditioning is used; when the building is empty; and so forth. Such details become critical when the objective is to place a smart bomb on the building or to take out the building's electrical power.

For collaboration to work—for the extended team to share part of the data overload and to provide the needed target detail, team members have to have a wealth of mutual trust and understanding. Both require team building and extended social interaction. Some companies have been highly successful at collaboration; the U.S. government still is working at it, and most governmental intelligence services worldwide haven't even started.

It is important to note what the collaborative process is not. As Mark Lowenthal has stated, it is not a substitute for competitive analysis—the process by which different analysts present alternative views of the target.[10] Collaboration, properly handled, is intended to help competitive analysis by ensuring that the competing views share as much information about the target as possible.

The Target

In Norfolk, Virginia, a young intelligence officer controls a Predator Unmanned Aeronautical Vehicle on patrol over Afghanistan. The Predator's video display shows a vehicle racing along a mountain road. Moving the Predator closer for a better view, the officer identifies the vehicle as a BMP, a type of armored personnel carrier. He calls in an AC-130 Spectre gunship on patrol nearby. As the AC-130 appears on the scene, the BMP lurches to a stop. The rear doors open, and the BMP disgorges Taliban soldiers running for cover. The Spectre's guns open up. In the Predator's video, the soldiers crumple, one by one, as the stream of gunship fire finds them.

The intelligence officer was able to order the attack by the AC-130 Spectre gunship because he had a mental picture of potential Taliban targets, and the BMP fit the picture in its location and characteristics. The BMP in Afghanistan was a specific operations target; the intelligence view of the target was much larger. It included details of the road network in Afghanistan that could support the BMP and maps delineating areas of Taliban control. A good mental model is essential when intelligence provides such close support to operations. The intelligence officer is under intense pressure to distinguish quickly between a troop carrier and a bus full of villagers, and the consequences of an error are severe.

The Target as a Complex System

As the BMP example suggests, the typical intelligence target is a *system*, not a single vehicle or building. Intelligence analysis therefore starts by thinking about the target as a system. A system comprises *structure, function,* and *process,* and the analyst has to deal with each of the three iteratively in systems thinking.[11] The structure of a system is defined by its components and the relationships among those components. Function involves the effects or results produced by the system, that is, the system outputs. Process refers to the sequence of events or activities that produce results.

The Escobar drug cartel is (or was) an example of a system. Figure 1-3 is a macro level picture of a cocaine cartel's structure, showing the major components and the relationships among the components. Each of these components has a structure of its own comprising subcomponents and their relationships. The coca supply component, for example, has subcomponents such as the farmers, land, seed, and farm equipment. A cocaine cartel also has several major functions, such as survival in the face of state opposition, making a profit for its stakeholders, and providing cocaine to its customers. Each component again has additional functions that it performs. The transportation and

Figure 1-3   Example Target: Cocaine Cartel Network

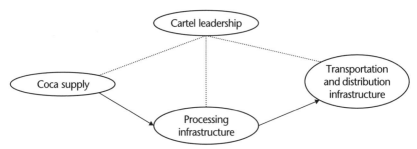

Note: Dotted lines represent the control that leadership exerts; arrows represent movement.

distribution infrastructure has the functions of getting cocaine from the processor to the customer, selling the drugs, and obtaining payment for them. As this example illustrates, most intelligence targets are systems that have subordinate systems, also called subsystems. The Escobar leadership comprised a subsystem with a structure that included components such as security and finance; it had a function (to manage the cocaine network) and a process for managing it.

As a counterexample, a geographical region is not a system. A geographical region is much too abstract a concept to be treated as a system. It does not have structure, function, or process, though it contains many systems having all three. Consequently, a geographical region could not be considered an intelligence target. The government of a region *is* a system—it has structure, function, and process.

All intelligence targets are systems. Furthermore, these targets are *complex systems* because:

- They are dynamic and evolving.
- They are nonlinear, in that they are not adequately described by a simple structure such as a tree diagram or the linear structure previously illustrated for the traditional intelligence cycle.

A cocaine supply network is a complex system. It is constantly evolving, and its intricate web of relationships does not yield easily to a hierarchical breakout. It can, however, usually be described as a network. Most complex systems of intelligence interest are, in fact, networks. The following section discusses the complex target as a network.

The Complex Target as a Network

Though intelligence has always targeted opposing systems, it has too often tended to view them as individual entities rather than as connected entities. This narrow focus downplays the connections among organizations and individuals—connections that can represent the real strength or weakness of an opposing system taken as a whole. This is why we focus on networks.

Networks, by definition, comprise *nodes* with *links* between nodes. Several types of networks have been defined, and they differ in the nature of the nodes and links. In *communications networks,* the nodes are points in the network, usually geographically separated, between which the communications are transmitted. A communications satellite and its ground terminals are communications nodes. The links are the communications means, for example: fiber optics, satellite communications, and wireless (cellular) telephones. In *social networks,* the nodes are people. The links show relationships between people and usually characterize the nature of the relationship. A social network exists at a cocktail party or within an investment club.

In this book, unless otherwise specified, *network* means a *generalized network* in which the nodes are entities and can be almost anything—people, places, things, concepts. A cocaine supply system is a generalized network. The links define relationships among the nodes. Sometimes the links quantify the relationship. Whereas communications and social networks are useful concepts in intelligence, the more powerful generalized network is the preferred and widely used concept for intelligence analysis.

In intelligence, the opposing generalized network typically is some combination of governments; individuals; NGOs, such as environmental, human rights, and religious groups; commercial firms; or illicit organizations, all tied together by some purpose, as suggested by Figure 1-4. In such conflict, intelligence has the goal of developing an understanding of the opposing network to make the analyst's own network as effective as possible and to render the opponent's network ineffective.

Analysts responsible for assessing the capabilities of an air defense network, a competing commercial firm or alliance, or a narcotics production and distribution network must take a network view. As an example, intelligence organizations concerned with the balance of power in the Middle East sometimes look at Iran and Iraq each in isolation. Yet no assessment of the future of the Middle East should ignore the continuing hostility between the two—the constraining effects of that hostility on likely future actions of either

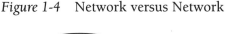

Figure 1-4   Network versus Network

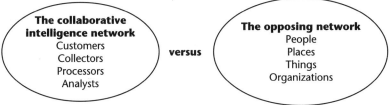

country and the opportunities that it provides for opponents. The two countries are part of a larger target network bound by ties of mutual mistrust and suspicion.

It is also important to look at both sides from a network context. It may be easier, especially in a bureaucracy, to look at the opponent's side as a network than to see that one's own intelligence assets form a network and to fully exploit its strengths. The collaborative collector-analyst-customer, target-centric approach creates an effective network to deal with the opposing network. Figure 1-5 shows the example of a cocaine supply target network with some components of the opposing (that is, U.S. and Colombian) intelligence customer network. As the figure indicates, U.S. law enforcement would logically target the transportation and distribution infrastructure, because much of that infrastructure is located within U.S. borders. U.S. law enforcement would not normally be able to target the cartel leadership in Colombia. Colombian law enforcement, on the other hand, could target both the cartel leadership and its transportation and distribution infrastructure, but would probably find the leadership a more profitable target. The customer network shown here is far from complete, of course, but it might include political leadership in the

Figure 1-5   Intelligence Customer Network versus a Target Cocaine Network

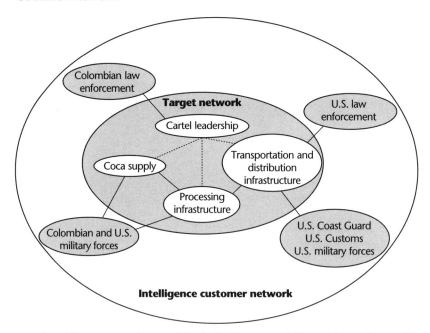

Note: Dotted lines represent the control that leadership exerts; solid lines indicate where an element of the intelligence customer network is targeting an element of the target network.

United States and Colombia, for example, or regional and European government elements concerned about the cocaine trade.

John Arquilla and David Ronfeldt of RAND Corporation have described the network target in their discussion of the impact of new communications and information technologies on military structures, doctrines, and strategies. They coined the term *netwar* and defined it as a form of *information-related conflict,* where opponents form a network. Specifically, Arquilla and Ronfeldt use the term to describe the "societal struggles" that make use of new technologies.[12] The technologies are available and usable anywhere, as demonstrated by the Zapatista "netwar" in Chiapas, Mexico, during 1994. The Zapatista insurgents skillfully used a global media campaign to create a supporting network of nongovernmental organizations (NGOs) and embarrass the Mexican government in a form of asymmetric attack.[13]

Netwar is not the same as information warfare, though the two may overlap in some problems. Information warfare, also called information operations, encompasses the use of information systems including computers, communications networks, and databases for competitive advantage against an opponent. Thus information warfare can be one of the "levers" pulled in netwar; computer networks may be a part of the target. But one can engage in netwar without attacking the opponent's information systems.

Within the U.S. Department of Defense, netwar is currently referred to as network-centric warfare.[14] Defense planners have identified three themes:

- A shift in focus from the single node target to the network target.
- A shift from viewing actors as independent to viewing them as part of a continuously adapting system.
- The importance of making strategic choices to adapt or just to survive in the changing system.

This concept of network-centric warfare is not new to the business world.[15] Companies such as Royal Dutch Shell were creating such networks, including allied outsiders, more than a decade ago. Participants in that network found it a powerful mechanism for bringing a wide range of expertise to bear on a problem.[16] The World Wide Web has speeded the formation of such networks, and the network-centric approach has been adopted widely in the commercial world. Companies such as Cisco Systems and Wal-Mart have made the collaborative network a key part of their business strategy. In Wal-Mart's network-centric retailing approach, sales information is shared with suppliers in near-real time so that they can better control production and distribution as well as manage their own supply chains for Wal-Mart products.[17] Another example is the network-centric securities trading system, Autobahn, created by Deutsche Morgan Grenfell.[18] Autobahn replaces the traditional trader-centered (hierarchical) system of securities trading with a network system where participants have equal access to securities pricing information. The network-centric approach gives companies such as Wal-Mart and Deutsche Morgan Grenfell an edge, forcing competitors to adopt similar approaches or lose out in competition.

Business intelligence might be ahead of government intelligence in applying the netwar strategy. Even military organizations, with their traditions of a hierarchical structure, are considering the advantages of a network structure.[19] Thus, where national intelligence efforts must deal with commercial entities, as they do in economic issues, weapons proliferation, and funds laundering issues, intelligence analysts increasingly must understand network-centric conflict. Furthermore, NGOs are increasingly involved in military, economic, political, and social issues worldwide, and the involvement of NGOs usually makes any conflict network centric, as it did with the Zapatistas in Mexico.

Summary

Intelligence is about reducing uncertainty in conflict. In that role it supports operations, and it is always concerned with a target. Traditionally, intelligence has been described as a cycle: from requirements to planning or direction, collection, processing, analysis and production, dissemination, then back to requirements. This traditional view has several shortcomings. It separates the customer from the process and intelligence professionals from each other. A gap exists in practice between dissemination and requirements. The traditional cycle is useful for describing structure and function and serves as a rationale for organizing and managing a large intelligence community. But it does not describe how the process works or should work.

Intelligence as a process is becoming a nonlinear and target-centric network, that is, a collaborative team of analysts, collectors, and consumers collectively focused on the intelligence target. This transition is being aided by the rapid advances in information technology.

All significant intelligence targets of this target-centric network are complex systems in that they are nonlinear, dynamic, and evolving. As such they can almost always be represented structurally as dynamic networks—opposing networks that constantly change with time. Conflict with such networks has been called netwar or network-centric conflict. In dealing with opposing networks, the intelligence network must be highly collaborative; but large intelligence organizations such as those in the United States provide disincentives to collaboration. If these disincentives can be removed, U.S. intelligence will increasingly resemble the most advanced business intelligence organizations in being both target centric and network centric.

The target of this target-centric approach for intelligence purposes is always represented as a model. The next chapter examines this model-oriented approach.

Notes

1. A *dead drop* is a temporary concealment place for material that is in transit between two clandestine intelligence operatives who cannot risk a face-to-face meeting. A tin can next to a park bench or the interior of a personable robot are classic examples of dead drops.
2. Walter D. Barndt Jr., *User-Directed Competitive Intelligence* (Westport, Conn.: Quorum Books, 1994), 21–22.
3. David Kennedy and Leslie Brunetta, "Lebanon and the Intelligence Community," case study C15-88-859.0, Kennedy School of Government Case Program, Harvard University.
4. Sherman Kent, "Producers and Consumers of Intelligence," in *Strategic Intelligence: Theory and Application,* 2d ed., ed. Douglas H. Dearth and R. Thomas Goodden (Washington, D.C.: U.S. Army War College and Defense Intelligence Agency, 1995), 129.
5. Stew Magnuson, "Satellite Data Distribution Lagged, Improved in Afghanistan," *Space News,* September 2, 2002.
6. V. Joseph Broadwater, "I Would Make the T-PED Pain Go Away," memorandum for the record (U.S. National Reconnaissance Office, Washington, D.C., August 3, 2000, photocopy).
7. Mark Bowden, "A 15-Month Manhunt Ends in a Hail of Bullets," *Philadelphia Inquirer,* December 17, 2000.
8. Magnuson, "Satellite Data Distribution."
9. Robert D. Steele, "The New Craft of Intelligence," advance review draft intended for general circulation, July 6, 2001, available from the author at bear@oss.net.
10. Mark M. Lowenthal, "Intelligence Analysis," address to the intelligence community officers' course 6-02, July 19, 2002.
11. Jamshid Gharajedaghi, *Systems Thinking: Managing Chaos and Complexity* (Boston: Butterworth-Heinemann, 1999), 110.
12. John Arquilla and David Ronfeldt, "Cyberwar Is Coming," in *Athena's Camp: Preparing for Conflict in the Information Age,* ed. John Arquilla and David Ronfeldt (Washington, D.C.: RAND Corporation, 1997).
13. David Ronfeldt and Armando Martinez, "A Comment on the Zapatista "Netwar," in *Athena's Camp,* 369.
14. Arthur K. Cebrowski and John J. Garstka, "Network-Centric Warfare: Its Origin and Future," *Naval Institute Proceedings,* www.usni.org/Proceedings/Articles98/PROcebrowski.htm, 1998.
15. Liam Fahey, *Competitors* (New York: John Wiley and Sons, 1999), 206.
16. Peter Schwartz, *The Art of the Long View* (New York: Doubleday, 1991), 90.
17. James F. Moore, *The Death of Competition: Leadership and Strategy in the Age of Business Ecosystems* (New York: HarperBusiness, 1996).
18. Cebrowski and Garstka, "Network-Centric Warfare."
19. Qiao Liang and Wang Xiangsui, *Unrestricted Warfare* (Beijing: PLA Literature and Arts Publishing House, 1999), 57.

2

A Synthesis/Analysis
Approach to the Target

*If we are to think seriously about the world, and act effectively in
it, some sort of simplified map of reality . . . is necessary.*
Samuel P. Huntington, *The Clash of Civilizations
and the Remaking of World Order*

The target-centric approach naturally leads to the creation of a model of the target.

Models are so extensively used in intelligence that analysts seldom give them much thought, even as they use them. For example:

- Imagery analysts can recognize a nuclear fuel reprocessing facility because they have a mental model of typical facility details, such as the use of heavy reinforced concrete to shield against intense gamma radiation.

- In signals intelligence (SIGINT) a communications or radar signal has standard parameters—it can be recognized because it fits an existing model in its radio frequency, its modulation parameters, its modes of operation.

- Clandestine or covert radio communications signals can be recognized because they fit a specific model: They use techniques to avoid intercept, such as very short (burst) transmissions or jumping rapidly from one radio frequency to another.

Analysis Principle ●————————————————————————————

Box 2-1   The Essence of Intelligence

All intelligence involves creating a *model* of the target and extracting knowledge therefrom. (So does all problem solving.)

- Economic analysts recognize a deteriorating economy because they have a checklist (a simple form of model) of indicators, such as budget deficit, balance of payments, and inflation.

The synthesis/analysis paradigm—synthesis being the creation of a model, analysis the extracting of knowledge from it—is a powerful tool in many disciplines. As political scientist Samuel P. Huntington noted, "if we are to think seriously about the world, and act effectively in it, some sort of simplified map of reality, some theory, concept, model, paradigm, is necessary."[1] In this book, the map, theory, concept, or paradigm is merged into a single entity called a *model*.

Modeling is usually thought of as being quantitative and using digital computers. However, all models start in the human mind. Modeling does not require a computer, and many useful models exist only on paper. Models are used widely in fields such as operations research and systems analysis. With modeling, one can analyze, design, and operate complex systems. One can use simulation models to evaluate real-world processes that are too complex to analyze with spreadsheets or flowcharts (which are themselves models, of course) to test hypotheses at a fraction of the cost of undertaking the actual activities. Models are an efficient communication tool for showing how the target functions and stimulating creative thinking about how to deal with an opponent.

Models are essential when dealing with complex targets. Without a device to capture the full range of thinking and creativity that occurs in the target-centric approach to intelligence, an analyst would have to keep in mind far too many details. Furthermore, in the target-centric approach, the customer of intelligence is part of the collaborative synthesis process. Presented with a model as an organizing construct for thinking about the target, customers can contribute pieces to the model from their own knowledge—pieces that the analyst might be unaware of. The supplier of information can do likewise.

Because the model concept is fundamental to everything that follows, it is important to define it.

The Concept of a Model

A model is a replica, or representation, of an idea, an object, or an actual system. It often describes how a system behaves. Instead of interacting with the real system, an analyst can create a model that corresponds to it in certain ways. For example, results of a political poll are a model of how a population feels about a topic; today's weather map is a model of how the weather is expected to behave.

Figure 2-1 shows a hierarchy of models and forms the basis for the discussion that follows. As the figure indicates, models can be classified as physical or conceptual (abstract).

Figure 2-1   The Model Hierarchy

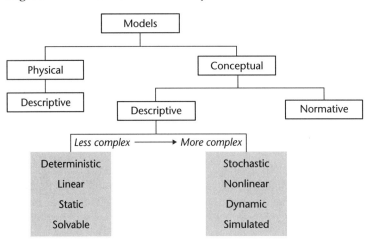

A *physical model* is a tangible representation of something. A map, a globe, a calendar, and a clock are all physical models. The first two represent the earth or parts of it, and the latter two represent time. Physical models are always descriptive.

Conceptual models—inventions of the mind—are essential to the analytical process. They allow the analyst to describe things or situations in abstract terms both for estimating current situations and for predicting future ones. A conceptual model is not a tangible item, although the item it represents may be tangible. Mathematical models are conceptual. A conceptual model may be either descriptive or normative. A normative model may contain some descriptive segments, but its purpose is to describe a best, or preferable, course of action. A decision-support model—that is, a model used to choose among competing alternatives—is normative.

In intelligence analysis, the models of most interest are conceptual and descriptive. Some common traits of these conceptual models follow.

- *Descriptive models can be deterministic or stochastic.* In a deterministic model the relationships are known and specified explicitly. A model that has any uncertainty incorporated into it is a stochastic model (meaning that probabilities are involved), even though it may have deterministic properties.[2] Consider the anecdote about drug kingpin Pablo Escobar in Chapter 1. A model of the home in which Escobar was located, and the surrounding buildings, would have been deterministic—the details were known and specified exactly. A model of the people expected to be in the house at the time of the attack would have been stochastic, because the presence or absence of Escobar and his family could not be known in advance; it could only be estimated as a probability.

- *Descriptive models can be linear or nonlinear.* Linear models use only linear equations (for example, x = Ay + B) to describe relationships. It is not necessary that the situation itself be linear, only that it be capable of description by linear equations. The number of automobiles produced in an assembly line, for example, is a linear function of time. In contrast, nonlinear models use any type of mathematical function. Because nonlinear models are more difficult to work with and are not always capable of being analyzed, the usual practice is to make some compromises so that a linear model can be used. It is important to be able to justify doing so, because most real-world intelligence targets are complex, or nonlinear. A combat simulation model is nonlinear because the interactions among the elements are complex and do not change in ways that can be described by linear equations. Attrition rates in combat, for example, vary nonlinearly with time and the status of remaining military forces. A model of an economy is inherently nonlinear; but the econometric models used to describe an economy are simplified to a set of linear equations to facilitate a solution.

- *Descriptive models can be static or dynamic.* A static model assumes that a specific time period is being analyzed and the state of nature is fixed for that time period. Static models ignore time-based variances. For example, one cannot use them to determine the impact of an event's timing in relation to other events. Returning to the example of a combat model, a snapshot of the combat showing where opposing forces are located and their direction of movement at that instant is static. Static models do not take into account the synergy of the components of a system, where the actions of separate elements can have a different effect on the system than the sum of their individual effects would indicate. Spreadsheets and most relationship models are static.

  A dynamic model, on the other hand, considers several time periods and does not ignore the impact of an action in time period 1 on time period 2. A combat simulation model is dynamic; the loss of a combat unit in time period 1 affects all succeeding time periods. Dynamic modeling (also known as simulation) is a software representation of the time-based behavior of a system. Where a static model involves a single computation of an equation, a dynamic model is iterative; it constantly recomputes its equations as time changes. It can predict the outcomes of possible courses of action and can account for the effects of variances or randomness. One cannot control the occurrence of random events. One can, however, use dynamic modeling to predict the likelihood and the consequences of their occurring. Process models usually are dynamic because they envision flows of material, the passage of time, and feedback. Structural and functional models are usually static, though they can be dynamic.

- *Descriptive models can be solvable or simulated.* A solvable model is one in which there is an analytical way of finding the answer. The performance model of a radar, a missile, or a warhead is a solvable problem. But other problems require such a complicated set of equations to describe them that there is no way to solve them. Worse still, complex problems typically cannot be described in a finite set of equations. In such cases—such as the performance of an economy or a person—one can turn to simulation. Rather than seeking the optimal solution, simulation requires the user to propose a set of possible solutions. These proposals are then introduced into the model, which typically is coded on a computer and verified for feasibility. From the courses of action chosen, the user can select the one with the best result.

  Simulation involves designing a model of a system and performing experiments on it. The purpose of these "what if" experiments is to determine how the real system performs and to predict the effect of changes to the system as time progresses. For example, an analyst can use simulation to answer questions like: What is the expected balance of trade worldwide next year? What are the likely areas of deployment for mobile surface-to-air missiles (SAMs) in country X? What is the expected yield of the nuclear warheads on country Y's new medium-range ballistic missiles?

The Synthesis/Analysis View

The target shown in Figure 2-2 comprises two parts: a knowledge base containing all the available information about the target, and a model of the target, constructed from the knowledge base. (The "model" is normally a

Figure 2-2   A Synthesis/Analysis View of the Target

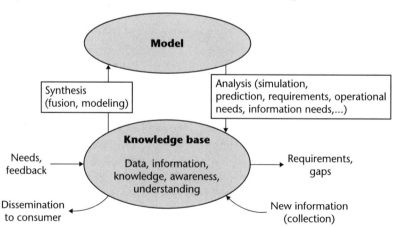

Figure 2-3   Generic Biological Weapons System Process Model

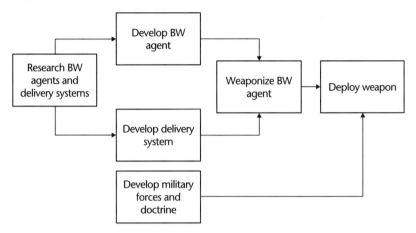

collection of interrelated models, as discussed later in this chapter.) The intelligence analyst moves back and forth between the model and the knowledge base, refining each in turn.

The creation of a model is referred to as *synthesis* (sometimes called fusion)—the creating of a whole out of its parts. *Analysis* is then the extraction of knowledge or understanding from the model. In practice, synthesis and analysis are often hard to separate and are often done concurrently. As a result, the two steps are frequently lumped together and simply called analysis, because analysts usually do both. To understand the process, though, it is important to keep a distinction between the two steps.

Let's start with an example on organizing available intelligence about a biological weapons (BW) threat. Our problem is to assess the ability of country X to produce, deploy, and use BW as a terror or combat weapon. One might start by synthesizing a generic model, or model template, based on nothing more than general knowledge of what it takes to build and use biological weaponry. Such a generic *process model* would probably look like Figure 2-3.[3]

But this generic model is only a starting point. From here, the model has to be expanded and made specific to the target (the country X BW program) in an iterative modeling process that involves the creation of more detailed models called submodels or collateral models. Let's start with a discussion of submodels and collateral models and then go into detail on the iterative nature of the process.

Submodels and Collateral Models

Like a Russian Matrushka doll, the overall target model can contain a number of more detailed component models. Participants in the target-centric process then can reach into the model set to pull out the information they need. The collectors of information can drill down into more detail to better

Figure 2-4   Biological Weapons System Test Submodel

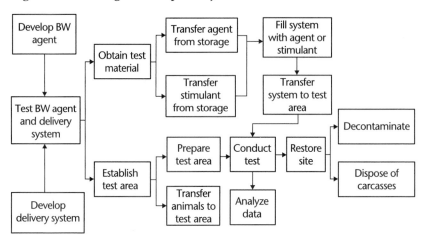

refine collection targeting and to fill specific gaps. The intelligence customer can drill down to answer questions, gain confidence in the analyst's picture of the target, and understand the limits of the analyst's work.

One type of component model is a submodel, a more detailed breakout of the top level model. Figure 2-4 illustrates a submodel of one part of the process shown in Figure 2-3.[4] In this scenario, as part of the development of the BW agent and delivery system, a test area has to be established and the agent must be tested on animals.

In contrast to the submodel, a collateral model may show particular aspects of the overall target model, but it is not simply a detailed breakout of a top-level model. A collateral model typically presents a different way of thinking about the target for a specific intelligence purpose. For example, suppose that the customer needs to know how the BW organization is managed, where the operations are located, and when the country will deploy biological weapons.

Figure 2-5 is a collateral model intended to answer the first question: How is the organization managed? The figure is a model of the BW development organization and, like most organizational models, it is structural.

Figure 2-5   Biological Weapons Development Organization Model

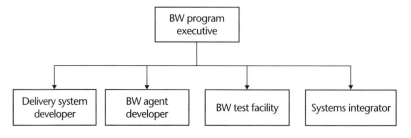

Figure 2-6 Collateral Model of Biological Weapons
Facilities in Country X

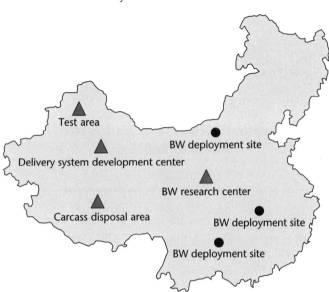

Figure 2-6 illustrates a spatial, or geographical collateral model of the BW target, answering the second question of where the BW operations are located. This type of model is useful in intelligence collection and in assessing likely usage of the deployed BW system.

Another type of collateral model of the BW target is shown in Figure 2-7—a chronological model of BW development designed to answer the question of

Figure 2-7 Chronological Model of Biological Weapons
Development

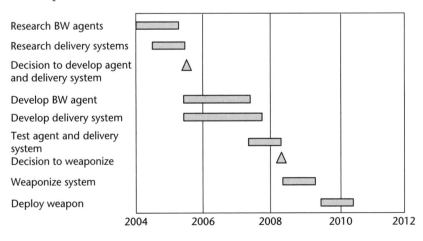

when the country will deploy biological weapons. This model also is of value to an intelligence collector for timing collection efforts and to the intelligence customer for timing political, economic, or military actions to halt or roll back the BW program.

The collateral models in Figures 2-5, 2-6, and 2-7 are examples of the three general types—structural, functional, and process—used in systems analysis. Figure 2-5 and Figure 2-6 are structural models. Figure 2-7 is both a process model and a functional model. In describing most complex intelligence targets, all three types are likely to be used.

Synthesis/Analysis as an Iterative Process of Refinement

Over time, the synthesis/analysis process of Figure 2-2 becomes an iterative process of extracting higher levels of knowledge from the target model and creating more refined models in turn. Systems synthesis/analysis must look at the three perspectives of structure, function, and process, especially in dealing with a complex system.[5] On repeating synthesis and analysis, one finds that each iteration brings out additional insights.

Figure 2-8 illustrates an example of this refinement process, progressing from raw data to intelligence as that process is defined by the National Security Agency. The idea is to progress through successively better models to a level of intelligence most useful to the intelligence customer.

As an example of how the iterative approach works, let us begin with the generic model of Figure 2-3. From this starting point, the analyst creates the test process submodel shown in Figure 2-4. Prompted by the recognition that a BW testing program must have a test site, the analyst asks

Figure 2-8   Synthesis/Analysis as an Iterative Process

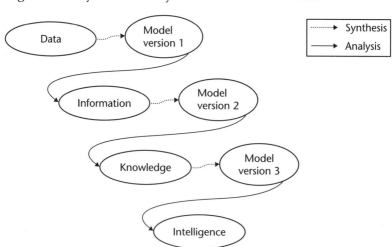

collectors to search for test areas having associated animal pens and certain patterns of biological sensor deployment near the site. The analyst also requests that the collectors search for a carcass disposal area. Assuming the collectors are successful, the analyst can create a collateral model—a map display like that shown in Figure 2-6. Based on observation of activity at the test site and disposal area, the analyst can refine the chronological model shown in Figure 2-7.

The hunt for Pablo Escobar was another example of an iterative synthesis/analysis process. The Colombian and U.S. intelligence teams created models of Escobar's cell phone communication patterns, his network of associates, and his financial structure. As new intelligence was gathered on his cartel members, cell phone numbers, bank accounts, and pattern of operations, all of these models were updated almost daily in a continuing iterative process.

Things That Should Never Go into the Model

Figure 2-2 indicates what should go into the target model. The following are some things that should be kept out. Misperceptions and biases have to be consciously examined and deliberately excluded:

- *Ethnocentric biases* involve projecting one's own cultural beliefs and expectations on others. It leads to the creation of a "mirror image" model that looks at others as one looks at oneself and to the assumption that others will act "rationally" as it is defined in one's own culture.
- *Wishful thinking* involves excessive optimism or avoiding unpleasant choices in model creation.
- *Parochial interests* cause organizational loyalties or personal background to affect the modeling process.
- *Premature closure* is a special danger in the model-based approach. Evidence that is consistent with one model does not automatically invalidate other models. In research, the experiment that doesn't turn out as expected, or the piece of data that doesn't fit with the rest, usually ends up being instructive. Information that doesn't fit into the model may be a clue that the model is wrong.[6]

Analysts have to accept that they may choose the wrong model to start with and be ready to adjust. Having competing models facilitates a successful synthesis/analysis process.

Summary

All intelligence involves creating a model of the target and extracting knowledge from that model. Models in intelligence are normally conceptual and descriptive. The easier ones to work with are deterministic, linear, static, solvable, or some combination. Unfortunately, in the intelligence business the target models tend to be stochastic, nonlinear, dynamic, and simulated.

The synthesis/analysis paradigm is the heart of the intelligence process. From an existing knowledge base, a model of the target is developed (synthesis). Then the model is analyzed to extract information for customers or for additional collection. The "model" of complex targets will normally be a collection of associated models that can serve the purposes of intelligence customers and collectors. Collateral models and submodels are examples. In an ongoing intelligence process, the analyst will continually incorporate new intelligence into the model for the purpose of refining it.

An analyst must keep the target model as close to reality as feasible. This means omitting such things as ethnocentric bias, wishful thinking, and parochial interests. The analyst must also avoid premature closure; that is, he or she must be ready to discard a model and turn to a new one if the evidence so dictates.

The number of potential models is large; the next chapter discusses the major types that intelligence analysts encounter.

Notes

1. Samuel P. Huntington, *The Clash of Civilizations and the Remaking of World Order* (New York: Simon and Schuster, 1996), 29.
2. A stochastic process is one in which the events of the process are determined by chance. Such processes are therefore analyzed using probability theory.
3. Michael G. Archuleta, Michael S. Bland, Tsu-Pin Duann, and Alan B. Tucker, "Proliferation Profile Assessment of Emerging Biological Weapons Threats," research paper, Directorate of Research, Air Command and Staff College, April 1996.
4. Ibid.
5. Jamshid Gharajedaghi, *Systems Thinking: Managing Chaos and Complexity* (Boston: Butterworth-Heinemann, 1999), 112.
6. Douglas H. Dearth, "The Politics of Intelligence," in *Strategic Intelligence: Theory and Application,* 2nd ed., ed. Douglas H. Dearth and R. Thomas Goodden (Washington, D.C.: U.S. Army War College and Defense Intelligence Agency, 1995), 106–107.

3

Creating the Model

One picture is worth more than ten thousand words.
                                                    Chinese proverb

Synthesis entails putting together parts or elements to form a model of the target. It is what intelligence analysts do, and their skill at it is a primary measure of their professional competence. The previous chapter introduced the concept of models in intelligence and provided some examples of how analysts use them. This chapter details the types of models that are commonly used to describe intelligence targets. It also discusses how the model types are created, how they are used, and some strengths and weaknesses of each type.

Creating a Conceptual Model

The first step in creating a model is to define the relevant "system" that encompasses the intelligence issues of interest. The system could be something as simple as a new fighter aircraft, a data processing center, an opium poppy field, or a new oil pipeline. However, few questions of intelligence can be answered using such a narrowly defined system. For complex targets, the analyst typically will deal with a complete system, such as an air defense system that will use the new fighter aircraft; a narcotics growing, harvesting, processing, and distribution network that the opium poppy field is part of; or an energy production system that goes from oil exploration through drilling, pumping, transportation (including the oil pipeline), refining, distribution, and retailing. Many intelligence problems will require consideration of related systems as well. The energy production system, for example, will give rise to intelligence questions about related companies, governments, suppliers and customers, and nongovernmental organizations (such as environmental advocacy groups). The questions that customers pose should be answerable by reference only to the target system, without the need to reach beyond it.

A major challenge in defining the relevant system is to use restraint. The definition must include *essential* subsystems or collateral systems, but nothing more. Part of an analyst's skill lies in being able to include in a definition the relevant components and only the relevant components. The Introduction to this book discusses the analytic abilities that help an analyst in this area.

A system, as noted in Chapter 1, can be examined structurally, functionally, or as a process. The systems model can therefore be structural, functional, process oriented, or any combination thereof. A structural model includes actors, objects, and the organization of their relationships to each other. Process models focus on interactions and their dynamics. Functional models concentrate on the results achieved—models used to simulate the combat effectiveness of a naval task force are one example.

Generic Models

After defining the relevant system, the next step is to select the generic models, or model templates, to be used. These model templates then will be made specific, or *populated,* using evidence (see Chapter 5). The generic biological weapons development model shown in Figure 2-3 is one example of a model template. This section discusses the most common types of generic models used in intelligence.

Lists

Lists and outlines are the simplest examples of a model. Benjamin Franklin favored a *parallel list* as a model for problem solving. He would list the arguments pro and con on a topic side by side, crossing off arguments on each side that held equal weight to reach a decision. The parallel list works well on a wide range of topics and remains very effective for conveying information to the customer. It is often used in intelligence for comparative analysis—for example, comparing the performance of a Russian fighter aircraft with its U.S. counterpart or contrasting two cultures.

Curves

Curves are a simple model that can be synthesized both for analysis and for presenting the results of analysis. More curves are introduced and used in later chapters, but here I will discuss one of the most common: a type of curve that projects changes over time. When experts extrapolate into the future, they often concentrate on one (or a few) forces that affect an entity, such as the economy or the environment. They then usually extrapolate some kind of disaster based on models that use the variables, leading to the *exponential* or *disaster curve* shown in Figure 3-1. The creators of the disaster curve tend to ignore or discount the ability of other variables, especially responsive or limiting factors such as human adaptivity and technology, to change at the same rate or faster. A classic older example is the exponential extrapolation of growth in telephones around 1900 that predicted that by 1920 the entire U.S. population would be working as telephone operators.[1]

Figure 3-1   The Exponential (or Disaster) Curve

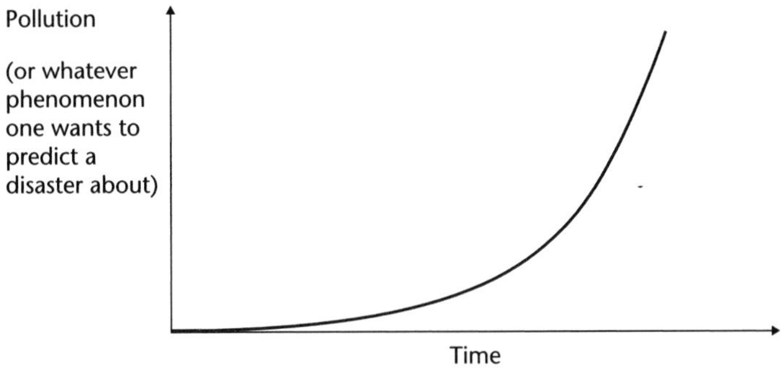

Pollution

(or whatever
phenomenon
one wants to
predict a
disaster about)

Time

Of course, the disaster curve never actually happens. An opposing reaction, feedback, contamination, or some other countervailing force steps in and retards the exponential growth curve so that an *"S" curve* results (see Figure 3-2). "S" curves occur so often in synthesis that they are revisited in Chapter 13.

Many phenomena can be modeled by the *Gaussian* or *normal curve,* shown in Figure 3-3. The intelligence of a population, variation in imagery quality, atmospheric dispersion of a chemical release, variation in securities pricing—all these and more can be represented by the normal curve. To illustrate, take the quality of a photograph. The quality of a photograph has an average value, indicated by the zero axis where the curve in Figure 3-3 peaks. But if many (say, two hundred) photographs of a scene are taken with the same camera and their quality plotted, a curve like that of Figure 3-3 results; and a few photographs will be exceptional (falling on the far right side of the curve), and a few will be poor (falling on the far left side of the curve).

Figure 3-2   The "S" Curve

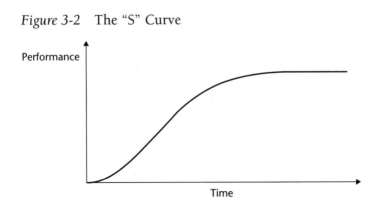

Performance

Time

Figure 3-3   The Gaussian (or Normal) Curve

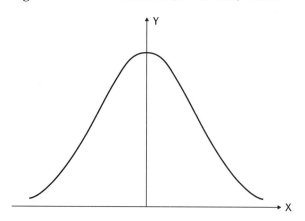

Comparative Modeling (Benchmarking)

Comparative techniques, like lists and curves, are another simple but useful form of modeling that typically do not require a computer simulation. Comparative techniques are used in government, mostly for weapons systems and technology analyses. In both governmental and business intelligence, comparative techniques are used to evaluate a competitor's operational practices, products, and technologies and are called *benchmarking.*

A powerful tool for analyzing a competitor's developments is to compare them with your own organization's developments. The analyst's own systems or technologies can provide a benchmark for comparison. One pitfall of comparative modeling is that analysts tend to rely on models that they are familiar with, such as their country's organizational or industrial process models, instead of those of the target country. Such so-called "mirror imaging" leads to many erroneous estimates. Other pitfalls of comparative techniques are discussed in Chapter 5.

Comparative models have to be culture specific to help avoid mirror imaging. A classic example of a culture-specific organization model is the *keiretsu.* The keiretsu is unique to Japan, though similar organization models exist elsewhere in Asia. A keiretsu is a network of businesses, usually in related industries, that own stakes in one another and have board members in common as a means of mutual security. A network of essentially captive (dependent on the keiretsu) suppliers provide the raw material for the keiretsu manufacturers, and the keiretsu trading companies and banks provide marketing services. Keiretsu have their roots in prewar Japan, which was dominated by four large conglomerates called Zaibatsus: Mitsubishi, Mitsui, Sumitomo, and Yasuda. The Zaibatsus were involved in areas such as steel, international trading, and banking and were controlled by a holding company.

Six keiretsu—Sumitomo, Mitsubishi, Mitsui, Dai Ichi Kangyo, Sanwa, and Fuyo—dominate Japan's economy. Most of the largest one hundred Japanese corporations are members of one or another of these "Big Six" keiretsu.[2]

An intelligence analyst who "mirror images" the keiretsu culture onto Western business practices would underestimate the close keiretsu cooperation between the supplier and manufacturer and the advantages it gives in continual product development, quality improvements, and reductions in cost. But the analyst also would miss the weaknesses inherent in a dependency relationship that shields the partners from competitive pressures, slows innovation, and eventually erodes the market position of all the keiretsu parties.

To avoid the problem of mirror imaging, it may help to create parallel models, side by side, for comparative modeling. This helps to highlight the differences between one's own company or country model and that of the target and helps to catch potential areas of mirror imaging.

Pattern Models

Many types of models fall under the broad category of pattern models. Pattern recognition is a critical element of all intelligence.[3] Most criminals and terrorists have a *modus operandi,* or standard operational pattern. Most governmental and industrial organizations (and intelligence services) also prefer to stick with techniques that have been successful in the past. An important aspect of intelligence synthesis, therefore, is recognizing patterns of activities and then determining in the analysis phase whether (a) the patterns represent a departure from what is known or expected and (b) the changes in patterns are significant enough to merit attention. The computer is a valuable ally here; it can display trends and allow the analyst to identify them, which is particularly useful in cases where trends would be difficult or impossible to find by sorting through and mentally processing a large volume of data. Pattern analysis is one way to effectively handle complex issues.

One danger in creating a pattern model is that the analyst may be tempted to find a pattern too quickly. Once a pattern has been settled on, it is easy to emphasize evidence that seems to support the pattern and to overlook, extenuate, or explain away evidence that might undermine it. The Introduction discusses how an intelligence analyst can avoid such missteps.

Here are some of the main types of pattern models used by intelligence analysts.

Statistics. Much of pattern synthesis is statistical. Intelligence deals with a wide variety of statistical modeling techniques. Some of the most useful are easy to learn and require no previous statistical training.

Almost all statistical analysis now depends on the use of digital computers. The statistical software used should provide both a broad range of statistical routines and a flexible data definition and management capability. The statistical software should have basic graphics capabilities to visually display such data as trend lines.

Figure 3-4   Histogram of Opium Production, 1988–1996

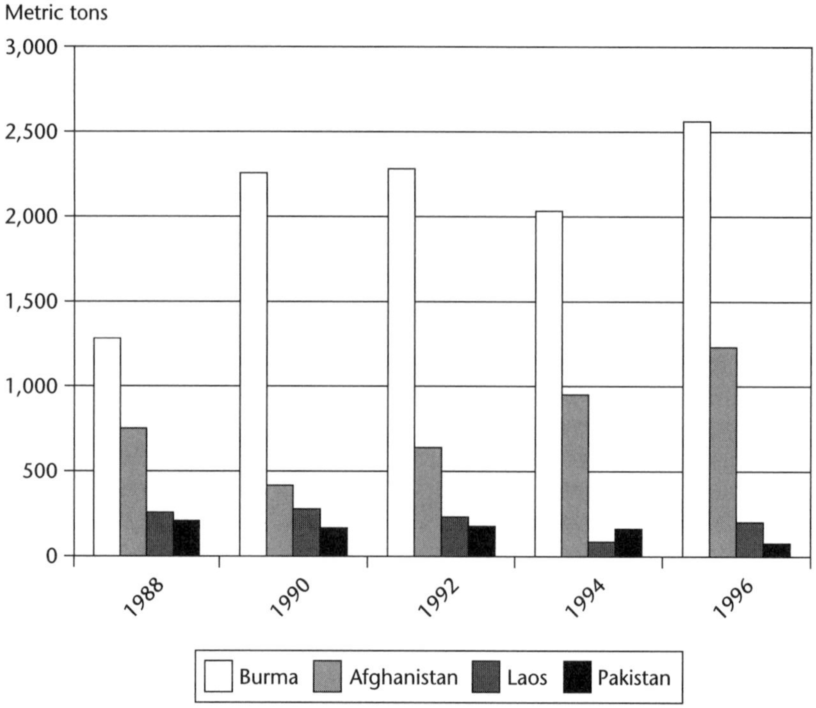

Histograms, which are bar charts that show a frequency distribution, are one example of a simple statistical pattern. An example that might be used in intelligence analysis is shown in Figure 3-4; it permits an analyst to examine patterns of opium production over time in the major producing countries.[4]

Chronological. Patterns of activity over time are important for showing trends. Pattern changes are often used to compare how things are going now with how they went last year (or last decade). Predictive analysis often relies on chronological models.

Timing shapes the consequences of planned events. In sales campaigns, military campaigns, and political campaigns, among others, timing is critical to making an impact. An opponent's strategy often becomes apparent only when seemingly disparate events are placed on a timeline.[5] Consider, for example, the chronological model shown in Figure 3-5. The timeline shows the expected actions of a hypothetical European electronics manufacturer that is building a missile guidance system destined for shipment to a Middle Eastern country.

Such a model can be used to predict an opponent's actions and to time future counteractions. In the example of Figure 3-5, the model could be used by the analyst country's government to block shipment of the guidance system or to disrupt the payment arrangements.

Figure 3-5   Chronological Model of a Firm's Expected
External Actions

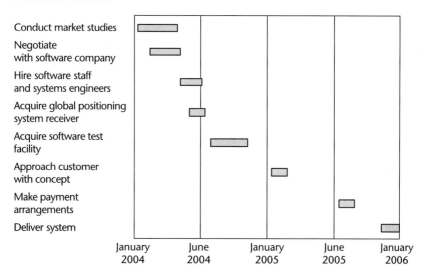

Event-time patterns such as Figure 3-5 tell analysts a great deal; they allow analysts to infer relationships among events and to examine trends. Activity patterns of a target network, for example, are useful in determining the best time to collect intelligence. An example is a plot of total telephone usage over twenty-four hours—the plot peaks around 11 a.m., which is the most likely time for a person to be on the telephone.

Figure 3-6 shows an example of a type of time series data analysis that is useful in satellite-based SIGINT or imagery intelligence (IMINT) collection planning. The horizontal axis is calibrated in months over the period of one year; the vertical axis is calibrated in hours of the day over a twenty-four-hour period (in Greenwich mean time). The dark areas show the visibility from a specific low orbiting satellite to Bermuda during the year, and the horizontal curved lines near 1100 and 2300 GMT show the points of sunrise and sunset at Bermuda during the year, establishing the limits of daylight. If the satellite were carrying a visible-imaging camera, then the shaded areas during daylight would indicate opportunities for imagery collection (or conversely, the unshaded areas would indicate when operations on Bermuda could be carried out unobserved). Such time pattern correlations are best done with the help of computers. Several commercial software packages are well designed for computing and displaying time series data.

Geospatial. Another way to examine data and to search for patterns is to use geospatial modeling. Geospatial modeling typically uses electronically stored maps (of the world, of regions, of cities) to display geographically oriented data. These displays are valuable for visualizing complex spatial

Figure 3-6   Satellite Visibility over Bermuda by Month and Hour

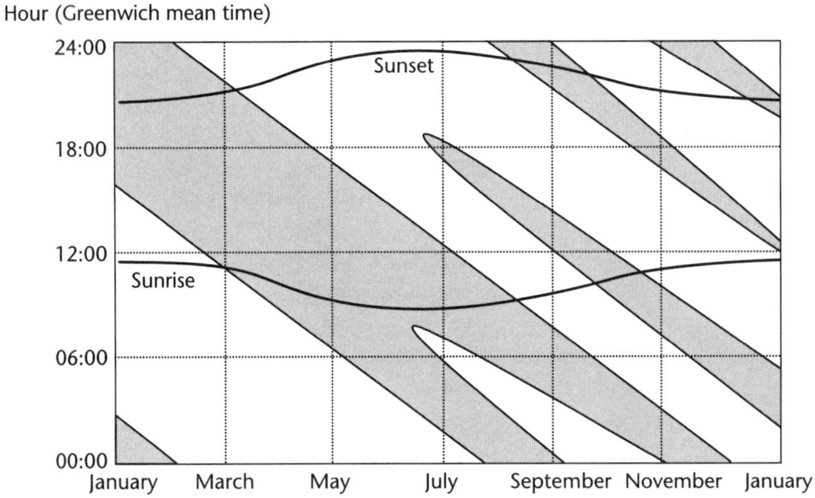

Hour (Greenwich mean time)

Note: Shaded areas mark days and times when activity on Bermuda is visible from a typical low-orbit satellite.

relationships. Networks often can be best understood by examining them in geospatial terms. Target movement patterns often show best on such a display. Figure 3-7 shows a hypothetical example of a Pakistani communications network map that might be used for analysis of network vulnerability points.

Geospatial displays of local areas, such as cities, facilitate a number of analytic inferences. For example, two buildings located within a common security fence can be presumed to have related functions; whereas, if the two buildings were protected by separate security fences, no such presumption would follow.

Spatial modeling can be used effectively on a much smaller scale. Within a building, computer aided design/computer aided modeling, known as CAD/CAM, can be a powerful tool for intelligence synthesis. Layouts of buildings and floor plans are valuable in physical security analysis and in assessing production capacity, for example. CAD/CAM is useful both in collection and in counterintelligence on a facility. CAD/CAM can be used to create a physical security profile of a facility, allowing an analyst to identify vulnerabilities by examining floor plans, construction details, and electronic and electrical connections.

Relationship Models

Relationship models among entities—people, places, things, and events—are perhaps the most common subject of intelligence synthesis. The most

Figure 3-7   Geospatial Model of a Pakistani Communications Network

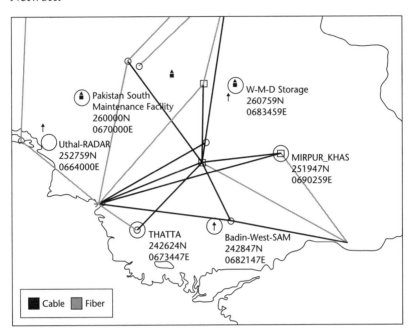

general intelligence problem is to define and analyze relationships among target elements—organizations, people, places, and physical objects—over time.

There are four levels of relationship models, each using increasingly sophisticated analytic approaches: hierarchy, link, matrix, and network models. The four are closely related and in fact represent the same fundamental idea of relationship modeling at increasing levels of complexity. The hierarchy model is a simple tree structure. A link model allows the view of relationships in more complex tree structures. Matrix models show the interrelationship of two or more tree structures at a given level. A network model can be thought of as a flexible interrelationship of multiple tree structures at multiple levels.

Relationship models require a considerable amount of time to create, and maintaining the model (known to those who do it as "feeding the beast") demands much effort. But such models are highly effective in analyzing complex problems, and the associated graphical displays are very powerful in persuading customers to accept the results.

Hierarchy Models. Hierarchies are used extensively and almost intuitively in synthesis and analysis. Their primary application is to deconstruct a large or complex object—such as a project, an organization, or a weapons system—into its component parts. One example of a hierarchy model of a project is

Figure 3-8   A Hierarchy Target Model

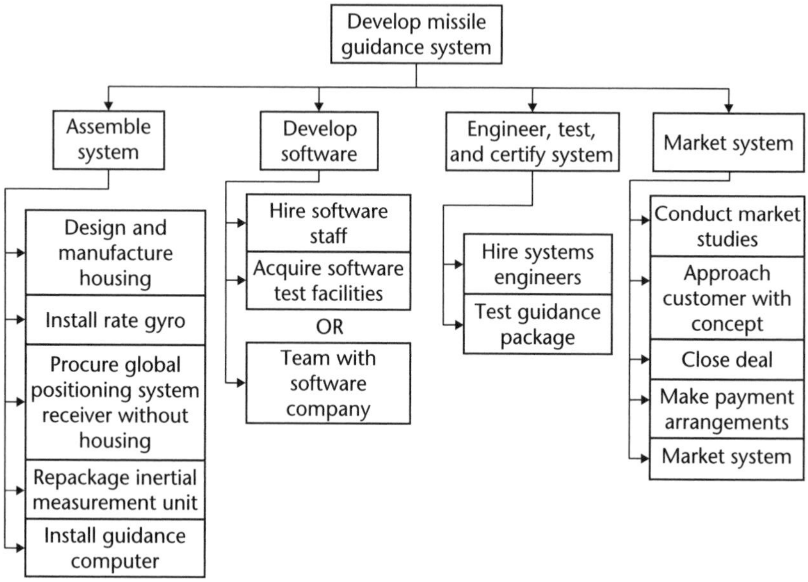

shown in Figure 3-8. It is drawn from a target that was introduced earlier in this chapter—an electronics manufacturer developing a missile guidance system. The objective is to develop a missile guidance system, as indicated by the highest box. In the second tier are four major tasks that an intelligence analyst has identified as necessary for system development and sale to the Middle Eastern country. Below that are a number of lower-level tasks that would be the subject of intelligence collection and synthesis.[6]

Organizational modeling naturally lends itself to the creation of a hierarchy, as anyone who ever drew an organizational chart is aware. A natural extension of such a hierarchy is to use a weighting scheme to indicate the importance of individuals or suborganizations in the organizational hierarchy.

A more sophisticated version of the hierarchy is the relevance tree, which is used in technology forecasting. Figure 3-9 shows an example of a relevance tree that subdivides chemical warfare agents according to their physiological effects.

This particular type of relevance tree is referred to as *object oriented*—a term that now is widely used in software programming and which has much the same meaning in both disciplines. Here, *object oriented* means that the tree is subdivided into distinct objects (in Figure 3-9, specifically, types of chemical warfare agents). Relevance trees have many varieties: objectives trees, decision trees, alternatives trees, and resource allocation trees. Examples of some of these are discussed elsewhere in the book.

Figure 3-9   A Chemical Warfare Relevance Tree

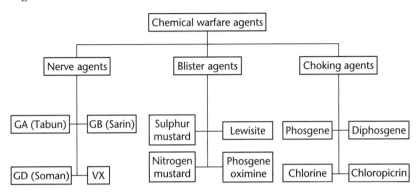

Link and Social Network Models. One of the most powerful tools in the analyst's toolkit is link modeling and analysis, along with its more sophisticated cousin, network modeling and analysis. Link models have demonstrated their value in discerning the complex and typically circuitous ties between entities. Link models are closely related to hierarchy models; in fact, some types of link diagrams are referred to as *horizontal relevance trees.*[7] Their essence is the graphical representation of:

- Nodes and their connection patterns, or
- Entities and relationships.

Link modeling has a long history; the Los Angeles police department reportedly used it first in the 1940s as a tool for assessing organized crime networks. Its primary purpose was to display relationships among people or between people and events. Today link modeling is routinely used in government intelligence and law enforcement to identify narcotics trafficking groups, terrorists, and espionage groups. It has been applied in sociology, anthropology, law enforcement, and in the analysis of communications networks.

Most humans simply cannot assimilate all the information collected on a topic over the course of several years. Yet a typical goal of intelligence synthesis/ analysis is to develop precise, reliable, and valid inferences (hypotheses, estimations, and conclusions) from the available data for use in strategic decisionmaking or operational planning. Link models directly support such inferences.

Before the 1970s link modeling was an arduous and time-consuming endeavor because graphical "trees" had to be constructed on paper. Computer software has contributed to the recent expansion of link synthesis/analysis. Software tools simplify the process by allowing the relational storage of data as it comes in and by graphically displaying different types of relationships among the entities.

The primary purpose of link modeling is to facilitate the organization and presentation of data to assist the analytic process. A major part of many assessments is the analysis of relationships among people, organizations, locations, and things. Once the relationships have been created in a database system, they can be displayed and analyzed quickly in a link analysis program. Figure 3-10 illustrates part of a link display that was drawn from an actual case study on funds laundering operations involving Citibank private bank accounts belonging to Mohammed, Ibrahim, and Abba Sani Abacha. The three men are sons of General Sani Abacha, the dictator who controlled Nigeria from 1993 until his death in 1998. General Abacha is believed to have taken more than $3.5 billion from the Nigerian treasury during the five years that he was in power.[8] The figure illustrates some of the relationships involved in laundering the funds the general stole. As with generalized network models, this is a generalized link model; it includes people, banks, companies, government organizations, and bank accounts.

Figure 3-10 shows the importance of being able to see second- and third-order links in pattern synthesis/analysis. Relationships that are not

Figure 3-10   Financial Relationships in a Link Model

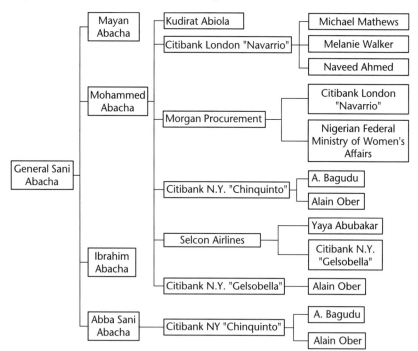

Note: These entities are persons, organizations, and bank accounts whose relationships are defined in Figure 3-11.

apparent when each piece of evidence is examined separately become obvious when link displays are used.

To be useful in intelligence analysis, the links should not only identify relationships among data items but should show the nature of the relationships (see Figure 3-11). A subject-verb-object display has been used in the intelligence community for several years to show the nature of relationships, and it is sometimes used in link displays. A typical subject-verb-object relationship from Figure 3-10 would read: "Mohammed Abacha (subject) owns (verb) Selcon Airlines (object)." This is a positive relationship, and needs to be distinguished from negative relationships such as the one between Mohammed Abacha and Kudirat Abiola (Abacha was charged with Abiola's murder).

Quantitative relationships and time (date stamping) relationships are also used when the link software has a filtering capability. Filters allow the user to focus on relationships of interest and can simplify by several orders of magnitude the data that is shown in a link display. For example, the user could select Morgan Procurement as the root (the start, or left side, of the link diagram) in Figure 3-10 and display a link chart of all the group and personal associations of Morgan Procurement. The user could then use the filters and display the Morgan Procurement network of associations for a specific date range (say, 1995–1998) and only associations with Swiss banks.

Matrix Models. When attempting to analyze the relationships between two hierarchies, one typically takes each hierarchy to the necessary level of detail and then arrays the two in a two-dimensional matrix. The result is the interaction matrix, a valuable analytic tool for certain types of synthesis. It appears in various disciplines and under different names and is also called a parametric matrix or a traceability matrix.[9] An interaction matrix has been used successfully, for example, to analyze the likely effect of electronics warfare techniques against specific systems. Consider a surface-to-air missile (SAM) system. It typically has a target acquisition radar that identifies hostile air targets; a target tracking radar that pinpoints the aircraft location, speed, and direction of movement; a sensor on the missile to help it home in on the target; and transmitters and receivers on the ground and on the missile so that guidance commands can be sent to the missile and missile status information returned to the ground. One can identify a set of possible countermeasures that might defeat the SAM system: jammers, aircraft maneuvers, decoys, and antiradiation missiles. The two sets are combined in a matrix of countermeasures against target system components, sometimes called a vulnerability matrix. An example interaction matrix is shown in Table 3-1, where a checked box indicates that the countermeasure can be effective against the indicated component of the SAM system.

An interaction matrix can also be quantitative, where the checked boxes in the matrix of Table 3-1 might be replaced with color coding, numbers, or some other indicator of magnitude of interaction. A quantitative interaction

Table 3-1   Interaction Matrix for Electronic Warfare

	Surface-to-air missile system components				
Countermeasure	Target acquisition radars	Target tracking radar	Missile seeker	Missile guidance uplink	Missile data downlink
On-board jammers		x	x		x
Maneuvers and tactics	x	x	x		
Expendables (decoys or chaff)	x	x	x		
Antiradiation missiles	x	x		x	

Note: Checked boxes indicate where a countermeasure would be effective against a missile system component.

matrix naturally fits into many of the commercially available decision support software packages. It is typically used to ensure that all possible alternatives are considered in problem solving.

In economic intelligence and scientific and technical intelligence, it is often important to assess the impact of an industrial firm's efforts to acquire other companies. One model for assessing the likely outcome of a merger or acquisition uses the five criteria that Cisco Systems uses to look at possible acquisitions. The criteria are listed in the first column of Table 3-2.[10] In this

Table 3-2   Matrix for Merger and Acquisition Analysis

	Score (0–9)		
Merger and acquisition criteria	Company A	Company B	Company C
Shared vision of where the industry is heading and complementary roles each company wants to play in it	3	7	1
Similar cultures and chemistry	5	5	0
A winning proposition for acquired employees, at least over the short term	2	1	8
A winning proposition for shareholders, employees, customers, and business partners over the long term	5	4	6
Geographic proximity, particularly for large acquisitions	0	9	4

Note: Higher scores equate to better performance against the criteria.

interaction matrix model, the three candidates for acquisition are ranked 0 to 9 on how well they meet each criterion (0 is the lowest score, 9 the highest). This merger and acquisition model has potential applications outside the commercial world. In 1958 it would have been a useful tool, for example, to assess the prospects for success of the "merger" that year between Syria and Egypt that created the United Arab Republic. The proposed "merger" would not have fared well against any of the criteria in Table 3-2—even the one on similar cultures.

Network Models. The key limitation of the matrix model is that it can deal with the interaction of two hierarchies at a given level, but being a two-dimensional representation, it cannot deal with interactions at multiple levels or with more than two hierarchies. Network synthesis is an extension of the link or matrix synthesis concept that can handle such complex problems. There are at least three types of network models.

- *Communications network models* are used by communications engineers to design and predict the performance of telecommunications networks. The nodes are communications terminals, and the links are channels through which data flow (for example, microwave point-to-point, fiber optic, or radio frequency cable lines).
- *Social network models* show patterns of human relationships. The nodes are people, and the links show that some type of relationship exists.
- *Generalized network models* are most useful in intelligence. The nodes can be any type of entity—people, places, things, concepts—and the links show that some type of relationship exists between entities.

Figure 3-11 is a modified version of Figure 3-10, redrawn as a network model with some additional information that has analytic value. Nodes are shaded to indicate type—bank accounts and bank employees in dark gray, other persons unshaded, and organizations in light gray. Relationships are shown as either positive (solid links) or negative (dashed links). Strength of relationship is shown by the thickness of the linkage line. Additional techniques can convey more information—making the links dotted to indicate a suspected relationship, for example, or making nodes larger or smaller to indicate relative importance in the model. Of course, many of the same techniques can be used in link models, too.

Link and network modeling have been successfully applied in the U.S. intelligence community to assess counterterrorism, counternarcotics, clandestine arms traffic, weapons proliferation, associating research and development groups with foreign weapons systems development, and similar relationship

Figure 3-11   Financial Relationships Network Model

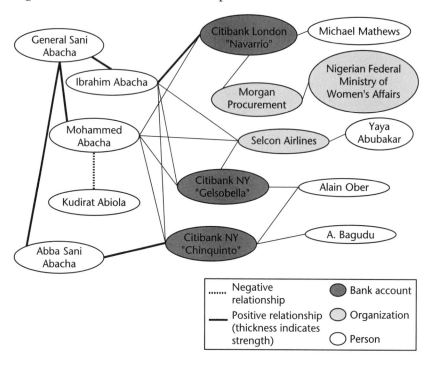

synthesis and analysis problems. Link and network modeling are indispensable tools in military intelligence for targeting and for planning combat strategies and tactics. Simpler problems are appropriate for link modeling; complex problems usually demand network models.

Profiles

Profiles are models of key individuals—heads of government or top executives in an organization. The purpose of creating profiles usually is to help predict what the key person will do in a given set of circumstances.[11] Chapter 12 discusses the use of profiles for prediction.

The pattern of mental and behavioral traits shared by adult members of a society is referred to as the society's *modal personality.* Several modal personality types may exist in a given society, and their common elements are often referred to as *national character* (see Box 3-1).

Defining the modal personality type is beyond the capabilities of the journeyman intelligence analyst, and one must turn to experts. This section contains only a brief overview of the topic of behavioral profiles to indicate its importance in the overall decision modeling problem, discussed in Chapter 12.

Box 3-1   National Character

A recurring story that reflects widely held—if tongue-in-cheek—views of national character goes:

Paradise is where	*Hell is where*
the cooks are French	the cooks are British
the mechanics are German	the mechanics are French
the police are British	the police are German
the lovers are Italian	the lovers are Swiss
and the Swiss organize everything.	and the Italians organize everything.

The modal personality model usually includes at least the following elements:

- Concept of self—the conscious ideas of what a person thinks he is, and his frequently unconscious motives and defenses against ego-threatening experiences such as withdrawal of love, public shaming, guilt, or isolation,
- Relation to authority—how an individual adapts to authority figures.
- Modes of impulse control and expressing emotion.
- Processes of forming and manipulating ideas.

Three model types are often used for studying modal personalities and creating behavioral profiles.

- *Cultural pattern models* are relatively straightforward to analyze (see Chapter 12) and are useful in assessing group behavior. They have less value in the assessment of an individual. Cultural patterns are derived from political behavior, religious idea systems, art forms, mass media, folklore, and similar collective activities.
- *Child-rearing systems* can be studied to allow the projection of adult personality patterns and behavior. They may allow more accurate assessments of an individual than a simple study of cultural patterns, but they cannot account for the wide range of possible pattern variations occurring after childhood.
- *Individual assessments* are probably the most accurate starting points for creating a behavioral model, but they depend on detailed data about the specific individual. Such data is usually gathered from testing techniques; the Rorschach (or "Inkblot") test—a projective personality assessment based on the subject's reactions to a series of ten inkblot pictures—is an example.

However, test data is seldom available on individuals of interest to the intelligence business; usually, fragmented data such as anecdotal evidence, graphology (handwriting analysis), or the writings and speeches of individuals (*Mein Kampf, The Thoughts of Chairman Mao*) must be used to construct a modal personality picture.

Another model template for individual personality assessments is the Myers-Briggs Type Indicator. It assigns people to one of sixteen different categories or types. There are four different subscales of Myers-Briggs that purport to measure different personality tendencies. As with other test-based assessments, the trick is to get test results on the target individual.

Process Models

A process model—one that describes a sequence of events or activities that produce results—can be an open or closed loop. Feedback is the difference, as Figure 3-12 illustrates. Most processes and most process models have feedback loops. Feedback allows the system to be adaptive—that is, to adjust its inputs based on the output. Even simple systems such as a home heating/air conditioning system provide feedback via a thermostat. For complex systems, feedback is essential to prevent the process from producing undesirable output. Feedback is such an important part of both synthesis and analysis that it receives detailed treatment in Chapter 11.

Business process reengineering uses process models like that shown in Figure 3-13. In this display, the process nodes are separated by function into "swim lanes" to facilitate analysis. This model is based on the example, previously introduced, of an electronics manufacturer developing a missile guidance system.[12]

Chapter 2 introduced the iterative process of model improvement using new intelligence. Figure 3-14 shows a hypothetical example of this sort of iterative modeling that can be done using a business process model. In this example, the original model envisioned the electronics manufacturer as hiring software staff to support software development and purchasing a global

Figure 3-12   A Simple Process Model

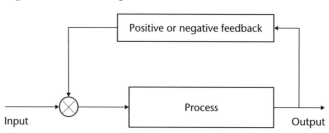

Note: The encircled X shows where the input and the feedback combine before they feed into the process.

Figure 3-13   Business Process Model for a Missile Guidance System

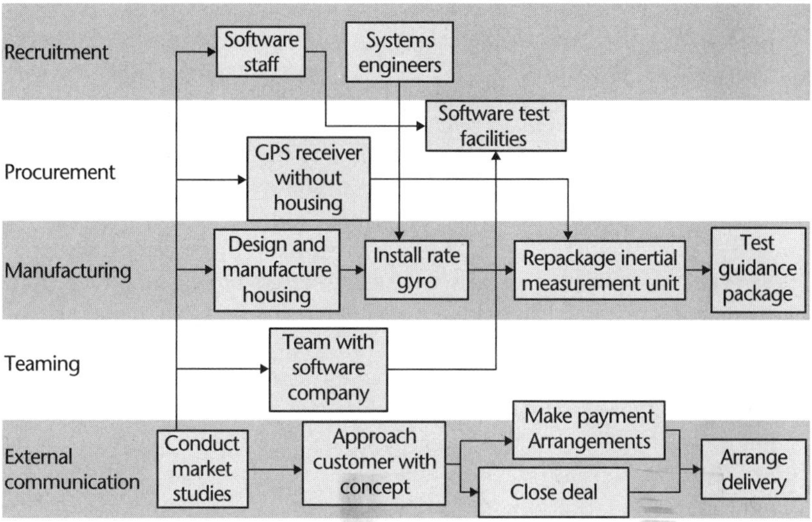

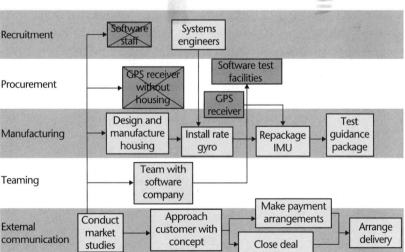

Note: GPS stands for *global positioning system.*

positioning system (GPS) receiver from an external source. Suppose that the analyst later receives evidence that the company is neither hiring software staff nor trying to acquire a GPS receiver externally. The analyst then revises the model to delete these two blocks and add a new one showing the analyst's estimate of internal manufacture of a GPS receiver. The analyst then must

Figure 3-14   Analysis Using the Business Process Model

estimate whether software test facilities will be procured or whether the manufacturer will rely on those of its partner software company.

Simulation

Simulation models are mathematical descriptions of the interrelationships believed to determine a system's behavior. As noted earlier, simulations
differ from other types of models in that the equations they comprise cannot
be solved simultaneously. One usually goes to simulation modeling when it is
impossible or impractical to write or measure all of the variables necessary to
solve the set of simultaneous equations that would fully describe a system.

In general, simulation models are most useful in making long-range forecasts where exact numerical estimates are not needed. Simulation models usually are most effective when used to compare the impact of alternative scenarios
(of policy decisions or natural phenomena, for example).

Simulation may be used in either a stochastic or a deterministic situation.
A simple spreadsheet is a deterministic model; the inputs are fixed by the
numbers in the spreadsheet cells, only one solution appears, and the input
numbers must be changed to get another answer. Where there is uncertainty
about the proper input numbers, stochastic simulation is used. The computer
"rolls the dice" to assign a value to each uncertain input and obtain an answer;
then many repeated "dice rolls" are made to obtain a range of answers. The resulting simulation model has been named a "Monte Carlo" model, after the
gambling capital of Monaco.

The challenge of the Monte Carlo simulation is to select the right type of
uncertainty for the input variables. All uncertain variables have a probability
distribution. A single six-sided die roll has what is called a uniform distribution; the chance of a 1 coming up is the same as the chance of a 2, or a 3.
When two dice are rolled, the distribution is not uniform; 7 is much more
likely to occur than 2 or 12. If the wrong probability distribution is chosen for
the input, the stochastic simulation will produce the wrong answer.

Simulation models are typically classified as either continuous, discrete
event, or hybrid continuous and discrete event.

- In *continuous simulations* the system changes with time. A driverless
  automobile rolling down a hill is an example of a continuous system;
  changes in the speed of the automobile occur continuously with
  time. This would also be a deterministic simulation, since the automobile speed at any time can be predicted by standard equations.

- In *discrete event models,* the system changes state as events occur in
  the simulation. An automobile parked on a hill could be modeled
  as a series of discrete events. The first discrete event would be
  when the parking brake spontaneously releases and the automobile begins moving down slope. The second discrete event would
  be when the automobile hits a tree and stops. This is also a

stochastic simulation, since it requires establishing the probability that the parking brake will spontaneously release and the probability of hitting the tree.

- *Hybrid models* are a combination of the two. A hybrid model of the automobile case would have two discrete event simulations—the beginning and end of the automobile's travel downhill—with a continuous event simulation of the travel in between.

Equations as Models. The most common modeling problem involves solving an equation. The equation is perhaps the simplest form of a simulation model. Most problems in engineering or technical intelligence are single equations of the form

$$f(x, y, z, t, ..., a, b, c, ...) = 0$$

or are systems of equations of this form. Systems of equations are particularly prevalent in econometric synthesis/analysis; single equations are common in radar, communications, and electronic warfare performance analysis.

Most analysis involves fixing all of the variables and constants in such an equation or system of equations, except for two variables. The equation is then solved repetitively to obtain a graphic picture of one variable as a function of another. A number of software packages perform this type of solution very efficiently. As an example, as a part of radar performance analysis, the radar range equation is solved for signal-to-noise ratio as a function of range, and a two-dimensional curve is plotted. Then, perhaps, signal-to-noise ratio is fixed and a new curve plotted for radar cross-section as a function of range.

Often the requirement is to solve an equation, get a set of ordered pairs, and plug into another equation to get a graphic picture rather than solving simultaneous equations.

The computer is a powerful tool for handling the equation solution type of problem. Spreadsheet software has provided us with an easy-to-use capability to create equation-based models. The rich set of mathematical functions that can be incorporated in a spreadsheet, and the spreadsheet's flexibility, make spreadsheet models possibly the most widely used models in intelligence.

Econometric Modeling. An econometric model is a quantitative description of an economic system. It incorporates a number of hypotheses on how economic systems function. Econometric models are sets of simultaneous linear equations used for macroeconomic analysis, and the number of equations can be very large. The models are widely used in both the financial and intelligence communities. Intelligence applications include trade, balance of payments, and worldwide energy analysis models.

Economic modeling also makes use of input-output modeling, a procedure in which the output product of an industrial sector is set equal to the input consumption of that product by other industries and consumers. Unlike many other models, input-output models are often very disaggregated and can, therefore, show more cause-effect relationships. Input-output models can be interpreted in terms of block diagrams and matrix algebra techniques. Input-output modeling has been applied to a variety of economic policy analysis and forecasting problems.

Combination Models

Most of the models described in the previous sections can be merged into combination models. One example is a relationship-time display: a dynamic model where link or network relationship lines become thicker (strengthen) or thinner (weaken) over time, and nodes change size or disappear.

A widely used combination is the space-time model. Many activities, such as the movement of a satellite, a ship, or an aircraft, can best be shown spatially. A combination of geographic and time synthesis/analysis can show movement patterns, such as those of people or of ships at sea. For example, merchant ships radio their geographic positions least daily. If a ship begins to transmit false position data, as revealed by independent means such as electronic intelligence (ELINT) or radar geolocation, it becomes a target of intelligence interest. If the ship's track does not fit a normal operating profile, for example, if it takes several days to move only a few miles, then alert analysts will begin to investigate whether the ship could have reached a nearby port for an unscheduled stop in that time frame.

Figure 3-15 shows an example of a ship tracking display for the Russian ship *Akademik Tupolev* during part of a voyage in 1990. The positions of the

Figure 3-15   Ship Tracking—A Combination (Space-Time) Model

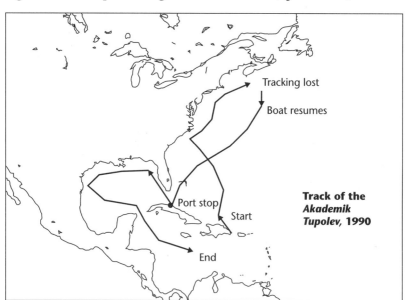

ship, taken alone, have no special significance; but the pattern of its movements close to the U.S. coastline, the delays in its progress, its "disappearances," and a correlation of the ship's position with other intelligence reports might reveal much. The *Turpolev* started its journey in the Dominican Republic, then moved north along the East Coast of the United States. Tracking was lost for about two days at the ship's northernmost point near Nova Scotia but resumed when the ship turned south toward Havana for a port stop, then moved on to the Caribbean.

The most widely used combination model, and probably the most important for intelligence purposes, is the scenario. Chapter 9 discusses this very sophisticated model.

Summary

Creating a target model starts with defining the relevant system. The system model can be a structural, functional, or process model, or any combination. The next step is to select the generic models or model templates.

Lists and curves are the simplest form of model. In intelligence, comparative models or benchmarks are often used; almost any type of model can be made comparative, typically by creating models of one's own system side by side with the target system model.

Pattern models are widely used in the intelligence business. Chronological models allow intelligence customers to examine the timing of related events and plan a way to change the course of these events. Geospatial models are popular in military intelligence for weapons targeting and to assess the location and movement of opposing forces.

Relationship models are used to analyze the relationships among elements of the target—organizations, people, places, and physical objects—over time. Four general types of relationship models are commonly used: hierarchy, link, matrix, and network models. The most powerful of these, network models, are increasingly used to describe complex intelligence targets.

Simulation models are also extensively used to describe complex targets. Simulation modeling can range in complexity from the simple equation to a sophisticated econometric model.

Profiles of leaders and key executives are used to predict decisions. Such profiles rely on the ability of the analyst to define the modal personality type. Process models, which describe a sequence of events or activities that produce results, are often used to assess the progress of a development project. The next two chapters discuss how to populate the model templates defined in this chapter.

Notes

1. In one sense, this turned out to be an accurate prediction. By the 1970s almost all telephones were either dial or pushbutton operated. As a result, almost all Americans over the age of ten are part-time telephone "operators" in the sense of the original extrapolation.
2. "Facts from the Corporate Planet: Ecology and Politics in the Age of Globalization," www.wired.com/news/business/0,1367,8918,00.html, October 23, 2002.

3. M.S. Loescher, C. Schroeder, and C.W. Thomas, *Proteus: Insights from 2020* (Utrecht, Netherlands: Copernicus Institute Press, 2000), 25.

4. U.S. State Department, "Estimated Worldwide Potential: Illicit Drug Net Production, 1987–1998, www.state.gov/www/global/narcotics_law/1998_narc_report/wdprod98.xls, August 2, 2002.

5. Loescher, Schroeder, and Thomas, *Proteus,* 24.

6. Michael C. O'Guin and Timothy Olgivie, "The Science, Not Art, of Business Intelligence," *Competitive Intelligence Review,* 12 (4): 15–24, 2001.

7. William L. Swager, "Perspective Trees: A Method of Creatively Using Forecasts," in *A Practical Guide,* ed. Bright and Schoeman, 165.

8. Minority Staff Report for Permanent Subcommittee on Investigations—Hearing on Private Banking and Money Laundering: A Case Study of Opportunities and Vulnerabilities, November 9, 1999, http://levin.senate.gov/issues/psireport2.htm.

9. Theodore J. Gordon and M.J. Raffensperger, "The Relevance Tree Method for Planning Basic Research," in *A Practical Guide,* ed. Bright and Schoeman, 134.

10. Michelle Cook and Curtis Cook, "Anticipating Unconventional M&As: The Case of Daimler-Chrysler," *Competitive Intelligence Magazine,* January-February 2001.

11. Carolyn M. Vella and John J. McGonagle, "Profiling in Competitive Analysis," *Competitive Intelligence Review,* 11 (2), second quarter 2000: 20.

12. Michael C. O'Guin and Timothy Olgivie, "The Science, Not Art, of Business Intelligence," *Competitive Intelligence Review,* 12 (4), 2001: 15–24.

4

Sources of Intelligence Information

Stand by your sources; they will repay you.
R. V. Jones, assistant director of Britain's Royal Air Force Intelligence Section during World War II

Adding substance to the models discussed in the previous chapter is a matter of information gathering and synthesis. This chapter focuses on the sources of data and how to use the information from those sources.

The automation of data handling has been a major boon to intelligence analysts. Information collected from around the globe arrives at the analyst's desk via the Internet or in electronic message form, ready for review and often presorted based on keyword searches. A downside of this automation is the tendency to treat all information in the same way. In some cases the analyst does not even know what collection source provided the information; after all, everything looks alike on the display screen. Furthermore, analysts tend to rely too much on what shows up "automatically." They too seldom try to stimulate collectors, and thereby they restrict the breadth or focus of what flows to them.

Information must be treated differently depending on its source. Analytical success requires understanding where to acquire data and the limits and pitfalls of the information available from the sources discussed in this chapter. A single data source seldom provides everything an analyst needs to synthesize a model of a complex target. Rather, a wide range of classified and unclassified sources must be called on—in part to reduce the chances of being misled by a single source.

Information gathering begins with the existing knowledge base. Before starting an intelligence collection effort, analysts should ensure that they are aware of what has already been found on a subject. Finished studies or reports on file at an analyst's organization are the best place to start any research effort. There are few truly new issues. The databases of intelligence organizations include finished intelligence reports, the full text of raw intelligence reporting, as well as many specialized data files on specific topics. Large commercial firms typically have comparable facilities in house or they depend on commercially available databases. Once the finished reports are in hand, the analyst should review all of the relevant *raw* data that already exists. Few things can ruin an analyst's career faster than sending collectors after information that is already in the organization's files. This does not mean that existing intelligence should be accepted as fact. Few experienced analysts would blithely accept the results of earlier studies on a topic, but they would know exactly what the studies found.

Introduction to Intelligence Sources

For bureaucratic reasons or because of historical precedent, most texts organize their discussion of intelligence sources according to the current U.S. perspective on intelligence collection that is depicted in Box 4-1. This chapter presents an alternative view of the sources of intelligence, one that has more relevance for intelligence analysts.

Collection organizations in large intelligence communities (United States, United Kingdom, Russia, China) are of necessity specialized; that is, they are optimized to collect information from one specific class of sources—imagery, radio signals, or human sources, for example. Because of this specialization, collection organizations are often called *stovepipes,* invoking the metaphor of a tightly controlled channel that has only one function. The metaphor is best not followed too far, because the only product that a stovepipe disgorges is smoke.

The U.S. intelligence community has divided the collection methods using the "INT" (short for *intelligence*) guilds to protect equities—that is, to define the areas of collection responsibility of large collection organizations such as the National Imagery and Mapping Agency and the National Security Agency. The current U.S. taxonomy is shown in Box 4-1.

Box 4-1   The U.S. Collection Taxonomy

Signals Intelligence (SIGINT): Intelligence comprising either individually or in combination all communications intelligence, electronics intelligence, and foreign instrumentation signals intelligence.

Imagery Intelligence (IMINT): Intelligence derived from the exploitation of collection by visual photography, infrared sensors, lasers, electrooptics, and radar sensors such as synthetic aperture radar wherein images of objects are reproduced optically or electronically on film, electronic display devices, or other media.

Human Intelligence (HUMINT): Intelligence derived from information collected and provided by human sources.

Measurements and Signatures Intelligence (MASINT): Scientific and technical intelligence obtained by quantitative and qualitative analysis of data (metric, angle, spatial, wavelength, time dependence, modulation, plasma, and hydromagnetic) derived from specific technical sensors.

Open Source Intelligence: Information of potential intelligence value that is available to the general public.

Figure 4-1   An Analyst's View of the Collection Taxonomy

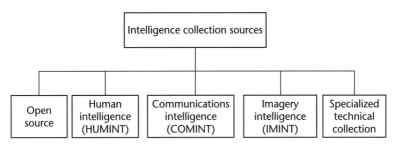

In this taxonomy, signals intelligence (SIGINT) is divided into three distinct "INTs": communications intelligence (COMINT), electronic intelligence (ELINT), and telemetry interception; the latter is typically called foreign instrumentation signals intelligence, or FISINT. The lumping of COMINT, ELINT, and FISINT together as SIGINT is usually defended as being logical because they have in common the interception of some kind of signal transmitted by the target. But some measurements and signatures intelligence (MASINT) and imagery intelligence (IMINT) sensors rely on a signal transmitted by the target, as well. *SIGINT* is in fact too general a term to use, when in most cases it means *COMINT.*

The taxonomy of Box 4-1 is based on resource control ("turf") considerations and, from an analyst's standpoint, is artificial. The taxonomy approach in this book is quite different. Instead of following the U.S. stovepipes, this book tries for a logical breakout that focuses on the nature of the material collected and processed, rather than on the collection means. Figure 4-1 illustrates this view of collection sources. Each of the dominant and widely used sources of intelligence—open source, HUMINT, COMINT, and IMINT—is covered, along with some of the advanced techniques that intelligence encompasses. The remainder of the chapter covers some specialized technical collection and processing techniques, many of which tend to be described as "MASINT"—another term, like "SIGINT," that is too general to have much value.

Although the perspective of Figure 4-1 has more utility for analysts, no separation of collection methods is completely satisfactory, or "clean." Overlaps will occur no matter what taxonomy is selected. In the sections that follow, a number of these overlaps are identified.

The Dominant Intelligence Sources

Four sources of intelligence dominate in volume and impact: open source, plus the three classified sources—HUMINT, IMINT, and COMINT. All have a history in intelligence that goes back hundreds of years. The use of open source in intelligence probably dates back to the beginnings of written language. HUMINT efforts are described in the Old Testament ("Moses sent them to spy out the land of Canaan, and said unto them, Get you up this way southward, and go up into the mountain").[1] COMINT dates back at least to reading signal flags and smoke signals. IMINT predates the camera, if sketches of castles and towns by spies in the Middle Ages can be considered IMINT.

Open Source

After exhausting the existing internal knowledge base, analysts can go to the easiest external sources (open literature, online databases). Open source information has traditionally meant published material that is publicly available—newspapers, books, and magazines. As such it is sometimes referred to as literature intelligence (LITINT) or open source intelligence (OSINT). Today open source intelligence covers much more than traditional published sources. Large volumes of imagery, for example, are becoming publicly available from commercial imaging satellites. Commercial databases hold vast economic data that are available for the price of a subscription. All fit the "open source" category, though they are not "published" in the traditional sense.

One problem of open source intelligence is that it is so abundant; an analyst cannot possibly take advantage of all the available material. In fact, an analyst cannot even learn about all of the available capabilities for obtaining open source materials. Tracking the data sources is a full time job. The solution is to turn to experts on research. Reference librarians can help search and retrieve documents from many different databases, including commercial databases. As these databases become available worldwide, almost any country or commercial company should have an excellent research capability available to its analysts.

Open source material is perhaps the most valuable source of intelligence and is typically the most easily overlooked by government intelligence organizations in favor of classified information. Its chief value is that it is relatively easy to obtain. Analysts should not turn to more expensive collection resources until exhausting the potential of open source intelligence; and analysts should keep coming back to it as the expensive sources provide new leads.

Political analysis draws heavily on open source intelligence. The statements of government leaders tell us much about their attitudes, their personalities (for personality profiling), the stresses that may exist within their government, and many other things. Their statements always have to be analyzed in context (who they are talking to, what agendas they have, for example) and have to be assessed with a good understanding of the leaders' national and organizational cultures. Fine nuances in public statements can convey a lot to an experienced political analyst. Economic analysis also relies heavily— in fact, primarily—on open source material, especially the very large databases on international trade and national economies that have been assembled by international organizations such as the United Nations.

A common misconception is that open source material is less useful for military intelligence because the "good" material is classified. On the contrary, one of the major intelligence successes of World War II was based on the skillful use of open sources. Although the Germans maintained censorship as effectively as anyone else, they did publish their freight tariffs on all goods, including petroleum products. Based on these tariffs, a young U.S. Office of Strategic Services analyst, Walter Levy, was able to pinpoint the exact location of the German refineries, which were subsequently targeted by allied bombers.[2]

Scientific and technical intelligence makes extensive use of open source information. No other source contains the technical detail that open source material can provide. No matter how classified a foreign project may be, the technology involved in the project eventually appears somewhere in open literature; scientists and technologists want to publish their results, usually for reasons of professional reputation. This rule holds true even against targets that heavily censor their open publications; one merely has to know where to look. For example, a collector can trace even the most sensitive U.S. defense or intelligence system developments simply by following the right articles over an extended period of time in journals like *Aviation Week* and *Space Technology*. In tracing such developments, one will soon become aware of the bathtub curve.

Figure 4-2 shows an example of the well-known (in the analysis business) "bathtub" curve. This curve, in its various forms, describes several trends or patterns that are important in intelligence. One example is the tracking of foreign weapons systems development. The basic research on weapons is usually accessible, as scientists and engineers need to communicate their findings. As this research is applied to a military system or moves toward production, the work becomes more secret. Finally, as a weapons system emerges from the research and development stage and enters testing, the program becomes visible again.

Figure 4-2   The Bathtub Curve

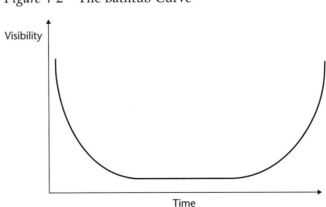

Keeping track of a technology on the bathtub curve requires skillful combination of open literature and classified sources. This technique has enabled analysts to determine the capabilities of a technology and the time phasing of technical developments and innovations even when the program was at the bottom of the "bathtub."

Analysts use technical details derived from open literature to evaluate the performance of a specific technology—that is, how well it will perform in a given role. Equipment nomenclature derived from open literature is of special value in COMINT analysis. Open literature is a good potential source of details on the devices and technologies that will be used in sensors, the sensing techniques used, and the results of research efforts.

Open source intelligence also has proven useful for tracking key individuals and research groups that have been identified by classified sources, for following key technologies and research results, and for associating test facilities with certain organizations or key research and development groups. Open literature seldom explicitly identifies a military sponsor of research that has classified applications, for example, but it may provide clues that lead to sponsor identification.

The key to using open source material in scientific and technical intelligence lies in identifying and analyzing the relationships among programs, persons, technologies, and organizations. A number of powerful computer-based tools are available for this purpose, and the methodology for relationship or "network" analysis is covered in Chapter 12.

In all areas of intelligence, the general rule for open source is this: What is said is not so important as who said it. Statements by a head of government typically carry more weight than those of a head of state. A finance minister's statements on budgetary issues carry more weight than do the same statements made by a minister of the interior.

Historically, most open source material came in printed ("hard") copy. Today, the most commonly used sources are online.

Online Data Sources. A wide variety of online databases can help in open source research. Most of these are now available through the World Wide Web. The number and availability of unclassified commercial databases is changing so rapidly that this book makes no attempt to catalog them. The rapid expansion of global information networks provides analysts with large volumes of information that were previously unavailable.

A persistent problem with online data sources remains the inability to extract relevant information from the mass of data. The analyst inevitably encounters information overload. Both government and commercial development projects continue to work toward the goal of creating a human-computer team that would dramatically improve the capability of human analysts to make inferences in complex, data-intensive domains. Such a team would vastly increase the ability to identify key facts hidden in immense quantities of irrelevant information, to assemble large numbers of disparate facts to reach valid conclusions, and to produce new patterns that assist in further analyses. We can reasonably expect to see steady improvement in the problem of extracting relevant information from the morass.

In the interim, specialized databases offer some relief from the search problem. For example, one of the more useful sources of technology information for both government and business intelligence is in online patent databases. These have consistently proven to be one of the most valuable sources of technology information. For many organizations that perform classified research, patents are the only way to publish their results openly. Some tips for searching patent databases follow:

- Obtain the names of all coauthors and any institute affiliations in a patent. In sifting through the great volume of patents, the first search an experienced open literature analyst usually makes is on names or institutes; this preliminary screening allows relevant work to be identified. The second screening is on the specific technology discussed in the patent.

- Abstracts are useful for screening and identifying patents of interest. The full text is essential for technology evaluation. The full text also may contain indicators that a patent is of interest to the military or to a particular company.

- Some patent literature describes patented devices that have been introduced into industry. These provide a filtered set of the most interesting patents—those that are applications-oriented enough to be used by a given industry.

Hard Copy Sources. Some open source material still is not available through the Web. Hard copy open source literature can be obtained from libraries, commercial databases, and from scientists and business people who have frequent dealings with their foreign counterparts. Valuable sources include newspapers, telephone books, monographs, journals, patents, and technical literature.

The most useful journals are the closed, restricted, and semiclassified journals (known as *gray literature*). State ministries and large research and manufacturing organizations publish journals that contain sensitive or proprietary information. Some such journals are classified. Most of them are controlled, and access is restricted, so it is a bit of a stretch to call them "open source." However, some may be found in public libraries due to errors in document control or distribution, and they can often be obtained by clandestine collection (for example, by agents). The in-house publications of many research organizations, even when not restricted, are often more valuable than normal trade journals; they tend to present more detail on work being carried on within the organization. Conference proceedings, which also fit into the gray literature category, usually have more value than the widely distributed journals and magazines.

Many openly available technical journals are commercially translated. However, these commercial translations have several shortcomings for intelligence analysis: Commercial translation delays range from months to years, depending on the language, and the translations can omit ancillary information that is critical for intelligence assessments. For example, several journals in the original language may contain lists of the first and middle names, affiliations, titles, positions, and education of all authors; these lists often are omitted in the translated version. Notes of the authors' thanks to superiors and senior scientists, which often provide valuable leads to the composition of research groups, are also often omitted.

Reference journals contain abstracts of some of the most important papers that are not routinely translated. Often, such journals provide the only evidence that work has been done in a certain area.

Abstracts of dissertations for higher degrees will typically show the project sponsor and the association of researchers and institutes involved. "Preprints" may contain similar information. These papers contain much of the unprocessed data, only a subset of which is published in open technical literature. Also, concepts and experiments not yet of quality for formal publication are published in this format.

Human Intelligence

Human intelligence, or HUMINT, encompasses a variety of means for gathering information on foreign developments; its focus is people and their access to information on topics of interest. HUMINT is best used to provide information that is not otherwise available. It typically is the best source of an adversary's plans and intentions. It usually is the best method of dealing with illicit networks.

Compared with the other "INTs," HUMINT takes more time to collect due to the need to contact the source, even when that source has already been developed (that is, recruited). HUMINT is not always on target; collectors have to provide their best shot working with the sources they have. But HUMINT is more flexible—information that is not available from one source may be available from another source or from piecing together several sources. HUMINT is best used to go after targets such as an opponent's plans, trade secrets, political stability, or for negotiation support. It also provides critical leads for further targeting by HUMINT or other INTs.

Governmental HUMINT activities include embassy officers' assessments, information elicited from contacts, information from paid agents, or documents or equipment clandestinely acquired by purchase or theft. The human sources can be diplomats and defense attachés, international conference attendees, defectors, émigrés, or refugees. (An attaché is a technical expert on the diplomatic staff of his or her country at a foreign capital. An emigré is a person who was forced to emigrate, usually for political or economic reasons.)

Cooperating private individuals and organizations also can supply privileged information that they encounter in the course of their work. Nongovernmental organizations have proliferated in recent years and are increasingly useful sources about foreign developments.

HUMINT is a major source of intelligence information for many commercial organizations, and many governments also use HUMINT for commercial purposes. Most corporations do not use clandestine HUMINT (for example, agents in the employ of their competitors) for ethical reasons. Where ethics do not constrain corporations, they usually avoid clandestine HUMINT because of the costs associated with exposure. Two recent examples illustrate the exposure hazards of clandestine commercial HUMINT. In 2001 Proctor and Gamble engaged in information collection against rival Unilever that included "dumpster diving"—sifting through Unilever's off-property trash for documents. Once exposed, Proctor and Gamble reportedly agreed to pay Unilever $10 million as part of a settlement.[3] In 2000 Oracle Corporation admitted that it had hired an investigator to find documents embarrassing to Microsoft; the tactics used reportedly included covert searches of Washington, D.C., political organizations and payment to janitors for trashed documents showing improper Microsoft activities.[4] Both incidents resulted in damaging media coverage of the offending companies.

HUMINT collection can cover all phases of a development program, from concept development to production or deployment and operations of systems. HUMINT sources have provided biographic reporting and information on research scientists, identification of research institutes, assessments of systems under development, trends in research programs, identification of key sites and equipment, and photographs of sites and platforms. HUMINT data also improves the effectiveness and comprehension of data collected by COMINT, IMINT, and open source intelligence and yields important insights into data collected by the technical collection systems described later in this chapter. Access to equipment or technical documentation collected through HUMINT gives an analyst an inside view into performance capabilities or production techniques that, in turn, supplements data collected by technical sensors.

The following sections detail HUMINT techniques that utilize liaison relationships, elicitation, emigrés and defectors, clandestine sources, sampling, and materiel acquisition. Their common theme is that the intelligence is collected by one person interacting with another person to obtain information.

Liaison Relationships. National intelligence organizations typically have liaison relationships with intelligence and law enforcement groups in other countries, sometimes even when official relationships between the two countries are cool. Corporate intelligence groups have their own liaison networks to share information about, for example, terrorist threats to corporate executives abroad.

Intelligence liaison also is not uncommon among governmental and non-governmental groups. Nongovernmental organizations provide many opportunities for government or commercial firms to conduct liaison for intelligence gathering. One of the better known historical examples was the World War II liaison set up by the U.S. Office of Naval Intelligence with Mafia groups for counterespionage operations using dock workers' unions and by the Office of Strategic Services for subsequent operations against the Fascist government in Sicily. Mafia chief "Lucky" Luciano was released from prison, reportedly for his assistance in counterintelligence and to help with the Sicilian operation.[5]

The effectiveness of the Mafia liaison has been hotly debated over the years, and many intelligence officers argue that intelligence groups should not cooperate with criminal organizations. Their reservations are often summed up with the adage "If you go to bed with dogs, expect to wake up with fleas!" The contrary argument is that one should use a nonjudgmental approach when choosing liaisons—if they can help more than they hurt, use them.

Liaison has a number of associated risks, one being the problem of false corroboration. It is not uncommon for several intelligence services to unwittingly use the same agent. (After all, if one service will pay you for what you know, others may be willing to do so.) When the agent's information is shared among intelligence services via liaison, it will seem to come to the analyst from different sources—the liaison service and the analyst's own HUMINT service. As a result, a single agent's information will be given added credibility that it does not deserve.

Elicitation. Elicitation is the practice of obtaining information about a topic from conversations, preferably without the source knowing what is happening. Elicitation is widely practiced in gatherings of diplomats and military attachés and in the commercial sector during business executives' social hours and sales conventions. Because the participants are all aware of the game, the information that is elicited may be tainted; but the gatherings are also valuable avenues for sending signals. Businesses in particular use this channel to signal competitors informally about their intentions, especially where use of more formal channels would violate antitrust law.

Making direct contact with knowledgeable sources in their home country or organization is often difficult, and the setting can be unfavorable for elicitation. However, these sources often publish their work or discuss it at international conferences and during visits with other professionals. Elicitation is an effective tactic to use at such professional gatherings, particularly where economists, trade specialists, scientists or engineers convene to present papers. These professionals are a valuable source of HUMINT, and the greater their egos, the more information—and the more valuable information—they are likely to impart. These professionals are connected to other professionals in their home country and in their organizations. Analysts, where they possess the appropriate credentials, often attend such meetings and do their own collection by elicitation.

The challenge in getting information from an elicitation source is to ask the right questions. Experts have advantages in elicitation because of their knowledge of the subject matter and because the elicitation appears to be a natural part of their interaction with other experts. Experts, however, bring their biases to the process, as noted in Chapter 5.

A variation on elicitation is to trade for information. While Peter Schwartz was at Royal Dutch Shell, he made regular use of scenarios (a sophisticated type of model) as a medium of exchange by presenting talks on the scenarios to selected groups—for example, insights on airline fuel futures to airline executives. In return, he received information from the executives on airline planning that he could use to refine his scenarios.[6]

Emigrés and Defectors. Government intelligence routinely makes use of emigrés and defectors. Emigrés have departed a country legally, but in some countries would not have been allowed to leave if they had information of significant intelligence value. Defectors have departed the country illegally and often have information of value.

However, both emigrés and defectors voluntarily cut their ties with their native lands, usually for economic or political reasons. As a consequence, their objectivity on such issues is in question, and their information must be carefully screened. As with elicitation sources, asking the right question is important; defectors want to please their new friends, and they may give answers that do that.

Corporate intelligence routinely makes use of a different type of emigré or "defector"—one who formerly worked for the competition—to get information about trade secrets such as marketing strategies, costs, and proprietary processes. Corporate emigrés and defectors typically have the same problems with objectivity as governmental defectors. In addition, these people carry the added baggage of former employment agreements and legal issues that the traditional emigré or defector is not forced to carry. Additionally, when changing corporate loyalties within a country, a corporate emigré or defector cannot expect governmental protection if accused of stealing trade secrets. Internationally, however, such protection may be available. During 1993 and 1994 the international automobile industry was the stage for the dramatic defection of J. Ignacio Lopez de Arriortua and six other senior managers from General Motors (GM) to Volkswagenwerk AG. Lopez and his colleagues apparently took a number of sensitive GM documents with them, as any defector should do if he wishes to increase his value to his new organization. Lopez was accused of masterminding the theft of more than twenty boxes of documents on research, planning, manufacturing, and sales when he left GM to become a Volkswagen executive in 1993. The German government followed the time-honored tradition of providing governmental protection for defectors; they at first refused to prosecute Lopez, and a subsequent prosecution was dropped.[7] Volkswagenwerk AG eventually paid GM damages in a civil suit. Corporate defectors to a country having less cordial relations with the United States would likely gain more protection, as would the company they defected to.

Clandestine Sources. Clandestine HUMINT sources (the classical spies, moles, or agents of spy fiction) are possibly the highest cost source for the quantity of information obtained. Therefore, targeting must be done carefully. Clandestine HUMINT may be the best way to determine plans and intentions.

In normal times the tight security that must surround and protect the clandestine source means that substantial time delays will exist from the time the source finds out about something until the information reaches an intelligence analyst. Fast communication of perishable data is important in crisis or wartime, but speed tends to increase the risk that the source will be exposed.

Sampling Techniques. Sampling techniques are best known for their use in public opinion polls. When analysts need to know something about the parameters of a large population (such as the mean sensitivity and standard deviation of sensors deployed worldwide in large numbers, or the attitudes on Middle East issues among the Arab population), they do not undertake the difficult or impractical task of surveying each member of the population. Instead analysts make estimates based on a small subset of the population. Sampling theory makes the estimative process more efficient. It does this by suggesting strategies for selecting the subset to be used in making an estimate, by defining alternative methods for making estimates from the subset data, by helping to reduce the cost of taking samples, and by providing techniques for quantifying (in a predictive sense) the size of the estimative error associated with a given sampling or estimation algorithm.

Sampling techniques in intelligence require additional skills that are not required in conventional public opinion polling as it is done in many countries. If one wanted to know the attitudes of narcotics couriers regarding a pending change in the United Kingdom's drug enforcement policy, for example, telephone polls or direct interviews would not work well. Clandestine polling, using indirect approaches to elicit responses, might work. In a well-run clandestine sample, the target audience is never aware that it has been polled—at least not about the issues that the pollster is focusing on.

Materiel Acquisition. Materiel acquisition and exploitation is presented here as part of HUMINT, because the acquisition is usually a clandestine effort that uses human sources. Materiel acquisition (materiel is the equipment, apparatus, and supplies used by an organization or institution) has long been practiced in commercial intelligence. Throughout recorded history, manufacturers have acquired samples of a competitor's product for evaluation as part of planning sales tactics, to copy good ideas, or even for reverse engineering. The Hittites of Asia Minor were early targets of materiel acquisition efforts. (Middle Easterners, at the time using bronze, acquired iron weaponry from the Hittites.)[8] Today most materiel acquisition by governmental intelligence agencies is by purchase, usually through middlemen to conceal the intended destination. Many commercial firms (all automobile manufacturers, for example) purchase their competitors' new products for evaluation.

The Soviet intelligence services were very good at clandestine acquisition. On one occasion they acquired a new IBM computer before it was officially on the market. The result must have been less than satisfactory for the Soviets, however, because none of the IBM sales or maintenance people they subsequently contacted knew how to make it work.

Materiel acquisition can also be done by special operations. One of the best known materiel acquisition efforts was the Bruneval Raid of World War II.[9] In the fall of 1941, Dr. R.V. Jones, assistant director of Britain's Royal Air Force Intelligence Section, was zeroing in on a new German antiaircraft fire control radar that was believed to transmit on a frequency of 570 MHz. One of the more daring British reconnaissance pilots finally brought back a picture of a new radar located near Bruneval, France. The British quickly noted that the new radar was located less than 200 yards from the coast, and they settled on a commando raid to obtain detailed information about the radar. The British assembled a company of paratroops to make an airborne assault. A naval assault was too risky because of the high cliffs around Bruneval, but a light naval force was assembled to handle the evacuation. Dr. Jones, in the meanwhile, had identified the German radar by name—*Würzburg*—but still could not confirm that the radar was the source of 570 MHz signals.

Jones specified in detail the parts he wanted his selected acquisition team—Royal Engineers and a radar mechanic—to bring back. They included the feed antenna for the radar dish, which would establish the operating frequency of the radar; and the receiver and display equipment, which would reveal whether any antijamming circuits existed. The transmitters would establish German technology for generating 570 MHz signals. Two radar operators were to be taken prisoner, if possible, so that they could be interrogated about radar operation. Finally, if equipment could not be removed, the labels and inspection stamps were to be taken, because these would provide valuable background information.

On the night of February 27, 1942, the raid, codenamed Operation BITING, took place. The raid was an unqualified success; the Bruneval force made off with the radar receiver, modulator, transmitter, and the feed element, which they sawed off the antenna. They brought back exactly what Jones asked for, except that only one radar operator was captured.[10] With the knowledge gained from this raid the British were able to develop successful countermeasures to the Würzburg.

The Bruneval raid was a success because the British, like the Soviets during the cold war, knew exactly what they wanted. The acquisition team had an expert analyst intimately involved at every step. Most successes in materiel acquisition since that time have involved carefully focused teams closely tied to analytical expertise. Most failures have resulted in cases where the acquirers, separated from the analysts, had no real idea what they were trying to get or why.

The most expensive single materiel acquisition effort may have been the Glomar Explorer's effort to bring up a Soviet submarine. In April 1968 a Soviet

Golf-class submarine on patrol northwest of Hawaii was racked with explosions and sank in 17,000 feet of water, carrying all ninety men aboard down with it. Soviet salvage vessels were unable to locate the sunken craft, but the U.S. Navy pinpointed its location using more sophisticated search equipment. At this point the CIA entered the picture with a proposal to recover the submarine. This was the beginning of the project that was reportedly codenamed Jennifer.

The CIA contracted with Howard Hughes' Summa Corporation to build a 620-foot-long deep-sea recovery vessel equipped with huge derricks, along with a companion barge to conceal the submarine when it was recovered. The Glomar Explorer was built under the cover of a deep-sea mining mission and was completed in 1973 at a cost of $200 million.

During July and August 1974 the Glomar Explorer located the submarine and began recovery operations. Cables were looped around the submarine and the winches began slowly pulling the submarine up toward the barge. About halfway up, the hull broke apart and two-thirds of the submarine fell back to be lost on the bottom. The remaining third was recovered and yielded valuable intelligence, but the sought-after prizes—the code books and nuclear warheads—were reportedly lost.[11]

Although Project Jennifer did not totally succeed, it provided a valuable illustration of the combination that makes for collection success: innovation and doing the unexpected. U.S. intelligence collection's single biggest asset—and possibly its single biggest advantage over other collection services—is the innovation and unpredictability of Americans. In materiel acquisition, as in HUMINT generally, U.S. intelligence officers have tried things that other services are too unimaginative or too conservative to try, relying heavily on the U.S. technological edge. Of course, U.S. collection services also have taken more risks and consequently gotten into more trouble. It remains an open question whether a more cautious approach is taking hold in U.S. intelligence.

Communications Intelligence

Communications intelligence, or COMINT, is the intercept, processing, and reporting of an opponent's communications. "Communications" in this definition includes voice and data communications, facsimile, Internet messages, and any other deliberate transmission of information. COMINT is collected by aircraft and satellites, overt ground-based sites, a limited number of seaborne collectors, and some covert and clandestine sites.

COMINT is traditionally considered the province of governments and is generally illegal when conducted by a private entity. Regardless, some countries use COMINT for business intelligence. And COMINT collection equipment is readily available in the commercial market worldwide. The best commercial units are not cheap, but they rival the best units that government COMINT organizations can supply.

COMINT collection, like HUMINT collection, can provide insights into plans and intentions. It can contribute information about people, organizations, equipment, facilities, procedures, schedules, budgets, operations, testing, deployment, and environmental conditions. COMINT gives clues as to relationships, organizations, and perhaps to sensitive or classified projects. The chief constraint on its use today is that it is human labor–intensive, relying on trained linguists. Eventually, machine translation of speech can be expected to ease this bottleneck. In the past, COMINT seldom provided much detail because it dealt primarily with brief conversations. This is no longer the case, as large volumes of material are now transmitted by data communications or facsimile.

Targets of COMINT could include government leadership, research and design organizations, test facilities, economic activities such as international funds transfers, participants in test and operational activities, and executive policy discussions. COMINT gives insights into research organizations, their projects, and their networks that support development programs or operations.

Military services conduct the bulk of COMINT efforts worldwide using trained linguists to monitor the mobile radio communications of opposing forces. COMINT that supports ongoing operations, known as *tactical COMINT,* is used heavily in law enforcement work and in countering illicit networks generally. The case of Pablo Escobar (see Chapter 1) is a typical example of this heavy reliance on tactical COMINT. Military COMINT is used extensively against air-to-ground, ground-to-ground, and naval communications. Most such COMINT involves the intercept of radio communications, though the use of underwater sound communications for submarines has spurred the development of COMINT capabilities in underwater acoustics.

COMINT has had a number of successes in wartime. During World War II the United States scored its Midway victory over the Japanese navy largely because U.S. cryptanalysts had cracked the Japanese naval codes and were able to identify Midway as the Japanese target. In Europe the British success at breaking the German ENIGMA cipher codes contributed to several World War II successes, including the Normandy landing.[12] But one of the earliest and most significant successes for COMINT came in World War I at the Battle of Tannenberg.

The Battle of Tannenberg occurred late in August 1914 during the opening moves of World War I. The Russian First and Second Armies were advancing through Eastern Prussia toward the German Eighth Army. Communications among the Russian headquarters were handled by high frequency radio, which can be received over a wide geographic region. Some of these communications were not enciphered. On the night of August 25, German radio units intercepted messages that gave the deployment and missions of the two Russian armies. Over the next few days, further intercepted messages gave away the strength, positions, and movements of the Russian armies. It quickly became apparent to the German commanders that General Samsonov's Second Army was being placed in an exposed position near the German town of Tannenberg, and that Russian General Rennenkampf's First Army was not in a position to provide support if Samsonov's army were attacked.

General von Hindenberg, commander of the German Eighth Army, positioned his entire force for an attack on the Russian Second Army. On August 26 he began the attack, and over the next three days deployed his units in response to Russian countermoves, being forewarned by additional intercepts of Russian radiograms. The result was a spectacular German victory; the Russian Second Army was decimated, General Samsonov committed suicide, and the eastern front ultimately settled into a stalemate.[13]

An interesting footnote of Tannenberg was the unanimous declarations of all key German participants that the intercepted information, although useful, was not critical to the outcome. Von Hindenberg himself, in his writings, gives the impression that he had no such information on the Russian dispositions.[14] In World War II Gen. Omar Bradley and Field Marshal Bernard Montgomery treated the intercepts of the German ENIGMA cipher machine in similar fashion, crediting their own operational skill for their victories.[15] Such statements deserve a certain amount of skepticism. They are standard disclaimers made by successful generals, statesmen, and corporate executives who have good intelligence support. In the intelligence business, openly crediting sources can cause the loss of those sources. Also, a leader does not want to give too much credit to his intelligence information, because the logical implication is that the leader with the best intelligence—not the best leadership skills—will win. The truth probably lies somewhere in the middle.

Encryption technology has outpaced cryptanalysis in the decades since World War II, and it would be very difficult, if not impossible, to repeat the Allied successes of that war. The lessons of the war were learned by all countries, and most cryptanalysis successes now come from radio operator mistakes such as those made by the Russians at Tannenberg. Of course, a large amount of military and civilian radio traffic remains unencrypted, but the trend is to encrypt highly sensitive communications. The following are some of the primary techniques for COMINT collection.

Microphones and Audio Transmitters. The microphone-and-wire is an old technology, still widely used by some intelligence services. It is cheap, reliable, and long lasting. Unfortunately, it is also relatively easy for counterintelligence units to find.

The audio transmitter, popularly known as the "bug," also has been a useful technical intelligence tool for decades. Because it transmits a radio signal rather than using a wire, it is simpler to emplace than the microphone-and-wire. Also, it is cheap and requires no great technical skill to use, so it is particularly popular among the less sophisticated intelligence organizations and in industrial espionage. The audio transmitter typically uses low radiated power to avoid detection, has its own power supply (unless it can tap into the building power system), and is small enough to be effectively concealed.

Advancing technologies in electronic miniaturization, power sources, and transmission techniques have provided these capabilities. Burst transmissions (very short, usually one second or less, radio signals), spread spectrum (typically signals that look like noise), and other techniques are available to reduce the probability of signal intercept. Increasingly, video as well as audio can be provided by "bugs." Difficult-to-detect infrared links are also available. Remote command and control techniques have been employed to switch transmitters on and off, reducing the probability of detection and conserving battery life.

Telephone Surveillance. Telephone conversations are perhaps the most common source of COMINT. The traditional approach is to monitor the telephone of interest via a telephone tap. In addition to monitoring normal telephone conversations, some devices take advantage of the fact that telephone instruments can transmit room conversations (audio) along telephone lines when the telephone handset is resting in its cradle (on hook). Some telephone instruments, as designed, pass audio while on hook; others, through faulty installation or damage, may inadvertently pass audio. The introduction of new and sophisticated digital and computer-based telephone systems has greatly expanded the possibilities of this technical surveillance technique.

Telephone conversations also can be intercepted in bulk by COMINT equipment if the equipment is properly positioned to collect microwave point-to-point transmissions from the telephone company's trunk lines. Unencrypted cellular telephone networks are also an easy target for COMINT. A major problem of such intercepts on civil systems is that the quantity of conversations that must be processed can swamp the COMINT processors—especially if the language must be translated. Some means of specific telephone recognition must be found to allow selection of the conversations of interest. In modern telephone systems, this can be difficult indeed.

Much international telephone and data traffic is carried over communications satellites. This traffic can be intercepted by many unintended recipients. Such activity for commercial intelligence purposes is likely to increase in the future, though it is illegal under international law. A number of governments routinely intercept satellite communications, sifting it for information of value—including information that will permit their own companies to compete in international markets.

Other COMINT Techniques. Where an intelligence service cannot gain access to a facility for a microphone and wire or audio transmitter installation, they can sometimes use one of several remote acoustic monitoring techniques. All such techniques depend on the ability of structural or emplaced objects in a room to pick up sound and mechanically vibrate.

When used as a specialized type of microphone, the *accelerometer* picks up mechanical vibrations directly from the building structure and transmits the audio out of a facility via wire or a radio transmitter. Whether the vibrations are from voice or machine noise, the accelerometer can effectively receive sound from several rooms away. Typically, the accelerometer is placed in a structural beam that runs into the area to be monitored. The vibrations from conversations in that room will travel along that structural beam and be picked up by the accelerometer.

Fluidics, as a method of surreptitiously collecting audio information, exploits the way in which acoustic energy travels with relatively low loss in liquids, or in gases if channeled. Thus, if a water pipe picks up acoustic energy, the audio signal will travel long distances within the pipe. Electrical conduit or air ducts will also propagate audio over substantial distances. The audio headsets used by passengers in many commercial airliners take advantage of this channeling effect in an air conduit.

Since the 1960s *radio frequency flooding* of installations has been used for intelligence data collection. The flooding signals usually operate in the microwave range and are used to collect data remotely, much as a radar senses its target. Flooding depends on the fact that objects, especially metal ones, vibrate slightly in response to audio in a room. A beam of microwave energy striking the metal object will be reflected from it with some weak modulation imposed by the audio vibrations. If the reflected energy can be collected and demodulated, conversations in the area can be monitored. Innocuous signals such as those emanating from a television or radio station can be used successfully to flood an installation. Flooding has also been directed at devices such as typewriters. Signals directed at the typewriters are modulated by the keystrokes and the modulated signal received by nearby antennas, thereby compromising the information typed.

Perhaps the best known instance of radio frequency flooding was that conducted by the Soviets against the U.S. Embassy in Moscow. The Soviets had concealed a passive sound pickup device in the great seal of the United States that they presented to the U.S. ambassador and that subsequently decorated the ambassador's study. The device was a small, U-shaped metal support for a strip of spring steel. The steel strip would vibrate slightly in response to sounds from within the office. When the seal was illuminated with a strong microwave signal from a nearby Soviet-controlled building, the U-shaped support acted as an antenna and would pick up the microwave energy and reradiate it, modulated by the audio signal from within the room. A nearby receiver would pick up and demodulate the reradiated signal.[16]

Laser radar techniques have been used to exploit audio vibrations from windows or similar fixtures within an office since the 1960s. The principle is the same as for radio frequency flooding. An infrared laser (which is invisible to the human eye) can be aimed at an office window from distances ranging up to hundreds of yards. If the proper infrared band is selected for the laser, the window glass will reflect the energy. Conversations inside the office will cause the windowpane to vibrate slightly, and these audio vibrations will modulate the reflected laser energy. An optical receiver located near the laser transmitter can then pick up the backscattered energy, demodulate it, and recover the audio. The technology to use such laser devices is now widely available.[17]

Imagery Intelligence

Imagery intelligence, or IMINT, is traditionally thought of as visible photography—whether with a handheld camera or airborne or spaceborne reconnaissance. Most imagery, in fact, is of this type. Increasingly, though, imagery from radar and from the infrared spectrum is important in intelligence.

IMINT can identify deployed military units, test facilities, and participants in exercises or operational missions. When used with COMINT and HUMINT, it has located research and development facilities and provided detailed information about equipment used at the test areas. It can tip off other collectors when aircraft or ships have left their home bases, have arrived at their staging bases, or are participating in tests, operational exercises, or operational missions. This tip-off allows the coordinated use of non–IMINT collection such as COMINT or specialized technical collection to cover the activity.

Commercial imagery—that is, imagery by either government or commercial organizations that is sold to the general public—is taking over a role formerly reserved for government intelligence agencies. It is steadily improving in quality and availability. Commercial satellite imagery increasingly is being treated as open literature. Governments and commercial firms know of its existence, its coverage, and the quality of imagery available from it. Almost anyone can buy it for any purpose, so imagery exploitation for a wide range of governmental and nongovernmental intelligence purposes has become an accepted practice.

In effect, this type of imagery—visible, radar, and multispectral—is available as "open source," and its quality is becoming good enough to be useful for a number of intelligence applications. The wide availability of satellite imagery has several effects, positive and negative:

- Fewer and fewer secrets are discovered by visible imagery; its capabilities are well known, and the number of visible imagery satellites is steadily increasing.

- The effect of this wide availability may be to drive government imagery intelligence into new technical areas or new capabilities. Governments will likely push the resolution or nature of their classified imagery so as not to duplicate commercially available images.

- On the plus side, commercial imagery can be shared among coalition forces without revealing sources and methods.

Photography and Video. The important role that short-range imagery—handheld photography and video cameras—plays in intelligence is often overlooked because remote sensing technologies, especially satellite imagery, tend to get more attention. Handheld imagery is nevertheless still important in a wide range of intelligence. Handheld imagery has provided details about industrial products and allowed performance analysis of aircraft, tanks, ships, and submarines, as well as permitted thorough examination of the instruments on board these vehicles. It is useful in getting sizes and characteristics of objects for technical evaluation and personal photographs ("mug shots") for counterintelligence and counternarcotics operations. Video is increasingly valuable for giving continuous surveillance of a target, and video shots of foreign leaders are useful in making physiological or behavioral assessments of those leaders.

Imaging Radar. When mounted on aircraft or spacecraft, radars can rapidly search large areas of the earth's surface. Microwave radars use frequencies that are not greatly affected by water vapor, and microwave radars are not affected by darkness, so they operate well at night and under most weather conditions. They have the added advantage of being able to see through vegetation, most camouflage netting, and sometimes even through the top layers of dry soil. They can penetrate nonmetallic walls and roofs of buildings.

Airborne or spaceborne imaging radars have the potential to detect and identify targets nearly as well as visible imagery can. The radar must, however, produce a high level of detail. As the resolution becomes poorer, the radar image blurs.

The *side-looking airborne radar (SLAR)* resolves targets by using an antenna that is as large as possible. The larger the antenna, the narrower the radar beam, and the better its resolution. Because the antenna must be large, it is usually mounted on the side of an aircraft and aimed perpendicular to the fuselage.

SLARs are an older technology seldom used now for reconnaissance applications because of the sensor resolution requirements and the size of the antenna needed to meet those requirements. An antenna that is 20 feet long, for instance, could be mounted on most aircraft or satellites. Such a SLAR antenna operating at 6 GHz would have a resolution of about 1 mile at a 120-mile range and 10 miles at a 1,200-mile range; neither resolution would produce an image good enough for analysis. SLARs are typically mounted on an aircraft, rather than a spacecraft, because the resolution of SLARs is better at the short ranges that aircraft can provide.

A *synthetic aperture radar (SAR)* is mounted on an airplane or satellite and takes advantage of the Doppler (motion) effect, and thus produces high-resolution images with a small antenna. In contrast with the SLAR, the SAR produces a clear, sharp picture that remains sharp at longer ranges. Whereas the SLAR uses a long antenna to improve resolution, the SAR creates, or "synthesizes," the equivalent of a very long antenna by using signal processing that relies on the Doppler effect.

With an antenna beam the radar illuminates a patch on the ground off to the side of the satellite or aircraft platform. As the SAR moves past a ground target, the frequency of the radar return from the target shifts downward due to the Doppler effect, much as the sound frequency (pitch) of a locomotive whistle drops as the train passes by. By tracking this shift in its signal processor, the SAR is able to create an image of the target. The image will have the same resolution if the antenna were as long as the distance traveled by the aircraft or spacecraft, within certain limits. This "synthetic antenna" distance can be five miles or more, giving a resolution of one meter or less independent of distance from the radar to the target.

In the first SAR systems the antenna used the same polarization for transmitting pulses and receiving their echoes. More recent SARs are called *polarimetric* SARs. That is, they transmit and receive on arbitrary (and different) polarizations to allow a multiplicity of images that contain different information—for example, transmitting vertical polarization or receiving horizontal polarization or circular polarization. Numerous intelligence advantages accrue from using polarimetric SARs: Choosing different transmit and receive polarizations can maximize the contrast between targets and background; land use classification and crop identification can be done more accurately; and better assessments of soil and vegetation parameters are possible.

At the time this book was written, Canada was providing commercially available SAR imagery via its RADARSAT. Commercially available SAR imagery will likely become widely available in the future at steadily improving resolutions.

Electrooptical Imaging Systems. Electrooptical imaging systems are attractive because they can cover large areas of earth's surface with resolutions sufficient for imagery interpretation. However, their optics do not function through clouds, haze, fog, or precipitation. The original spaceborne imaging sensors were cameras using film that was returned to earth by deorbiting "buckets." The U.S. KH-4 CORONA satellite used one such system. Today, electrooptical imagers use arrays of light-sensitive detectors that are much like those in digital cameras.

Electrooptical images are taken in both the visible spectrum and the *infrared* spectrum. Infrared imaging uses wavelengths somewhat longer than that of visible light and can function at night as well as in daylight. At wavelengths near that of visible light (called "near infrared"), the image depends on light reflected from the earth's surface, like visible imaging. Color infrared images using this near infrared light are often called "false-color" images. Objects that are normally red appear green, green objects (except vegetation) appear blue, and "infrared" objects, which normally are not seen at all, appear red. Color infrared imagery is used heavily in vegetation studies. Healthy green vegetation is a very strong reflector of infrared radiation and appears bright red on color infrared imagery.

At longer wavelengths, further removed from those of visible light ("far infrared"), the image is created by heat radiated from the earth and objects on it, rather than from reflected light. Far infrared is useful for detecting human-made objects such as vehicles and power plants at night.

Multispectral and hyperspectral sensors use the reflected or emitted light from the surface of an object or feature to identify the object or feature. They operate mostly in the infrared spectrum, but may include the visible spectrum as well.

The *multispectral imager* is widely used in spaceborne imaging of the Earth's surface. This is a type of electrooptical imager that receives independent images at several different frequencies or wavelengths (usually infrared, but extending to visible and even ultraviolet wavelengths) simultaneously, and compares the images. Multispectral sensors are simply passive optics devices operating simultaneously in different frequency bands (wavelengths). Multispectral imagery permits people to examine moisture patterns and locate buried objects. Different surface features will show up prominently on different frequency bands of the multispectral imager. If the proper wavelengths are selected, multispectral images can be used to detect camouflage, thermal emissions, and hazardous wastes, for example.

Hyperspectral imaging uses the same technique but samples a much larger set of spectral bands (in the hundreds), with much finer spectral resolution. Both multispectral and hyperspectral imaging allow us to discriminate, classify, identify, and quantify materials that are present in the image. But the increased sampling of the spectrum allows us to garner more intelligence information than is possible with multispectral imaging. A wide range of environmental intelligence and crop forecasting techniques use hyperspectral imaging. Detection of chemical or biological weapons, bomb damage assessment of underground structures, and foliage penetration to detect troops and vehicles are examples of the potential of hyperspectral imaging. Hyperspectral scanners appear to be capable of detecting submerged submarines at shallow depths.

Specialized Technical Collection

There are many specialized techniques for collecting and processing intelligence, most of which focus on specific classes of targets and provide specific intelligence answers. Most either use novel sensors or specially process raw data from conventional sensors. In the United States many of these techniques are lumped together under the name of measurements and signatures intelligence (MASINT)—a term that embraces a diverse set of collection and processing techniques. Others are designated as SIGINT. The range of techniques is too large for a complete list, and the field is constantly changing. The following sections provide a partial list of specialized collection techniques.

Specialized technical collection employs sensors such as radar, radio frequency antennas, lasers, passive electrooptical sensors, nuclear radiation detectors, and seismic or acoustic sensors for the purposes of gathering information. These instruments gather measurements such as radar cross sections, radiant intensities, or temperatures to characterize military operations and tactics; to assess missile, aircraft, and propulsion systems performance; to monitor research, development, testing and production facilities; and to understand cultural and economic activities, environmental effects, and naturally occurring phenomena. The collection sensors used divide broadly into either remote sensing or *in situ* sensing, though some sensors may blur the difference.

Remote Sensing

Remote sensing is often defined as sensing of the earth's surface from satellites or aircraft using some part of the electromagnetic spectrum. It also

Figure 4-3   Electromagnetic Spectrum of Remote Sensing

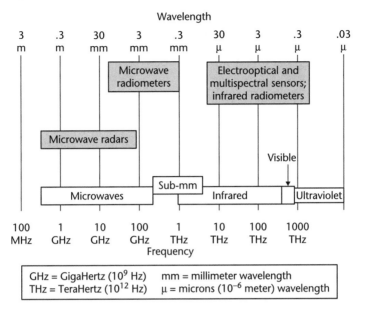

includes the sensing of aircraft or satellites from the earth. Figure 4-3 shows the segment of the electromagnetic energy spectrum that remote sensors use. Optical sensors work in the ultraviolet to infrared regions. Radars operate in the microwave and millimeter wave region.

As we move toward higher frequencies (to the right in Figure 4-3), moisture, clouds, and even darkness tend to decrease the sensor's effectiveness by reducing the amount of energy the sensor receives. For detection reliability, a sensor should operate under all weather and light conditions. But at higher frequencies the resolution of the sensor generally improves. Good resolution—the ability of the sensor to distinguish small objects—allows the identification of specific vehicles, for example. With poor resolution, the objects are blurred or indistinguishable.

Remote sensors' main advantage over other sensors is that they can cover a large area of the earth quickly. They achieve this because they can have a very wide swath width, allowing the sensor to search a wide area in one pass. Normally one faces tradeoffs between swath width and resolution. Good resolution is essential for detecting observables on the surface. However, sensors that have wide swath widths generally have poor resolution, and sensors with good resolution usually have small swath widths.

Remote sensors divide into two general classes: active and passive (see Figure 4-4). Active sensors (radars) transmit a signal and then interpret the signals that are reflected off the target. Passive sensors exploit natural emissions or

Figure 4-4   Categories of Remote Imaging Sensors

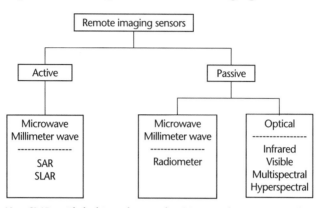

Note: SLAR = side-looking airborne radar; SAR = synthetic aperture radar.

use an alternative illumination source, such as the sun. Most of these sensors operate in the microwave, millimeter wave, or optical bands. Most remote sensors used in earth resources sensing create images, but a few do not. Each class and frequency band has unique advantages and disadvantages. And each class encompasses several specific sensor types, each of which has advantages and disadvantages.

In Situ *Sensors*

The alternative to remote sensing is to use devices that sense changes in the medium (air, water, earth) immediately surrounding the sensor. These *in situ* sensors measure phenomena within an object or at short ranges and typically detect sound, electrical currents, temperature, contaminants, radiation, or magnetic fields. Air sampling equipment, carried aloft by reconnaissance aircraft to monitor the debris from atmospheric nuclear tests, are examples of *in situ* sensors. Telemetry equipment provides readings about the radiation belts from *in situ* sensors located on spacecraft. The quantity and variety of these sensors make it impractical to discuss the technical details of each.

Most *in situ* sensors do not have the broad-area search potential of the remote sensors. Compared with sensors mounted on air and space vehicles, they have either relatively slow search rates or relatively small ranges, or both. Consequently, all of them are limited to covering much smaller areas than the remote sensors.

In situ sensors can be used to track ships or submarines. As ships or submarines move through the water, they leave behind trace chemicals. Metals are continuously deposited in the water by corrosion and erosion of the hull. Lubricants, waste flushed from sanitary tanks, hydrogen gas discharged from a submarine's life support system—all are deposited in a ship's wake. Neutron radiation from a nuclear power generator can cause detectable changes in seawater. All these contaminants leave a "track" in the ocean that can be followed by the appropriate sensors located on a trailing ship or submarine.

One class of *in situ* sensors—biosensors—have become much more prominent as a result of the growing worldwide threat of biological terrorism. Biosensors can identify specific pathogens such as anthrax and smallpox.

Electronic Intelligence

Electronic intelligence (ELINT) refers to the information gained from the remote sensing of noncommunications signals—including those emitted by radar, beacons, jammers, missile guidance systems, and altimeters. Though the acronym may be unfamiliar, ELINT is widely used in countries such as the United States: the radar detector that many motorists use to detect police radar is an ELINT device.

ELINT primarily targets radars. Radars are relatively easy to intercept since they typically transmit high power signals. The ELINT receiver begins with a substantial advantage over the radar, because whereas the radar signal travels directly from the radar to the ELINT receiver, it must travel to the target, be reflected, and return to the radar to be useful. However, typical ELINT sites or platforms are located at extreme ranges, many hundreds or thousands of miles from the radar. So, modern ELINT systems require very sensitive receivers to obtain enough signal details for analysis. ELINT divides broadly into two types: technical and operational.

Technical ELINT. Technical ELINT is used to assess a radar's capabilities and performance, to determine the level of technology used in building the radar, and to find weaknesses in the radar to help electronic warfare designers defeat it. Technical ELINT collection and processing typically concentrates on signals that already have been identified and on evolutionary modifications to these signals. However, the highest priority signals for ELINT collection are always new and unidentified signals, because they presumably represent the most advanced capability. Newly developed radars would radiate only for short periods in tests and only during times when it is believed that hostile intercept potential was at a minimum. Therefore, short duration intercepts are the best one can hope for on such radars.

Operational ELINT. Operational ELINT is primarily of interest to military field commanders and law enforcement officers for tactical intelligence. Operational ELINT involves geolocating deployed radars and determining their operational status. A ship, aircraft, or surface-to-air missile unit can often be tracked best by continuously pinpointing the location of the radar(s) it carries. Operational ELINT is used extensively in modern warfare to pinpoint targets for air attack and to locate threat radars so that attacking aircraft can avoid the defense the radars control.

Operational ELINT can also use fine-grain signatures of radar signals to identify and track specific radars. This technique is called specific emitter identification or "fingerprinting" because, as no two fingerprints are identical, no two radars have identical signal parameters, even though they may be physically identical otherwise.

Telemetry

Vehicles that are undergoing testing—missiles, aircraft, and even farm tractors and earth-moving equipment—carry instruments called transducers that monitor pressures, temperatures, and subsystems performance. The instrument readings are typically recorded for later laboratory analysis. In vehicles where the recorder might not survive a catastrophic failure (aircraft) or where recorder recovery is impractical (missiles and satellites), the readings are transmitted via radio back to a ground site. Such transmissions are called telemetry.

Complex and expensive systems such as missiles and satellites have a large number of instrument readings to transmit. It is impractical to devote a separate transmission link to each reading. Telemetry systems therefore combine the signals from the readings in a process called multiplexing for transmission using a single transmitter. Each signal occupies a "channel" in the multiplex system. At the receiver, the channels are separated (demultiplexed) and sent to separate displays or recorders.

Some telemetry systems, especially older ones, multiplex by allocating a different part of the radio frequency spectrum to each signal; this technique is known as frequency division multiplexing. A more complex approach is time division multiplexing, where each signal periodically gets to use the entire frequency bandwidth of the transmitter for a short time interval.

Interpretation of intercepted telemetry is difficult, in part because of the "scaling problem." The engineers running the instrumentation know the scales for the readings they receive and which channels of telemetry come from which instrument. The intercepting party must often infer both the nature of the instrument and the scale of the readings from external evidence— correlating the readings with external events such as aircraft or missile altitude or speed.

Because telemetry involves the deliberate transmission of information, its interception could be considered a part of COMINT. But because of its specialized nature and fairly narrow customer base, telemetry intercept is included as part of specialized technical collection.

As noted earlier, telemetry interception is also called foreign instrumentation signals intelligence, or FISINT. However, *FIS* does not accurately characterize the growing commercial collection efforts to collect telemetry on competitors' products. Some aircraft manufacturers have for years intercepted and analyzed the telemetry from their competitors' aircraft or missile tests.

Telemetry can be denied to an opponent by encryption. The digital telemetry that is typically sent by time division multiplexing is particularly amenable to encryption. Encryption denies the collector information on what are called telemetry internals; that is, the values of the readings themselves. Encryption therefore forces the collector to rely on what are called telemetry externals, that is, changes in the signal due to the flight profile of the vehicle that provide information about aspects of the vehicle's performance.

Radar Intelligence

Radar traditionally is used to locate and track a target in space. One special type of radar sensing, usually called RADINT, uses radars to collect intelligence regarding the physical characteristics and capabilities of radar targets. RADINT targets have included satellites, missiles, ships, aircraft, and battlefield vehicles. RADINT can image the target, determine its radar cross-section, identify and discriminate among targets, precisely measure components, divine the motion of the target or components, and measure the target's radar reflectance and absorption characteristics. Radar returns can be used to reconstruct the trajectories of missiles and convey the details and configuration of the missile reentry vehicle itself. One of the most significant RADINT applications is for space object identification.

Space Object Identification Radars. For several decades the United States and other countries have used high resolution microwave radars for remote identification of targets. Such radars have particular advantages in space object identification (SOI), as compared with optical imaging devices, which also are used for SOI. Microwave radars are able to operate through long atmospheric paths and in cloud or weather conditions that would render an optical system ineffective. Also, such radars offer a rich variety of waveforms and associated processing techniques that can be used both to create images of and to observe operations of satellites.

A satellite comprises several interconnected objects, each of which scatters radar energy back toward the radar. At certain orientations of the satellite relative to the radar, the arms that interconnect these centers also would scatter radar energy back toward the radar. For example, when the arm is in the plane of the radar wavefront, the arms themselves would become strong scatterers. Furthermore, each major scattering center, in turn, comprises several smaller scattering centers that can be separated (resolved) by a high resolution radar.

Imaging radar techniques attempt to resolve these scattering centers with the highest possible resolution so that the scattering centers form a detailed image of the satellite. Some SOI techniques also attempt to observe motion of the centers, such as the reorientation movement of antennas or solar panels. The combination of imagery and observation of component movements can reveal a great deal about the mission and operations of the satellite.

Radar imagery for SOI is difficult to achieve because conventional long-range search radars have a wide beamwidth (on the order of hundreds of meters) at satellite ranges, so that the scattering centers cannot be separated (resolved) in azimuth (perpendicular to the direction of travel of the radar signal). Normal radar pulse widths are on the order of tens to hundreds of meters, so that the scattering centers cannot be resolved in range. As a result, the satellite appears to such radars as a single large scattering center.

The usual approach to SOI imaging radar is to use very wide bandwidth radars, giving a pulse that can effectively separate scattering centers that are less than one meter apart. A technique called range-Doppler processing can then be used to obtain good azimuth resolution. In particular, a technique called inverse synthetic aperture radar can then be used to create an array that is effectively thousands of meters long in the direction of travel of the satellite. Such an array has a very narrow beamwidth along the direction of travel, so that scattering centers can be resolved in azimuth.

The combination of high-range resolution and high-azimuth resolution can be used to generate a radar image that resolves the scattering centers. Figure 4-5 shows a radar image of the space shuttle created using such techniques. SOI radars can obtain similar-quality images of aircraft. The quality of radar imaging does not nearly match that of optical imaging. The image requires interpretation and an understanding of how satellites are designed.

Figure 4-5   Radar Image of the Space Shuttle

The objects at the extreme right and left of the image are the wings, and the shuttle nose is at the top.

In strategic intelligence, radar for SOI appears to be the primary RADINT tool in use by countries other than the United States. Several countries have built or are planning high-performance radars that have a technical intelligence capability. Russia, Germany, Japan, the United Kingdom, and France are most notable for their developing capability.[18]

Laser Radar. Laser radar, also called optical radar or LIDAR, operates at a much higher frequency than microwave radars. Laser radars transmit using pulsed lasers whose wavelength can vary from the infrared band to the ultraviolet. Their high frequency allows the transmission of a very short pulse (a nanosecond or less), which is a difficult matter for a conventional microwave radar. Low power lasers that are adequate for short-range radar are available worldwide. Medium and high power lasers are increasingly available for use against long range (satellite, for example) targets.

The use of laser radars to exploit acoustic vibrations for COMINT was discussed earlier. RADINT uses laser radars because they are capable of transmitting very short pulses for high-range accuracy, because they can produce a narrow beam, and because they provide information about the reflectance of the target that microwave radars cannot provide.[19]

Radio Frequency Intelligence

A variety of equipment emits radio frequency energy: internal combustion engines, electrical generators, switches. These emissions are typically weak, but sensitive equipment can detect the signals and locate the emitter or use the characteristic "signature" of the emission to identify the target. In addition to highly sensitive receiving equipment, processors need highly sophisticated signal processing equipment to deal with unintentional radiation signals and derive useful intelligence from them.

Specific pieces of equipment can often be identified by their unique radio frequency signatures. The functions being performed within a factory building and the rates of production, for example, can sometimes be determined by monitoring the radio frequency emission patterns.

Furthermore, intentional radiation can sometimes be used to obtain target signatures, because moving parts on the target modulate a nearby radio frequency signal. A radar or radio mounted on an aircraft, for example, will have its signal modulated by the aircraft propellers or jet turbine blades. The modulation, though weak, can provide both the aircraft type and identification of the specific aircraft. The concept is similar to use of microwaves or lasers to illuminate an object and to pick up conversations as audio vibrations that modulate the signal.

Geophysical Intelligence

Geophysical intelligence involves the collection, processing, and exploitation of environmental disturbances transmitted through the earth (ground, water, or atmosphere). Magnetic sensing can detect the presence or motion of vehicles and ships or submarines by the weak changes they create in the earth's magnetic field. Magnetometers, mounted on aircraft, have been used to detect submerged submarines at short distances (on the order of a few hundred meters).

Unintentional emission or modulation of sound waves (acoustic energy) can provide the same types of intelligence information as those for radio frequency energy. This specialized area of unintentional emissions intelligence is called either ACINT (for underwater sound) or ACOUSTINT (sound in air). Acoustic energy collection works best where sound carries well over large distances, as underwater sound does. The use of passive sonar to obtain the signatures of submarines is well known. The submarine's turbines, propellers, and other on-board machinery generate acoustic noise that can be detected and used for identification at ranges of many kilometers in water.

Closely related to acoustic intelligence is seismic intelligence, the measurement of seismic waves that travel through the earth as a result of a major disturbance, such as an underground or underwater explosion. If a number of such *in situ* sensors are deployed around the globe, signal analysts can locate the source of such an explosion by comparing the time of arrival of the signal at each sensor.

Radiometry and Spectrometry

All objects at temperatures above absolute zero emit radio frequency energy. As the target becomes hotter, both the strength and frequency of emissions increase; very hot objects radiate in the visible range (a lamp filament, for example). Anyone who has ever watched iron being heated to red- or white-hot temperatures has observed this phenomenon.

Different objects radiate differently. Rock, earth, seawater, and vegetation all have different emission patterns. Factories or vehicles, when in use, tend to radiate more strongly, and the presence of "hot spots" on a building or vehicle provides information about the nature and status of the vehicle or the use of the building.

Radiometric sensors take advantage of this phenomenon to obtain information about ships, aircraft, missiles, and the environment (the natural background). These passive sensors receive and record the electromagnetic energy that objects naturally emit. The radiometer records the natural energy that is emitted in the radio frequency range by heated objects; the warmer the object, the more energy it radiates, and a good radiometer can sense temperature changes of less than one degree Celsius. However, the radiometer typically must view the target for a long period of time, compared with radar viewing, and therefore will have a comparatively poorer search rate at its maximum sensitivity. Radiometers are of two general types: microwave and infrared.

Radiometry is used to characterize weather; cloud conditions; vegetation and soil moisture; and the water content of snow, sea ice, missile plumes, and ship wakes. Objects near room temperature are usually investigated using microwave radiometers. Hot objects, such as missile plumes and high explosive and nuclear detonations, tend to be investigated using radiometers operating in the infrared bands.

Microwave radiometers are less attractive than infrared radiometers because of their poorer resolution, but, like radars, they are not much affected by clouds. Both can operate as either imaging or nonimaging sensors. Some microwave radiometers are designed to receive millimeter wave energy, which provides better resolution but somewhat poorer all-weather capability.

Nuclear Sensors

All nuclear reactions result in the emission of particles and waves—gamma rays, x-rays, neutrons, electrons, or ions. The radiation is strongest from a surface or atmospheric nuclear detonation, but nuclear power reactors also emit. The strength and type of radiation allows one to characterize the emitter. A number of nuclear radiation detectors have been developed; some are capable of detecting concealed nuclear devices at substantial ranges, and some are quite small, the size of a shirt button.

Materials Intelligence

Materials intelligence includes the collection and analysis of trace elements, particulates, effluents, and debris. Such materials are released into the atmosphere, water, or earth by a wide range of industrial processes.

Materials intelligence is important in analysis of nuclear, chemical, and biological warfare; factory production; and economic and environmental problems. It has long been practiced in law enforcement, and one of its premier practitioners is fictional: Sherlock Holmes, who, as he modestly admitted, could "distinguish at a glance the ash of any known brand either of cigar or of tobacco."[20]

Biometrics

Biometrics is the use of a person's physical characteristics or personal traits for human recognition. Its current popularity belies its age; Morse code operators have long been able to recognize other operators by their characteristic pattern of keying the code, known as their "fist." Digitized fingerprints and voiceprints have been used in human recognition for years, and their use is increasing. Iris and retinal scans, hand geometry, and keystroke dynamics are newer biometric technologies.

Today biometric facial recognition is probably the most rapidly growing area of biometrics. Facial recognition uses camera images, measuring distances and angles between points on the face—mouth extremities, nostrils, eye corners—to create a "faceprint" that can be recognized in scanning a crowd of people. Biometric facial recognition currently is being used to control access to facilities and to computers, to gaming casinos, and at border crossing points around the world.[21]

Information Operations

Collection that is undertaken against an information processing system does not fit under any of the traditional INTs. It typically has some connection with HUMINT, because it is often an extension of the technical collection efforts carried out by HUMINT operatives. It resembles COMINT, especially when collection from data communications networks is involved. Collection against publicly available information processing systems such as the World Wide Web falls into the category of open source. This section focuses on collection against protected systems, though the Web often is a channel for such attack.

Intelligence operations against computers are rapidly becoming the best known type of technical collection—and the most productive. Many groups are interested in collecting such information, including hostile intelligence services, organized crime groups, commercial competitors, and pranksters or "hackers." Increasingly these intelligence efforts are sponsored by government rather than nongovernment groups. In 1999 and 2000 unidentified hackers downloaded scores of "sensitive but unclassified" internal documents from computers in the Department of Defense and in the Los Alamos and Lawrence Livermore labs. The effort was traced to a foreign country whose officials denied being involved, but the intrusions suddenly stopped.[22]

Computer security programs to counter such attacks usually focus on vulnerability, because vulnerabilities are easier to measure. Very little analysis effort is devoted to assessing the threat to international commercial networks or to government and commercial computers and databases. Because of a lack of threat knowledge, companies and countries devote too many resources to nonexistent threats simply because they represent the realm of the possible; conversely, because threat assessments have not been made, they devote too few resources to areas under attack.

The threat of sophisticated penetration attempts, however, is increasing. The proliferation of computer capabilities around the world, and the development of commercial computer espionage capabilities, has resulted in the rapid expansion of the threat. Commercial computer espionage will continue to increase during this decade, and it will become even more difficult to distinguish such efforts from national security targeting. When a hacker enters a system, as the previous example illustrates, the victim usually cannot identify the real source of the attack. Although the use of computer attack for commercial espionage is illegal in most countries, such attacks are likely to grow more numerous.

Attacks on information processing equipment are possible by exploiting equipment emanations or by direct or indirect access to the equipment software. Networks can make remote access to data much easier. The following sections describe some commonly used techniques for exploiting computer systems in intelligence. Because this is a rapidly changing and highly technical field, these descriptions are only introductory and omit some of the more sophisticated collection methods.

Viruses and Worms. Viruses are well known in the computer business. They may have some application in information warfare, such as in actions against an opponent's computer networks, but they are not common tools for collecting intelligence. Because most computer systems have virus protection, the trend is to make a computer virus *polymorphic*—that is, stealthy and able to change its code and form to avoid detection.

Worms are more selective and focused than viruses. The distinguishing characteristic of a virus is its ability to replicate itself and spread through a network. A worm performs some type of illicit operation within a computer system but does not contain instructions to replicate itself. Worms are used, for example, to instruct a bank computer to transfer money to an illicit account. They can also be used to transmit controlled data to unauthorized recipients, and this is how they are used in intelligence collection.

Trojan Horses. The Trojan horse is a seemingly innocent program that conceals its primary purpose—to infiltrate the user's computer system for illicit purposes. A Trojan horse may contain a virus or worm, for example. Operating systems software and almost any applications software package—spreadsheets, word processors, database managers—could be Trojan horses. Trojan horses predate viruses and have been used for years to enter high level accounts that were protected by passwords. A simple Trojan Horse in a word processor might, for example, make a copy of all files that the word processor saves and store the copies in a location where the horse's "master" can access them later. Another simple Trojan horse, once activated, waits until the user attempts to log off. It then simulates a real logoff while keeping the user online. When the user next attempts to log on, the Trojan Horse captures the user's password for its "master" and simulates a logon.

Trapdoors. The trapdoor is a set of instructions that permits easy access to a computer's software or operating system. It normally bypasses the security routines so that it can be used to enter the system at any time for running tests, upgrading systems, or fixing problems. Normally, trapdoors are eliminated when the system becomes operational. However, trapdoors may be left open by mistake or to permit continuing maintenance. They may also be deliberately planted to permit access at a later date.

The best known trapdoor existed only in the movies. In the movie *WarGames,* the hero (a computer hacker) discovers a trapdoor called Joshua that allows him access to the North American Aerospace Defense Command's strategic defense software, starting a chain of events in which the war game becomes much too realistic.

The trapdoor is perhaps the primary tool for industrial computer espionage. In many systems a trapdoor gives unlimited access to data in the system. Valuable corporate proprietary information has been acquired time and again from competitors via trapdoors.[23]

Collecting Emanations. If the computer emits compromising electromagnetic signals, sensors placed close by can recover information being processed. Electronic and magnetic signals can radiate from the area both in space and through power lines or other conducting paths. Sensitive in detail and difficult to detect, these types of attacks are a capability of sophisticated adversaries. U.S. government concern for protection against the collection of emanations spawned a sizable industry known as TEMPEST. TEMPEST technology uses shielding and other electronic design techniques to reduce the radiated electromagnetic signals.

Protecting Intelligence Sources and Methods

It is axiomatic that if you need information, someone will try to keep it from you. In small governments and the business intelligence world, selective dissemination of and tight controls on intelligence information are possible. But a large government has too many intelligence customers to justify such tight restrictions. Thus these bureaucracies have established an elaborate system to simultaneously protect and disseminate intelligence information. This protection system is loosely called the compartmentation system, because it puts information in "compartments" and restricts access to the compartments.

There are two levels of protection for intelligence information. The levels distinguish between the *product* of intelligence and the *sources and methods;* usually the product is accorded less protection than the sources and methods. Why? The product, if lost, reveals only itself and not how it was obtained. Information about the product is typically classified "secret" or below, though "top secret" reports are used to protect especially sensitive information. Information that might reveal the identity of the source (the agent) is given the highest level of protection. Loss of this information usually results in someone being imprisoned or killed, wherein the source is lost permanently and other potential sources are discouraged from coming forward.

In the U.S. intelligence community, the system for protecting the intelligence product, sources, and methods is called the Sensitive Compartmented Information (SCI) system. The SCI system uses an extensive set of code words to protect sources and methods. Usually only the collectors and processors have access to the code word materials. The product is mostly protected only by standard markings such as "secret" and "top secret," and access is granted to a wide range of people.

Under the SCI system, protection of sources and methods is extremely high for two types of COMINT. Clandestine COMINT—usually acquired through taps on telecommunications systems—is heavily protected because it is expensive to set up, provides high-quality intelligence, and its loss has a severe and often permanent impact. COMINT based on decryption is the second highly protected type. Successes at breaking encryption are tightly compartmented because an opponent can readily change the encryption code, and breaking the new code is laborious.

IMINT, on the other hand, has no special controls, because the information needs to be made available quickly to field commanders. Very little protection of sources and methods is needed anyway, because when a reconnaissance aircraft flies overhead, it is obvious to the enemy that you are taking their pictures. Most aerial photography has been classified secret or below, and a substantial amount of satellite photography is now unclassified.

Open source intelligence has little or no protection because the source material is unclassified. However, the techniques for exploiting open source material, and the specific material of interest for exploitation, can tell an opponent much about an intelligence service's targets. For this reason, the National Security Agency has for years marked its translations of open source as "Official Use Only." A restrictive marking also allows a government to ignore copyright laws while limiting use of the material. Corporations make use of similar restrictive markings on material that is translated or reproduced for in-house use for the same reasons—concealment of interest and avoidance of copyright problems.

A more serious reason for protecting open source methods is that, if an opponent knows what the intelligence target materials are, it is easier for him to use countermeasures. The United States has long been aware that many intelligence services translate and avidly read *Aviation Week and Space Technology*. When the Defense Department wishes to mislead or deceive another country about U.S. aerospace capabilities and intentions, this magazine is the logical place to "plant" the misleading story.

The protection given to specialized technical collection varies greatly across the many "INTs" involved. ELINT is classified secret or below. When an opponent uses a radar, he has to assume that someone will intercept it, and denial is very difficult. In contrast, the ability to break out the telemetry channels and determine the meaning of each channel signal is the important method to protect. FISINT therefore resembles COMINT—the processing part is accorded tight compartmentation protection. Information operations are given a high degree of protection for a similar reason; they are easily defeated if their success becomes known to an opponent.

Compartmentation of all these types of intelligence affects synthesis/analysis in two ways. First, there is a constant tension between using information and risking loss of the source. Material from the "sources and methods" compartment has to be moved into the "intelligence product" compartment so that it can be used by the customer. There is no easy way to do this, and almost every intelligence service has lost collection assets because an intelligence customer gave the press information or acted in such a way that the collection source was "blown."

Second, there is the problem of analyst access to the information. A question that analysts often encounter during data research is: "What if I can't get access to critical data that I know exists?" This is a recurring problem in all government intelligence organizations, because sensitive material is often published in tightly held compartmentation channels. Intelligence community compartmentation is an abused and sometimes illogical system, often misused to protect turf rather than sources and methods. Critics of the U.S. intelligence

Analysis Principle ●————————————————————————

Box 4-2   Darwin's Law Applies Only in a Darwinian Environment

"The ultimate result of shielding men from the effects of folly is to fill the world with fools."
Herbert Spencer

Natural selection works only if allowed to take place without external interference. In a Darwinian information environment, freedom of information allows only the valid ideas to survive. The problem is that a large intelligence community is a compartmented one, so inaccurate target models are often protected from competition, wheras they would die quickly if exposed to criticism. Peer review and the voice of a devil's advocate are crucial during synthesis/analysis. During the 1970s the U.S. intelligence community had competing analysis teams prepare competing national intelligence estimates on the Soviet Union, partly to promote the formation of competing target models.

community have noted that the providers of intelligence are jealous of their powers and resist external review of their product.[24] All the collectors in a large intelligence bureaucracy want to present their data directly to the policymakers—without interference from a middleman—and receive credit for it. One of the extreme examples of this was the scramble of Nazi Germany's intelligence organizations to curry favor with Hitler by presenting choice tidbits of information.[25] Credit is also a factor in determining funding for a project or organization. All intelligence communities must deal with these same incentives.

The major penalty compartmentation imposes on the intelligence business is that it restricts critical review of the analytic product. A highly compartmented intelligence organization pays a significant price for such compartmentation in the quality of its product. As Box 4-2 notes, peer review is important in synthesis/analysis.

Summary

The traditional U.S. taxonomy of intelligence collection was created because of historical precedent or for bureaucratic reasons. It divides intelligence collection into open source, SIGINT, IMINT, HUMINT, and MASINT. This chapter presents an alternative view of the sources of intelligence, one that is more relevant for intelligence analysts. This alternative taxonomy includes the four sources that are used by most analysts: open source, COMINT, IMINT, and HUMINT; and specialized technical collection, which includes newer and very focused collection techniques that depend heavily on technology.

In gathering information for synthesizing the target model, analysts start with the more readily available and inexpensive sources (internal files and open source material) and move to the more obscure and expensive ones (HUMINT, COMINT, and IMINT).

Open source material is perhaps the most valuable source of intelligence and is typically the most easily overlooked by government intelligence organizations in favor of classified information. Open source information has traditionally meant published material that is publicly available—newspapers, books, and magazines. Increasingly it includes the Internet and commercially available imagery sources.

HUMINT includes clandestine sources (the traditional spy); liaison (the sharing of intelligence with other intelligence services or nongovernmental organizations); and materiel acquisition (acquiring and exploiting equipment or samples). It also includes acquiring information from emigrés and defectors and through clandestine polling. Elicitation—the practice of obtaining information about a topic from conversations, preferably without the source knowing what is happening—is widely practiced in both governmental and commercial intelligence.

COMINT, or communications intelligence, is the interception, processing, and reporting of an opponent's communications. It includes "bugs" and the traditional microphone and wire but also advanced technology to collect voice, data, and facsimile communications.

IMINT includes short range imagery—both still pictures and video—and remote sensing (from distances ranging from miles to thousands of miles). It ranges across the electromagnetic spectrum, including radar, infrared, and visible spectrum images. Newer technology such as multispectral and hyperspectral imaging uses information about the spectral signature of a target to provide insights that are not available otherwise.

For specialized intelligence needs, a wide range of sophisticated technical collection techniques is available. Electronic intelligence is perhaps the most widely used of these, especially in supporting the military and law enforcement. Telemetry collection is used to assess the performance of aircraft and missiles. Information operations (such as computer "hacking") are used to obtain intelligence from computers and data networks. The number of such technical collection techniques is substantial today, and new techniques continue to be developed as new technologies develop or evolve.

Collection sources and methods have to be protected or they will be lost. Names of HUMINT sources, the nature of COMINT or specialized technical collection, and the decryption of encrypted messages all fall into this category. The information a source provides is accorded less protection than the source's identity, because the information provided needs to go to many intelligence customers.

The next chapter describes how to evaluate the information that is gathered from these different sources. It also begins the discussion of fitting information into the target model, a discussion that will continue throughout the book.

Notes

1. Numbers 13:17, *King James Bible.*
2. Walter Laqueur, *The Uses and Limits of Intelligence* (Somerset, N.J.: Transaction Publishers, 1993), 43.
3. Arthur Weiss, "How Far Can Primary Research Go?", *Competitive Intelligence Magazine,* 4 November-December 2001): 18.
4. Ibid.
5. Richard Eels and Peter Nehemkis, *Corporate Intelligence and Espionage* (Old Tappan, N.J.: Macmillan, 1984), 59; Charles D. Ameringer, *U.S. Foreign Intelligence* (Lanham, Md.: Lexington Books, 1990), 170.
6. Peter Schwartz, *The Art of the Long View* (New York: Doubleday, 1991), 78.
7. Charlotte W. Craig, "Germany Drops Spy Case Against Lopez; Former GM Exec Must Give Money to Charity" *Detroit Free Press,* July 28, 1998, www.auto.com/industry/qlopez28.htm.
8. University of California at Davis, Department of Geology, "The Age of Iron," www.geology.ucdavis.edu/~GEL115/115CH5.html, March 22, 2003.
9. The full details of this real-life "spy thriller" can be found in Alfred Price's book, *Instruments of Darkness* (London: William Kimber, 1967), 80–87.
10. Ibid.
11. "Project Jennifer," http://web.ukonline.co.uk/aj.cashmore/.features/articles/jennifer-text.html, March 22, 2003.
12. F. W. Winterbotham, *The Ultra Secret* (New York: Dell, 1974).
13. For more information, see Wilhelm Flicke, *War Secrets in the Ether* (Laguna Hills, Calif.: Aegean Park Press, 1994), 4–12.
14. Ibid.
15. Douglas H. Dearth and Thomas R. Goodden, *Strategic Intelligence: Theory and Application,* 2d ed. (Washington, D.C.: U.S. Army War College and Defense Intelligence Agency, 1995), 111.
16. John Wingfield, *Bugging* (London: Robert Hale Ltd., 1984), 21–22.
17. Ibid., 52–53.
18. Tom Wilson, "Threats to United States Space Capabilities," Commission to Assess United States National Security Space Management and Organization, www.fas.org/spp/military/commission/report.htm.
19. *Reflectance* is defined as the fraction of the total radiant flux incident upon a surface that is reflected and that varies according to the wavelength distribution of the incident radiation.
20. Sir Arthur Conan Doyle, "A Study in Scarlet," in *The Complete Sherlock Holmes,* (London: Hamlyn, 1984), 26.
21. John D. Woodward Jr., "Super Bowl Surveillance: Facing Up to Biometrics," in *Intelligencer: Journal of U.S. Intelligence Studies,* Summer 2001: 37.
22. Association of Foreign Intelligence Officers (AFIO) Weekly Intelligence Note 36-02, September 9, 2002; available from the association by contacting afio @ afio.com.
23. John McAfee and Colin Haynes, *Computer Viruses, Worms, Data Diddlers, Killer Programs, and Other Threats to Your System* (New York: St. Martin's Press, 1989), 79.
24. Angelo Codevilla, *Informing Statecraft: Intelligence for a New Century* (New York: Free Press, 1992), 24.
25. David A. Kahn, *Hitler's Spies: German Military Intelligence in World War II* (New York: Perseus Books Group, 2000), 63.

5

Populating the Model

What is truth?

Pontius Pilate

M ost synthesis involves aggregating data or establishing data relationships in the target model using the data sources discussed in the previous chapter. This step in the intelligence process is often defined as *collation:* the organizing of relevant information in a coherent way, looking at source and context. It includes evaluating the information for accuracy, completeness, and meaning.

This chapter describes a collation methodology for synthesis. Synthesis normally starts with a model template or template set of the sort described in Chapter 3. Our job now is to fit the relevant information into the templates. We talk about templates in the plural because we wind up with several of them when dealing with complex problems—both collateral models, as discussed in Chapter 2, and alternative models. As David Schum has noted, "the generation of new ideas in fact investigation usually rests upon arranging or juxtaposing our thoughts and evidence in different ways."[1] To do this, multiple alternative models are needed.

Evaluating Evidence

The basic problem of weighing evidence is determining its reliability. In the end, weighing evidence involves subjective judgments that the analyst alone must make. Some helpful insights on reliability are contained in the preceding chapter—see the sections on COMINT and HUMINT for some analytical pitfalls.

Weighing evidence entails three steps: evaluating the source, evaluating the communications channel through which the information arrived, and evaluating the evidence itself. The communications channel is often ignored, but it is a critical piece in solving the reliability puzzle, as discussed later in this chapter.

At the heart of the evaluation process is one of the oldest analytic principles, Occam's razor. The name comes from William of Occam, who said that

Analysis Principle ●————————————————————————

Box 5-1   Occam's Razor

Explain your observations with the fewest possible hypotheses. In other words, choose the simplest explanation that fits the facts at hand.

"It is vain to do with more what can be done with fewer."[2] In modern-day English, we know this as the KISS principle: Keep it simple, stupid! Occam's razor is not an infallible principle; sometimes the correct explanation for a given set of facts is very complex or convoluted. However, analysts can make data fit almost any desired conclusion, especially if they selectively discard inconvenient facts. So the razor is a valuable part of the analyst's toolkit (see Box 5-1).

Evaluating the Source

Accept nothing at face value. Evaluate the source of evidence carefully and beware the source's motives for providing the information. Evaluating the source involves answering three questions:

- Is the source competent (knowledgeable about the information being given)?
- Did the source have the access needed to get the information?
- Does the source have a vested interest or bias?

In the HUMINT business, this is called determining *bona fides* for human sources. Even when not dealing with HUMINT, one must ask these three questions.

Competence. The Anglo-American judicial system deals effectively with competence—it allows people to describe what they observed with their senses because, absent disability, we are presumed competent to sense things. The judicial system does not allow the average person to interpret what he or she sensed unless the person can be qualified as an expert in such interpretation.

Source evaluators must apply the same criteria. It is too easy, in a raw intelligence report, to accept not only the observations of a source but also the inferences that the source has drawn. Always ask, "What was the basis for this conclusion?" If no satisfactory answer is forthcoming, use the source's conclusions with caution or not at all.

A radar expert talking about an airborne intercept radar performance is credible. If he goes on to describe the aircraft performance, he is considerably less credible. An economist assessing inflation prospects in a country might have credibility; if she goes on to assess the likely political impact of the inflation, be skeptical.

Access. Usually, the issue of source access does not come up or is not an issue, because it is assumed that the source had access. Where there is reason to be suspicious about the source, however, check whether the source might not have had the claimed access.

In the legal world, checks on source access come up regularly in witness cross-examinations. One of the more famous examples was the "Almanac Trial" of 1858, where Abraham Lincoln conducted the cross-examination. It was the dying wish of an old friend that Lincoln represent his friend's son, Duff Armstrong, who was on trial for murder. Lincoln gave his client a tough, artful defense; in the trial's highlight, Lincoln consulted an almanac to discredit a prosecution witness who claimed that he saw the murder clearly because the moon was high in the sky. The almanac showed that the moon was lower on the horizon, and the witness's access—that is, his ability to see the murder—was called into question.[3]

Vested Interest or Bias. In HUMINT analysts occasionally encounter the "professional source" who sells information to as many bidders as possible and has an incentive to make the information as interesting as possible. Even the densest source will quickly realize that more interesting information gets him more money.

Official reports from government organizations have a similar vested interest problem. Be skeptical of this information; it deserves no automatic credibility because of the source. One seldom finds outright lies in such reports, but government officials will occasionally distort or conceal facts to support their policy positions or to protect their personal interests. U.S. researchers have long provided to U.S. government intelligence organizations distorted information on the researchers' foreign contacts. The usual approach is to exaggerate the importance of their foreign counterparts' work as a ploy to encourage more funding for their own work. A report does not necessarily have more validity simply because it came from a citizen of one's own country rather than from a foreigner, as the following example illustrates.

It is no secret anymore that U.S. intelligence services used our academic experts to get information from their Russian counterparts in the days of the cold war. In one case a U.S. expert on ionospheric research came back from a Moscow conference with a report that his Russian counterpart was investigating the use of the ionosphere for a new form of long-range communications. The report caused some concern in the Defense Department, and to keep the Soviets from getting a jump up on the United States, the Defense Advance Research Projects Agency funded a U.S. research effort—some of the research money, of course, going to the expert who brought the report home.

In what became an unholy alliance, the Soviet scientist, in turn, called his government's attention to the new U.S. research work. The Soviet government, figuring that there must be something there if the Americans were working on it, funded the Soviet scientist to conduct similar research and experiments. The research never really provided anything of interest outside academia, except possibly a useful lesson on source evaluation for both sides.

Vested interest and bias are both common problems in dealing with experts in the comparative modeling and analysis (benchmarking) techniques that were introduced in Chapter 3. Comparative modeling—comparing your country's or organization's developments with those of an opponent—can involve four distinct fact patterns. Each pattern poses challenges about vested interest or bias. The first possible pattern is that Country A has developed a certain capability (for example, a weapon, technology, or factory process) and so has opponent Country B. In this case the analyst from Country A has the job of comparing Country B's capability with that of Country A. The other three possible patterns are that Country A has developed a particular capability, but Country B has not; that Country A has not developed a particular capability, but Country B has; or that neither country has developed the capability. In short, the possibilities can be described as:

- We did it—they did it.
- We did it—they didn't do it.
- We didn't do it—they did it.
- We didn't do it—they didn't do it.

There are many examples of the "We did it—they did it" sort of intelligence problem, especially in industries where competitors typically develop similar products. The United States developed intercontinental ballistic missiles (ICBMs); the Russians developed ICBMs. Both sides developed antiballistic missile systems and missile firing submarines. Many countries build aircraft, cruise missiles, tanks, electric power distribution systems, computers, and so on. In these cases the intelligence officer's analysis problem is not so difficult because he can turn to his own country's or organization's experts on that particular system or product for help.

For example, in World War II both the British and the Germans developed and used radar. So when in 1942 a British reconnaissance aircraft photographed a bowl-shaped antenna near the French coast, British intelligence could determine, with help from their experts, that it was a radar. Because the radar, which was later nicknamed the Würzburg, posed a threat to British aircraft attacks on Germany, the British undertook some rather direct technical collection means to gather additional information about the radar. The result was the Bruneval Raid, described in Chapter 4.

There can be some pitfalls, however, when a country uses its own experts, and analysis of the Würzburg is a good example. The Würzburgs were normally deployed in pairs, one radar in a pair having one to three searchlights collocated with it. British radar experts believed that the second radar was a spare, to be used when the first radar was inoperative, since this was the normal British practice. British intelligence officer R. V. Jones, however, argued that the Würzburg with searchlights was intended to track bombers, whereas the second radar had the job of tracking fighters that would be guided to the bomber. British experts disagreed, since this would require an accuracy in coordinate transformation that was beyond their technical skill at that time. They failed to appreciate the accuracy with which German radars operated as a matter of course. As it turned out, Jones, armed with a better understanding of the German way of building defense systems, was correct.

In the second case of "We did it—they didn't do it," the intelligence officer runs into a real problem: It is almost impossible to prove a negative in intelligence. The fact that no intelligence information exists about an opponent's development cannot be used to show the development does not exist.

After the British created the magnetron (a microwave transmitter tube widely used in radar) and discovered what wonders it could do for a radar system, their constant worry was that the Germans would make a similar discovery and that the British would have to face radars with capability equal to their own. In fact, the Germans only learned about the magnetron when they captured one from a downed British aircraft late in the war, but the threat kept British intelligence on edge.

The third pattern of "We didn't do it—they did it," is the most dangerous type that we encounter. Here the intelligence officer has to overcome opposition from skeptics in his country. R. V. Jones faced a case like this when he pieced together the operating principles of a new German aircraft navigation system called Knickebein.

Knickebein was a radio beam system that the Germans used to guide their bombers at night to their bomb drop point (usually London). At one point, when Jones was attempting to convince top government officials to send radio-equipped aircraft aloft to search for the Knickebein signal, he was opposed by Britain's leading authority on radio wave propagation—Thomas Eckersley of the Marconi Company. Eckersley argued that radio waves would not propagate sufficiently far at 30 megahertz to be observed over London. Fortunately for Jones, the ELINT search aircraft collected the signal before its flights could be halted.

"We didn't do it—they didn't do it." This seems to be a ridiculous case. After all, if we haven't developed a weapon and they haven't developed a weapon, who cares? The answer is that people do care, and intelligence analysts spend a great deal of their time on just this sort of problem.

Back in World War II, British intelligence received reports about classified testing going on at a secret installation inside Germany. According to the reports, automobiles driving near this installation would suddenly stall and could not be started again. After a while a German sentry would step out of the nearby woods, tell the automobile drivers they could proceed, and the automobiles would start and run normally again.

As one might imagine, the thought of a weapon that could stall internal combustion engines caused British intelligence some concern, since British tanks, trucks, and airplanes tended to rely on such engines. While the threat was a continuing concern to British intelligence, in the postwar period it was found that the order of events had become transposed in reports. What actually happened is that the Germans were testing very sensitive radio equipment that was vulnerable to automobile ignition noise. When testing was underway, German sentries throughout the area around the plant would force all automobiles to stop and shut down their ignition until testing was over.

This sort of transposition of cause and effect is not uncommon in human source reporting. Part of the skill of an intelligence analyst is in avoiding the trap of taking sources too literally. Occasionally, intelligence analysts must spend more time than they should on problems that are even more fantastic or improbable than that of the German engine killer. During the 1970s and early 1980s the United States expended loads of intelligence and scientific research effort on the threat that the USSR was building a particle beam weapon capable of destroying ballistic missile warheads in flight. In retrospect, the particle beam weapon appears to have been a classic case of "we didn't do it—they didn't do it"; the United States didn't build one and neither did the Soviets; in fact, no one could.

Where comparison of systems or technologies is used, the usual approach is to compare systems or technology performance, as measured in test and evaluation programs, with the performance data or estimates about the target's system. Test and evaluation have been essential parts of systems development. In assessing systems that use advanced technologies, test and evaluation is important because so many techniques work in theory but not in practice.

However, an intelligence organization faces a problem in using its own parent organization's (or country's) test and evaluation results: many have been contaminated. Some of the tests are faked, some contain distortions or omit key points. An honestly conducted, objective test may be a rarity. Several reasons exist for this problem. Tests are sometimes conducted to prove or disprove a preconceived notion and are thus unconsciously slanted. Some tests are faked because they would show the vulnerability or the ineffectiveness of a system and because procurement decisions often depend on the test outcomes. History provides many examples of this problem, though the majority of cases probably are never discovered.

During World War II both the British and the Germans conducted tests that were rigged to prove a point.[4] In the example of Sims' continuous aim naval gunnery system, which is discussed in Chapter 11, the U.S. Navy tested a proposed new technique for gunnery. The test was designed to confirm the preconceived notion that the technique would not work, not to test a concept.

A typical example of the problem is an electronics warfare test conducted a few years ago at one of the U.S. military test ranges. An airborne jammer was not performing as expected against a particular target-tracking radar. Investigation revealed that the radar had in fact been jammed, but the radar site personnel had tracked the jammer aircraft using a second radar that was not supposed to be part of the test.

In addition to recognizing that an organization's (or country's) test results may be contaminated, an analyst also must deal with the parallel problem: the target organization may have distorted or faked its tests for the same reasons. It is unwise to rely on test reports alone. It may be necessary to monitor the tests as well. In examining any test or evaluation results, begin by asking two questions:

- Did the testing organization have a major stake in the outcome (such as the threat that a program would be cancelled due to negative test results or would profit from positive results)?
- Did the *reported* outcome support the organization's position or interests?

If the answer to both questions is yes, be wary of accepting the validity of the test. In one industry, pharmaceutical testing, tests have been fraudulently conducted or the results skewed in some way to support the regulatory approval of the pharmaceutical.[5] The results could be similar in other industries.

Evaluating the Communications Channel

A basic rule of weighing evidence is to look at the communications channel through which the evidence arrives. In a large intelligence system, collection requirements must move through a bureaucracy to a requirements officer, from there to a country desk, a field requirements officer, a SIGINT collector or a HUMINT case officer (for instance), then to an agent; and response goes back through the reports chain. The message never gets through undistorted, and it's a wonder that it ever gets through at all. This distortion of the message is expressed in physics as the second law of thermodynamics (see Box 5-2). The law has been modified for the intelligence field: The accuracy

---

Analysis Principle ●————————————————————————————

Box 5-2 The Second Law of Thermodynamics

The second law of thermodynamics can be stated in several ways. Two of the simplest ways (these are equivalent) are:

- No physical process is perfectly reversible. There is no such thing as perpetual motion.[1]
- Entropy (randomness, chaos) always increases with time. This could also be stated as "the degree of randomness always increases in a physical system."

[1] A. D'Abro, *The Rise of the New Physics*, vol. 1 (New York: Dover, 1951), 344.

of a message through *any* communications system decreases with the length of the link or the number of intermediate nodes.

This same principle occurs in communications engineering; Claude Shannon described it in his communications theory exposition. Just as heat always flows so that entropy (chaos, randomness) increases, so on a digital communications line the originally crisp pulses will gradually lose their shape over distance and disappear into the noise, as illustrated in Figure 5-1.

Like an electronic communications channel that is being analyzed using Shannon's communications theory, some nodes in the intelligence communications channel contribute more "noise" than others. A communications pulse traveling down a noisy or distorted channel loses its shape and finally disappears in noise. The signal disappears completely or emerges as the wrong signal.

The same communications problem occurs in an organization. Large and complex systems tend to have more entropy. The result is often cited as "poor communication" problems in large organizations, and the effects can be observed in the complex project curve discussed in Chapter 12. Over a long chain of human communication, the equivalent of Figure 5-1 is that the original message eventually becomes little more than rumor.

In the business intelligence world, analysts recognize the importance of the communication channel by using the differentiating terms *primary sources* for firsthand acquisition of information (through discussions or other interaction directly with a human source) and *secondary sources* (information learned through an intermediary, a publication, or online). This division downplays the many gradations of reliability, and national intelligence organizations commonly do not use the primary/secondary source division. Some national intelligence collection organizations use the term "collateral" to refer to intelligence gained from other collectors, but it does not have the same meaning as the terms "primary" and "secondary" as used in business intelligence.

Neither the "primary" versus "secondary" distinction nor the "collateral" evidence distinction serves a useful purpose; it is more important to look at the communications channel itself. Ask about the channel: What was it? Is this

Figure 5-1   The Effect of Entropy on the Communications Channel

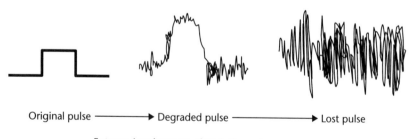

Original pulse ──────▶ Degraded pulse ──────▶ Lost pulse

Entropy (randomness, chaos) always increases

information being intentionally provided? If so, what part of it is true? Is it deception or sending a message or signal to the opponent? If it is a message or signal, what is the message and the reason for it?

The hearsay rule as applied in judicial proceedings is a recognition of the application of Shannon's theory and of entropy in human affairs. Under the hearsay rule, a witness cannot testify about what a person said to prove the truth of what was said; in the court's view, the message has traveled through too many intermediate nodes to be credible. As noted in the HUMINT and COMINT sections in the previous chapter, entropy has an effect on the credibility of some intelligence, and the credibility degrades in direct proportion to the number of nodes traversed.

Entropy has another effect in intelligence. An intelligence assertion that "X is a possibility" very often, over time and through diverse communication channels, becomes "X may be true," then "X probably is the case," and eventually "X is a fact," without a shred of new evidence to support the assertion. In intelligence, we refer to this as the "creeping validity" problem.

Earlier in this chapter we discussed bias in the source. Bias can also be a problem in the communications channel. Years back one U.S. intelligence organization had the good fortune to obtain an audio tap into a highly classified foreign installation. The problem with the tap was that the audio was very weak and in a foreign language. One could barely discern that it was speech. One translator with very sharp ears was able to produce transcripts, however, and the product was some exciting and very disturbing intelligence; several reports went to top levels of the U.S. government.

The transcribed material was very good—too good, in fact, and technically inconsistent. An investigation revealed that the translator wasn't translating; he was making it all up out of a fertile imagination and some knowledge of what was of current intelligence interest. The reports were withdrawn and the translator fired. On withdrawing them, we learned another basic rule of intelligence: The surest way to get a customer to read a report is to retract it.

Two lessons emerge from this example: First, if the source or a person in the communications channel has something to gain by providing interesting material, be wary. In this case the translator earned recognition and a promotion. Second, intelligence that has impact is more likely to be used. In this case the lesson comes from the customers, who would cite the reports for years because they were so interesting and provocative. When the customers learned that the reports were not valid their response was typically, "Well, they should be!"

Evaluating the Evidence

The major credentials of evidence are credibility, reliability, and inferential force. *Credibility* refers to the extent to which we can believe something. *Reliability* means consistency or replicability. *Inferential force* means that the evidence carries weight, or has value, in supporting a conclusion. The credibility of tangible evidence depends on its authenticity, accuracy, and reliability. The credibility of testimonial evidence depends on the veracity, objectivity (and memory), and observational sensitivity of the testifier.[6]

U.S. government intelligence organizations have come up with a set of definitions to distinguish levels of credibility of intelligence:

- Fact—verified information, something known to exist or to have happened.
- Information—the content of reports, research, and reflection on an intelligence issue that helps to evaluate the likelihood that something is factual and thereby reduces uncertainty.
- Direct information—information that can be considered factual because of the nature of the source (imagery, intercepts, observations).
- Indirect information—information that may or may not be factual because of some doubt about the source's reliability, the source's lack of direct access, or the complex (nonconcrete) character of the contents (hearsay from clandestine sources, foreign government reports, or local media accounts).[7]

This division sounds suspiciously like the "primary" and "secondary" source division used in business intelligence. It downplays the real-world situation: that intelligence has a continuum of credibility, and that direct information such as signal intercepts or imagery can be misleading or false due to denial and deception.

In weighing evidence, the usual approach is to ask three questions that are embedded in the oath that witnesses take before giving testimony in U.S. courts:

- Is it true?
- Is it the whole truth?
- Is it nothing but the truth? (Is it relevant or significant?)

Is It True? Is the evidence factual or opinion (someone else's analysis)? If it is opinion, unless the source quotes evidence to support it, question its validity.

How does it fit with other evidence? The relating of evidence—how it fits in—is best done in the synthesis phase. The data from different collection sources are most valuable when used together. The synergistic effect of combining data from many sources both strengthens the conclusions and increases the analyst's confidence in the conclusions.

- HUMINT and COMINT data can be combined with ELINT data to yield a more complete picture of a radar.

- HUMINT and open source are often melded together to give a more comprehensive picture of people, programs, products, facilities, and research specialties. This is excellent background information to interpret data derived from COMINT and imagery intelligence (IMINT).

- Data on environmental conditions during tests can be used with ELINT and COMINT data obtained during the same test event to evaluate the capabilities of active sensor systems.

- Identification of research institutes and their key scientists and researchers can be initially made through HUMINT, COMINT, or open source. Once the organization or individual has been identified by one INT, the other ones can usually provide extensive additional information.

- Successful analysis of COMINT data may require correlating raw COMINT data with external information such as ELINT and IMINT, or with knowledge of operational or technical practices.

One of the best examples of synthesis comes from the extensive efforts U.S. intelligence made during the 1960s through the 1980s to assess the performance of Soviet ballistic missiles. Satellite photography was compared with telemetry to check hypotheses about the weight and size of missiles. Photography of missiles on a launch pad could be used to alert telemetry collectors. Radar tracking of the boost phase could be cross-checked with telemetry to determine booster performance, and the same cross-checks on reentry vehicles could be used to more confidently estimate reentry vehicle size and weight.[8]

Is It the Whole Truth? When asking this question, it is time to do source analysis. In HUMINT, this means looking at such things as past reporting history or psychological profile (Is the source loose-lipped? A conniver? Or a straight shooter?). We all have *ad hoc* profiles on the people we deal with based on such things as first impressions or reputation. Sometimes we need more—a psychological profile, for example.

An incomplete picture can mislead as much as an outright lie. During the cold war, Soviet missile guidance and control experts regularly visited their counterparts in the United States to do some informal elicitation. Alerted to yet another impending Soviet visit, U.S. intelligence, working with a leading U.S. expert, set up an elaborate display of a new and highly accurate missile guidance system in the expert's office. The Soviet visitors were impressed with the new technology, and the entire visit centered on the details of the guidance system and how it was manufactured. What the U.S. expert did not mention was that for the system to work some components had to be machined to a precision that was beyond U.S. or Soviet capabilities. It was a failed design, but the problem would not become apparent until (as we heard later) the Soviets had spent many months and much money trying to replicate the design. The U.S. expert told no lies—he simply omitted a critical truth.

Is It Nothing but the Truth? It is worthwhile at this point to distinguish between data and evidence. *Data* becomes *evidence* only when the data is relevant to the problem or issue at hand. The simple test of relevance is whether it affects the likelihood of a hypothesis about the target. Does it help answer a question that has been asked? Or does it help answer a question that *should* be asked? The preliminary or initial guidance from customers seldom tells what they really need to know—another reason to keep them in the loop via the target-centric process.

Medical doctors often encounter the relevance problem. They must synthesize evidence (symptoms and test results) to make a diagnosis: a model of the patient's present state. The doctor encounters serious difficulties when she must deal with a patient who has two pathologies simultaneously. Some of the symptoms are relevant to one pathology, some to the other. If she tries to fit all of the symptoms into one diagnosis, she is apt to make the wrong call. This is a severe enough problem for doctors, who must deal with only a few symptoms. It is a much worse problem for intelligence analysts, who typically deal with a large volume of data, most of which is irrelevant.

The converse problem of fitting evidence into the model is the risk of discarding relevant evidence. Avoid discarding evidence simply because it doesn't seem to fit the model. Such anomalies may indicate that something is wrong with the model, or another model is more appropriate. Alternatively, as with the two pathologies problem above, the evidence should be partitioned and fit into two distinct models.

Pitfalls in Evaluating Evidence

There are at least seven pitfalls to avoid in weighing evidence.

Vividness Weighting. In general, the channel for communication of intelligence should be as short as possible; but when could a short channel become a problem?

If the channel is too short, the result is *vividness weighting*—the phenomenon that evidence that is experienced directly is strongest ("seeing is believing"). This is part of a continuing problem: Customers place the most weight on evidence that they collect themselves—a dangerous pitfall that senior executives fall into repeatedly and that makes them vulnerable to deception. Strong and dynamic leaders are particularly vulnerable: Franklin Roosevelt, Winston Churchill, and Henry Kissinger are examples of statesmen who did their own collection and analysis and occasionally got into trouble as a result.

There is a danger in judging any evidence by its presentation, yet we continue to do it. Statistics are the least persuasive form; abstract (general) text is next; concrete (specific, focused, exemplary) text is a more persuasive form still; and visual evidence, such as imagery or video, is most persuasive.

Of course, vividness can work for the analyst. She can use the impact of certain types of evidence to make the presentation of her conclusions more effective.

An example of the powerful impact that vivid evidence can have is the murder of *Wall Street Journal* reporter Daniel Pearl in Pakistan during February 2002. The videotape of the murder and decapitation of Pearl reportedly was shown to President George W. Bush and evoked a strong reaction. Decision-makers often are unduly affected by vivid evidence.

Weighing Based on the Source. One of the most difficult traps for an analyst to avoid is that of weighing evidence based on its source. HUMINT operatives repeatedly value information gained from clandestine sources—the classic spy—above that from refugees, emigrés, and defectors. COMINT gained from an expensive emplaced telephone tap is valued (and compartmented) above that gleaned from high-frequency radio communications (which almost anyone can monitor). The most common pitfall, however, is to downplay the significance of open source material; being the least classified, it is deemed to be the least valuable. This particular form of snobbery is rampant in government intelligence organizations, which have available to them highly classified sources. Using open sources well is a demanding analytic skill, but it can pay high dividends to those who have the patience to master it. Collectors may make the mistake of equating source with importance. Having spent a sizable portion of their government's budget in collecting the material, they may believe that its value can be measured by the cost of collecting it. No competent analyst should ever make such a mistake.

Favoring the Most Recent Evidence. Analysts often give the most recently acquired evidence the most weight. One caution on the danger of doing this is taken from the second law of thermodynamics, discussed earlier. For weighing evidence, the second law of thermodynamics has a different meaning. As Figure 5-1 suggests, the value of information or the weight given it in a report tends to decrease with time. The freshest intelligence—crisp, clear, and the focus of the analyst's attention—often gets more weight than the fuzzy and half-remembered (but possibly more important) information that has had to travel down the long telephone lines of time. The analyst has to remember this tendency and compensate for it. It sometimes helps to go back to the original (older) intelligence and reread it to bring it more freshly to mind.

Favoring or Disfavoring the Unknown. Most analysts have problems deciding how much weight to give to answers when little or no information is available for or against each one. Some analysts give an answer too much weight where evidence is absent; some give it too little. Former CIA analyst Richards J. Heuer Jr. cites this "absence of evidence" problem in the example of two groups of automobile mechanics who were given a choice of reasons why a car would not start, with the list of choices ending in "other." The mechanics were told to estimate what percentage of failures was attributable to each reason. One group was given a list that omitted several of the reasons; they tended to overweight the remaining reasons and underweight the category "other."[9]

Trusting Hearsay. The chief problem with HUMINT is that it is hearsay evidence; and as noted earlier, the courts long ago learned to distrust hearsay for good reasons, including the biases of the source and the collector. Sources may deliberately distort or misinform because they want to influence policy or increase their value to the collector; and the analyst doesn't have the nonverbal details of the conversation—the setting, the context, facial and body expressions—to judge.

COMINT, like HUMINT, is hearsay for two reasons. First, much interpretation goes into a COMINT report, and the COMINT analyst who translates and interprets the conversation does not do so objectively. COMINT analysts, like HUMINT sources, know that exciting or provocative reports are more likely to be published than mundane ones. Second, some COMINT targets know that they are being monitored and deliberately use the collector as a conduit for information. Intelligence analysts have to use hearsay, but they have to weigh it accordingly.

Trusting Expert Opinions. Expert opinion is often used as a tool for analyzing data and making estimates. The problem is that the expert is frequently wrong and frequently unobjective. With experts, an analyst gets all of the biases: the axes the experts have to grind and the ego that convinces them there is only one right way to do things (their way). Analysts and HUMINT collectors both have a long history of dealing with experts, especially scientists, who inflate reports on foreign developments to further their own research work. Most scientific experts consulted by intelligence organizations have been guilty of report inflation at one time or another. Experts used as evaluators have the same problem. Analysts should treat expert opinion as HUMINT and be wary when the expert makes extremely positive comments ("that foreign development is a stroke of genius!") or extremely negative ones ("it can't be done").

Negative comments might stem from what former British intelligence officer R. V. Jones described as "principles of impotence." An expert will find it more reassuring to decide that something is impossible than to decide that he merely failed to accomplish it. Having made such a judgment, an expert will always defend it vigorously, for the same reasons that intelligence analysts find it difficult to change their conclusions once made (see Box 5-3).

Jones encountered several examples of principles of impotence during his tenure, such as, "It is impossible to make a bulletproof fuel tank"; "radio waves cannot be generated in the centimeter band (above 3,000 MHz)"; and "photoconductive materials cannot be made to detect wavelengths longer than two microns."[10] All of these "impossibilities" later became realities. During 1943–1944 aerial photography of the German rocket test center at Peenemunde revealed the existence of a rocket about forty-five feet long and six feet in

Analysis Principle •————————————————————————————

Box 5-3   Impotence Principles

Fundamental limits are well known and valid in physics: It is generally accepted that one can neither travel faster than the speed of light nor reduce the temperature of an object to absolute zero. R.V. Jones described such postulates as "principles of impotence," and pointed out that they pose a special danger for scientific experts. Having tried an experiment or development and failed, the expert is strongly tempted to invoke a principle of impotence and say "It can't be done."

diameter. As was the case with many other interesting analytic problems of World War II, this one fell to R.V. Jones to puzzle through.

British experts of the time were familiar only with rockets that burned cordite in a steel case. A simple calculation showed that a cordite-burning rocket of this size would weigh approximately eighty tons and would have to have a warhead weighing on the order of ten tons to be worthwhile. To the British cabinet, the prospect of rockets as heavy as railroad locomotives carrying ten tons of high explosives and landing on London was appalling.

In June 1944 a V-2 rocket crashed in Sweden, and British intelligence officers had an opportunity to examine the fragments. They reported that two liquids fueled the rocket and that liquid oxygen was one of the fuels. Armed with this evidence, Jones was able to sort through the volume of conflicting HUMINT reports about the German rocket and to select the five reports that mentioned liquid oxygen. All five were consistent in attributing light weights to the rocket and warhead. Jones subsequently (and correctly) reported to the British war cabinet—over the objections of British rocket experts—that the V-2 weighed twelve tons and carried a one-ton warhead.[11]

Though experts have frequently led us astray, their contribution has on the whole been positive. Some say that experts are harder to deceive. In the words of one author, "It is hard for one specialist to deceive another for very long."[12] By this view, deception, as discussed later in this chapter, can be beaten more easily with expert help. Maybe. Many experts, particularly scientists, are not mentally prepared to look for deception, as intelligence officers should be. Some are naive—even gullible. A second problem is that experts are quite able to deceive themselves without any help from opponents.

Variations on the use of expert opinion attempt to combine the expertise of several experts to reduce the problems cited above. Using a panel of experts to make analytical judgments is a common method of trying to reach conclusions or to sort through a complex array of interdisciplinary data. The quality of the conclusions reached by such panels depends on variables such as the panel's:

- Expertise.
- Motivation to produce a quality product.

- Understanding of the problem area to be addressed.
- Effectiveness in group dynamics (process).

A major advantage of the target-centric approach is that it formalizes the process of obtaining expert opinions. It also lends itself readily to techniques, such as Delphi, for avoiding negative group dynamics. Delphi is a systematic version of the panel consensus designed to eliminate some of the traditional panel shortcomings. It uses anonymous inputs to help obtain an objective consensus from initially divergent expert opinion. One objective of the Delphi method is the encouragement, rather than the suppression, of conflicting or divergent opinions. Participants explain their views, and others review these explanations absent the personality, status, and debating skills that are brought to bear in conferences. The Delphi method arrives at a consensus by pooling the two separate items involved in any estimate:

- Expert information or knowledge.
- Good judgment, analysis, and reasoning.

Although a Delphi participant may not initially be well informed on a given question, she still can contribute judgment, analysis, and reasoning of the information and arguments provided by other respondents.

Where panels are used, several techniques are available to make the panel input more effective. In general, the techniques apply whenever collaborative analytic efforts are used, as they inevitably will be if the target-centric approach is applied.

If the analysis is a group effort and qualitative, a method for combining the various opinions must be determined in advance and approved by the participants. The analysis may be as simple as providing a list of all comments by participants, or as difficult as reducing variance among opinions to the point that one combined opinion can be generated. If the analysis is quantitative, decide whether each participant's vote will be averaged or whether the group will be asked to come to consensus.

In determining the voting method, consider the level of expertise of each voter. Often, analyses include persons from different organizations with varying viewpoints and levels of expertise. But it is rarely feasible politically to accord a greater weight to those voters who are better informed. Instead, seek consensus among voters. In this process, each person's vote is posted before the group. All votes are then viewed to determine a median or mode. If there appears to be great dispersion among the votes, a mediator intervenes and asks voters on opposing ends to explain their positions to each other. In many cases a disparity in knowledge was the cause of the polarized opinions.

Premature Closure and Philosophical Predisposition. When confronted with evidence (facts, opinions, suppositions, and so on) bearing on a problem, analysts too often make early judgments about the solution to the problem and then defend this initial judgment tenaciously. This can lead the analyst to se-lect (usually without conscious awareness) subsequent evidence that supports the favored hypothesis and to reject (or dismiss as unimportant) evidence that conflicts with it. This approach breaks several tenets of good problem solving procedures, in particular the tenet of postponing evaluation and judgment until all relevant data are available.

The primary danger of reaching conclusions too early (premature closure) is not so much in making a bad assessment because the evidence is incom-plete. Rather, the danger is that when a situation is changing quickly or when a major, unprecedented event occurs, the analyst will become trapped by the judgments already made. Chances increase of missing indications of change, and it becomes harder to revise an initial estimate, as intelligence analysts found out during the Cuban Missile Crisis.

Few intelligence successes make headlines. Failures make headlines. One exception was the Cuban Missile Crisis, in which U.S intelligence services ob-tained information and made assessments that helped policymakers act in time to make a difference. The assessments would have been made sooner, how-ever, except for the difficulty in changing a conclusion once reached and the tendency to ignore the Cuban refugees who cry "wolf" too often.

For some time before 1962, Cuban refugees had flooded western intelli-gence services, embassies, and newspapers with reports of missiles being hidden in Cuba. When the reports about the deployment of medium-range ballistic missiles began to sift into the CIA and the Defense Intelligence Agency in 1962, they were by and large disregarded—intelligence analysts had heard such false reports too many times. Only as the weight of evidence from several independent sources, including photographic evidence and ship movement patterns, began to grow was it possible to change the collective mind of the in-telligence community.[13]

The Cuban Missile Crisis illustrates the problem that Princeton University professor Klaus Knorr described as "philosophical predisposition": a situation in which expectations fail to apply to the facts.[14] Before 1962 the Soviets had never deployed nuclear weapons outside their direct control, and U.S. analysts assumed that they would not do so by deploying nuclear warhead-equipped missiles in Cuba. Thus the analysts discounted information that contradicted this assumption. The counterintelligence technique of deception (part of de-nial and deception) thrives on this tendency to ignore evidence that would dis-prove an existing assumption, as discussed later in this chapter. Furthermore, once an intelligence agency makes a firm estimate, it has a propensity to ig-nore or explain away conflicting information in future estimates. Denial and deception succeed if one opponent can get the other to make a wrong initial estimate.

Fortunately, there are several problem-solving approaches that help to sift data while preventing premature closure or overcoming the bias of philosophical predisposition. Sophisticated computer-based tools have been developed to support these problem-solving approaches.

Convergent and Divergent Evidence

Two items of evidence are said to be *conflicting* or *divergent* if one item favors one conclusion and the other item favors a different conclusion. Two items of evidence are said to be *converging* if they favor the same conclusion.

A HUMINT cable reports that the Chinese freighter *Kiang Kwan* has left Shanghai bound for the Indian Ocean. A COMINT report on radio traffic from the *Kiang Kwan* as she left port states that the ship's destination is Colombia. Ships seldom sail from Shanghai to Colombia via the Indian Ocean, so the two reports point to two different conclusions; they are divergent. Note that both items of divergent evidence can be true (for example, the ship could make an intermediate stop at an Indian Ocean port); they simply lead to differing conclusions.

In contrast, two items of evidence are *contradictory* if they say logically opposing things. A report says that Yasir Arafat was in Libya yesterday at 1200 hours; another report says that he was in Jordan yesterday at the same time. Only one report can be true.

Redundant Evidence

Convergent evidence can also be *redundant.* To understand the concept of redundancy in evidence, it helps to understand its importance in communications theory. Information comes to an analyst by several different channels. It often is incomplete, and it sometimes arrives in garbled form. As discussed in Box 5-2, entropy takes its toll on any information channel. In communications theory, redundancy is one way to improve the chances of getting the message right.

Redundant (duplicative) evidence can have corroborative redundancy or cumulative redundancy. In both types, the weight of the evidence piles up to reinforce a given conclusion. A simple example illustrates the difference.

Corroborative Redundancy. An analyst following clandestine arms transfer networks receives two reports. A COMINT report indicates that a Chinese freighter carrying a contraband arms shipment will be at coordinates 05-48S, 39-52E on June 13 to transfer the arms to another boat. A separate HUMINT report says that the Chinese freighter *Kiang Kwan* will rendezvous for an arms transfer south of Pemba Island on June 13. Both reports say the same thing; a quick map check confirms that the coordinates lie near Pemba Island, off the Tanzanian coast; so no new information (except the ship's name) is gained by the second report. The second report has value for confirmatory purposes and helps establish the validity of both sources of information.

The analogy in communications theory might occur when dealing with a noisy teletype channel. Message errors are not a concern when dealing with text only, because text has inherent redundancy; if "Chinese freighter will rendezvous," is sent, but the recipient gets the printout "Chinese freighter will rentezvous," the message will probably be understood in spite of the errors. The coordinates of the rendezvous point, however, have less inherent redundancy. Some redundancy does exist in geographical coordinates—a message that has the coordinates "5 degrees 88 minutes South," clearly has an error, since minutes of latitude and longitude never exceed 59. However, it is unclear what the correct latitude should be. It is common practice to spell out or repeat numbers in such a message, or even to repeat the entire message, if a chance of a garble exists; that is, the sender introduces *corroborative redundancy* to ensure that the correct coordinates are received.

Cumulative Redundancy. Now, suppose instead that the HUMINT report in the previous example says that a Chinese freighter left port in Shanghai on May 21 carrying AK-47 rifles and ammunition destined for Tanzanian rebels. The report does not duplicate information contained in the COMINT report, but it adds credibility to both reports. Furthermore, it leads to a more detailed conclusion about the nature of the illicit arms transfer.

The second report, in this case, adds cumulative redundancy to the first report. Both reports are given more weight, and a more complete estimate can be made than if only one report was received.

Rules for Combining Evidence

Drawing conclusions from evidence means that, in some way, an analyst must weigh the evidence and make a judgment as to which conclusions the evidence supports and to what extent. In most cases and for most analysts, this is a qualitative judgment. Formal numerical processes for combining evidence are time consuming to apply and are not commonly used in intelligence analysis. They are usually reserved for cases in which the customer demands them, either because the issue is critically important, because the customer wants to examine the reasoning process, or because the exact probabilities associated with each alternative are important to the customer. Bayesian analysis is the best known of the formal processes.

Bayesian analysis, based on Bayes' rule, is a formal method for using incoming data to modify previously estimated probabilities. It therefore can be used to narrow the error bounds on both estimates and predictions. Each new piece of information may be evaluated and combined with prior historical or subjective assessments of the probability of an event to determine whether its occurrence has now been made more or less likely and by how much. Bayesian analysis can also be used to compute the likelihood that the observed data are attributable to particular causes. One advantage claimed for Bayesian analysis is its ability to blend the subjective probability judgments of experts with historical frequencies and the latest sample evidence.

To explain Bayes' rule, let us assume that we know how often a given event normally occurs. We can assign that event a probability: $P(event)$. Assume also that we have previously made an intelligence conclusion and given it a likelihood, or probability, of P(conclusion). Finally, we are fairly sure that, if our conclusion is true, it changes the probability P(event). We call this changed probability P(event | conclusion), which is read as "probability that the event will occur, given that the conclusion is true."

Now, suppose that the event does occur. Its occurrence changes the probability of our conclusion to a new probability P(conclusion | event), which is read as "probability that our conclusion is true, given that the event has occurred." The new probability is given by Bayes' rule, which is expressed by the formula:

$$P(\text{conclusion} \mid \text{event}) = \frac{P(\text{event} \mid \text{conclusion}) \; P(\text{conclusion})}{P(\text{event})}$$

A simple illustration will help make Bayes' rule clear. Suppose an analyst has previously made an estimate based on existing evidence that a particular bank is laundering narcotics funds and has given the estimate a probability P(conclusion) = .4. The analyst knows that the probability of similar banks making profits in excess of 12 percent is .2 if the bank operates legally. The bank in question, however, recently made a profit of 20 percent, which certainly looks suspicious. The analyst concludes that there is a 30 percent (.3) chance of the bank making this much profit if it is in the fund-laundering business. The probability that the bank is laundering funds has increased:

$$P(\text{conclusion} \mid \text{event}) = \frac{(.3)\,(.4)}{(.2)} = .6$$

One problem with Bayesian analysis is that it does not deal well with ignorance. That is, if the analyst assigns probabilities to either conclusions or events based on very little knowledge, she can wind up with contradictions. The solution to this problem in Bayes' rule is to use a more formal methodology called the Dempster-Shafer approach to combining evidence. The Dempster-Shafer approach is mathematically complex and is not described in detail here.[15]

Both Bayes' rule and Dempster-Shafer rely on placing a numerical weight on bits of evidence. There are three approaches to numerical weighting: ordinal scale, interval scale, and ratio scale weighting. Ordinal scales simply indicate rank or order, but no mathematical operations are possible. Interval scales have equal intervals between numbers, but the lack of an absolute zero reference does not allow multiplication or division. Only ratio scaling, which has an absolute zero reference, allows the multiplication and division required for Bayesian or Dempster-Shafer analysis. Ratio scaling is discussed in detail in Chapter 14.

Denial and Deception

Denial and deception—significant challenges for collectors and analysts and sometimes referred to as cover, concealment, and deception—are major weapons in the counterintelligence arsenal of a country or organization. Denial and deception may be the only weapons available to many countries against highly sophisticated technical intelligence (especially against IMINT and SIGINT).

Denial and Deception Techniques

Denial and deception come in many forms. Denial is somewhat more straightforward. Communications and radar signals can be denied to SIGINT by operational practices such as intermittent operation, use of land lines instead of radio, encryption, or a wide range of technical approaches known collectively as low-probability-of-intercept (LPI) techniques. Signals can also be denied by the more aggressive tactic of jamming the SIGINT system with interfering signals. Denial against IMINT may take the form of camouflage netting, obscuring or masking techniques, or placing sensitive operations in underground facilities (protecting them against attack at the same time). Denial of technical intelligence collection could include scrubbing gas emissions and processing effluents to conceal the nature of the process at a plant.

Deception techniques are limited only by our imagination. Passive deception might include use of decoys or having the intelligence target emulate an activity that is not of intelligence interest—making a chemical warfare plant look like a medical drug production facility, for example. Active deception includes misinformation (false communications traffic, signals, stories, and documents), misleading activities, and double agents (agents who have been discovered and "turned" to work against their former masters), among others.

Deception can be very effective against an intelligence organization that, through hubris or bureaucratic politics, is reluctant to change its initial conclusions about a topic. If the opposing intelligence organization makes a wrong initial estimate, then long-term deception is much easier to pull off, as noted earlier. Project Jennifer, discussed in Chapter 4, succeeded in part because Soviet intelligence apparently accepted the cover mission of the *Glomar Explorer* as deep sea mining. If denial and deception are successful, the opposing organization faces an *unlearning* process: Its predispositions and settled conclusions have to be discarded and replaced. Highly adaptive organizations have the capacity to unlearn and are therefore less vulnerable to denial and deception. Large bureaucratic organizations find unlearning very difficult.

Detailed knowledge of an opponent is the key to successful denial and deception, as the *Farewell* operation showed. In 1980 the French internal security service Direction de la Surveillance du Territoire (DST) recruited Soviet KGB Lt. Col. Vladimir I. Vetrov, codenamed "Farewell." Col. Vetrov supplied some four thousand documents to the French detailing an extensive KGB effort to clandestinely acquire technical know-how from the West, primarily from the United States. In 1981 French president Francois Mitterrand shared the source and the documents (which DST named "the Farewell Dossier") with U.S. president Ronald Reagan.

The documents revealed a far-reaching and successful intelligence operation that had already acquired highly sensitive military technology on radars, computers, machine tools, nuclear weaponry, and manufacturing techniques. But the specific targets on the list provided the needed guidance for an effective counterstrike.

In early 1982 the Defense Department, the FBI, and the CIA began developing a counterattack. Instead of simply improving U.S. defenses against the KGB efforts, the U.S. team used the KGB shopping list to feed back, through CIA–controlled channels, the items on the list—augmented with "improvements"—that were designed to pass acceptance testing but would fail randomly in service. Flawed computer chips, turbines, and factory plans found their way into Soviet military and civilian factories and equipment. Misleading information on U.S. stealth technology and space defense flowed into the Soviet intelligence reporting. The effect of the deception campaign, accompanied by exposure and expulsion of KGB collection operatives in Europe, was to discredit the KGB's technology collection effort within the USSR.[16]

Mounting a deception campaign often requires extensive effort, but sometimes it is worth the payoff. The *Farewell* deception exacted high costs but reaped many benefits; it may have hastened the end of the cold war.

In contrast, a deception technique commonly practiced by contractors in large government proposals requires very little effort. The membership of competing teams is a valuable item of intelligence in planning the "win themes" of competitive proposals. To conceal membership, team members will, on instruction of the team leader, mislead competitors about which team they are on—for example, sitting with and conversing with another team in bidders' conferences. The surge of telephone calls among potential allies and potential competitors that accompanies such a proposal effort is rampant with bluffing, slow rolling (protracted bad-faith negotiations with a competitor to foster uncertainty and to delay the competitor's action), and misleading information to keep the competitor off balance.

Depending on the type of campaign, exposure of the deception can be bad news for either side. In *Farewell*, exposure would likely not have reduced the effectiveness of the deception, since it would have called into question all of the successful KGB technology acquisitions.

Governments carry out most deception. Commercial entities also engage in deception to mislead competitors, but the company must usually tread a fine line in conducting such deception. The objective is to mislead the competitor without misleading the public (in countries such as the United States, where misinformation can result in lawsuits) and without doing anything illegal. In a number of areas though, such as positioning for competitive contract bidding and in mergers and acquisitions, deception is a common and accepted part of the game.

Countering Denial and Deception

At one point in history, intelligence services did very well at countering denial and deception. During World War II both the British and the Germans had efficient systems for identifying the techniques and countering them. (The successful Allied deception about the 1944 Normandy invasion was a notable exception.) Few denial and deception tactics worked for very long. Britain and Germany owed this success to a tight feedback loop in their intelligence processes. Intelligence analysts interacted constantly with IMINT and SIGINT collectors to develop counter-countermeasures. As a result, there existed a constant action-counteraction process, much like what has existed in the electronic warfare and radar communities in the past sixty years.

Many of the standard techniques for countering denial and deception were developed back in World War II, and they continue to work with new twists and new technologies. However, when measures of collection performance measure the wrong things, or when collection becomes too predictable—as can happen in large intelligence organizations—tactics for countering denial and deception no longer work.

Measuring the Wrong Things. Intelligence organizations such as those in the United States and Russia do not have an efficient feedback loop connecting collectors and analysts, partly because of cumbersome bureaucracies. Instead, these organizations operate as open loop systems, meaning they don't have feedback. The U.S. agencies, in particular, have become too fixated on numbers—both on quality and quantity of collection—and insufficiently concerned with content. For example:

- If the COMINT collectors get continuous copy of a high priority communications channel for six hours, they probably get credit, even if no conversations of substance were carried on the channel during that time or if the entire channel was encrypted.
- If the IMINT collectors take one hundred pictures of a critical installation, they get credit for each image in their collection performance ratings, even if the last ninety-nine pictures contain nothing new.
- HUMINT collectors typically have their performance rated by the number of reports submitted, encouraging the submission of many short reports instead of a few complete ones.

A target-centric approach to the intelligence process, as described in Chapter 1, forces collection performance to focus on content, not on quantity. If collected material does not belong in any target model—that is, if it has no intelligence value—it quickly becomes obvious to all concerned, and the collector is more likely to take action to make future intelligence relevant to the targets.

Making Collection Too Predictable. If an opponent can model the collection process, he can defeat it. U.S. intelligence learned that lesson in HUMINT against numerous Soviet targets after some painful losses. The U.S. IMINT and

SIGINT communities may have yet to learn the lesson. There is a tendency to believe that overhead (satellite) IMINT and SIGINT are less vulnerable to countermeasures. However, critics have pointed out that not only denial, but also effective deception, is possible against both IMINT and SIGINT if the opponent knows enough about the collection system.[17] The effectiveness of hostile denial and deception is a direct reflection of the predictability of collection.

The best way to defeat denial and deception is for all of the stakeholders in the target-centric approach to work closely together. The two basic rules for collection, described below, form a complementary set. One rule is intended to provide incentive for collectors to defeat denial and deception. The other rule suggests mechanisms for defeating it.

First, establish an effective feedback mechanism. *Relevance* of the product to intelligence questions is the correct measure of collection effectiveness, and analysts and customers—not collectors—determine relevance. The system must enforce a content-oriented evaluation of the product, because content is the measure of relevance. This implies that a strong feedback system exists between analyst and collector and generally that collectors have established close links to the analysts. Another important step is to develop new techniques for sensor fusion or synthesis of intelligence data—something that analysts do well. An analyst can often beat denial and deception by simply using several types of intelligence—HUMINT, COMINT, and so on—in combination, simultaneously, or successively. It is relatively easy to defeat one sensor or collection channel. It is very difficult to defeat all types of intelligence at the same time. Hyperspectral imaging, for example, is a valuable weapon against IMINT deception because it can be used to measure so many different aspects (signatures) of a target.

The second rule is to make collection smarter and less predictable. Don't optimize systems for quality and quantity; optimize for content. One might, for example, move satellite-based collectors to less desirable orbits to achieve surprise or keep opponents off balance. In collecting discarded papers ("TRASHINT"), don't always look in the same dumpster.[18]

Apply sensors in new ways. Analysis groups typically have thought of ways to do this in their areas of responsibility. Also, techniques for defeating denial and deception that have been developed for one problem (counternarcotics, for example) may be applicable to others (weapons proliferation).

Use denial and deception to protect a collection capability. Military tacticians claim that the best weapon against a tank is another tank; and the best weapon against a submarine is another submarine. Likewise, the best weapon against denial and deception is to mislead or confuse opponents about intelligence capabilities and to disrupt their warning programs. Uncertainty is an effective weapon against any intelligence service.

Consider provocative techniques against denial and deception targets. In the U.S. Air Force airborne reconnaissance programs dating back to the 1950s, provocation was used effectively to overcome the practice of emissions control by the Soviets. In emissions control, one keeps all nonessential signals off the air until the SIGINT collector has left the area. The U.S. response was to send an aircraft on a penetration course toward the Soviet border, for example, and turn away at the last minute, after the Soviets had turned on their entire air defense network to deal with the threat. "Probing" an opponent's system and watching the response is a useful tactic for learning more about the system. The reaction to probing may have its own set of undesirable consequences: The Soviets would occasionally chase and shoot down the reconnaissance aircraft to discourage the probing practice.

Consider multifunctional collection platforms that carry several types of sensors but use them intermittently or unpredictably. If an opponent is unsure what sensors actually exist or are operational on a vehicle, denial and deception becomes more difficult.

Hit the collateral or inferential targets. If an opponent engages in denial or deception about a specific facility, then supporting facilities may allow inferences to be made or to expose the deception. Security measures around a facility and the nature and status of nearby communications, power, or transportation facilities may provide a more complete picture. A sequel to the successful British commando raid on the Bruneval radar, discussed earlier, was that the Germans protected all of their *Würzburg* radars near the coast with barbed wire entanglements. The barbed wire showed up clearly on aerial photography and made it relatively easy for R. V. Jones's photo interpreters to locate all of the radars that the Germans had successfully concealed until that time.

Finally, *do not ignore anomalies.* Evidence that doesn't fit into the model is a tip-off to look more closely at the evidence and at the model. When analysts don't take time to investigate anomalies, they become vulnerable to deception.

Summary

Once a model template has been selected for the target, it becomes necessary to fit the relevant information (collected from the sources discussed in the previous chapter) into the template. Fitting the information into the model template requires a three-step process of evaluating the source, evaluating the communications channel through which the information arrived, and evaluating the evidence itself.

This process is relevant to open source and HUMINT collection, as well as to COMINT, IMINT, and specialized technical collection. In evaluating the source and the evidence, an intelligence analyst must constantly be aware of the potential for denial and deception. A collaborative target-centric process helps to stymie denial and deception by bringing in different perspectives. In evaluating the communications channel, analysts should recognize that processors of collected information—as well as the source of the information—may have a vested interest or bias.

In the ongoing target-centric process, the picture will always be incomplete after the available information is incorporated into the target model. This means that gaps exist, and new collection has to be undertaken to fill the gaps. The next chapter offers a step-by-step process for defining the intelligence problem so that no important question goes unanswered.

Notes

1. David A. Schum, "On the Properties, Uses, Discovery, and Marshaling of Evidence in Intelligence Analysis," Lecture to the SRS Intelligence Analysis Seminar, Tucson, Ariz., February 15, 2001.
2. Bertrand Russell, *A History of Western Philosophy* (New York: Simon and Schuster, 1945), 472.
3. John Evangelist Walsh, *Moonlight: Abraham Lincoln and the Almanac Trial* (New York: St. Martin's Press, 2000).
4. Alfred Price, *Instruments of Darkness* (London: William Kimber, 1967).
5. John Braithwaite, *Corporate Crime in the Pharmaceutical Industry* (London: Routledge and Kegan Paul, 1984).
6. Schum, "On the Properties."
7. "The Skills of an Intelligence Analyst," North Carolina Wesleyan College, http//faculty.ncwc.edu/toconnor/392/spy/analskills.htm, March 29, 2003.
8. John Prados, *The Soviet Estimate* (Princeton: Princeton University Press, 1987), 203.
9. Richards J. Heuer Jr., *Psychology of Intelligence Analysis* (McLean, Va.: Center for the Study of Intelligence, Central Intelligence Agency, 1999), 119.
10. R. V. Jones, "Scientific Intelligence," *Research,* 9 (September 1956): 350.
11. Ibid.
12. Roy Godson, *Intelligence Requirements for the 1990s* (Lanham, Md.: Lexington Books, 1989), 17.
13. Prados, *The Soviet Estimate,* 133.
14. Klaus Knorr, "Failures in National Intelligence Estimates: The Case of the Cuban Missiles," *World Politics,* 16 (April 1964): 455–467.
15. Glenn Shafer, *A Mathematical Theory of Evidence* (Princeton: Princeton University Press, 1976), 3–34.
16. Gus W. Weiss, "The Farewell Dossier," CIA: Studies in Intelligence 39 (5), 1996, www.cia.gov/csi/studies/96unclass.
17. Angelo Codevilla, *Informing Statecraft* (New York: Free Press, 1992), 159–165.
18. TRASHINT is a widely used but not officially recognized term.

6

Defining the Intelligence Problem

Indeed, they disbelieve what they cannot grasp.

The Koran

The preceding chapters have focused on synthesizing a model of the intelligence target. In this chapter and the following chapter, the focus is on a transition to analysis of the model.

For any target, there are typically several people who are interested in receiving intelligence about it. And these customers typically have different interests or different intelligence problems to which they want answers. The U.S. State Department might be interested in Iraqi oil well activity to estimate sanctions violations; a field military commander might be interested in the same oil well activity to prevent the wellheads from being destroyed. Therefore, all intelligence analysis efforts start with some form of "problem" definition. The problem may come in the form of a request from the customer.

The initial guidance that customers give analysts about a problem almost always is incomplete, and it may even be unintentionally misleading. Therefore, the first and most important step an analyst can take is to understand the problem in detail. Determine why the intelligence analysis is being requested and what decisions the results will support. The success of analysis depends on an accurate problem definition. As one senior policy customer noted in commenting on intelligence failures, "sometimes, what they [the intelligence officers] think is important is not, and what they think is not important, is."[1]

In intelligence terms, this phase of the process is often called *establishing needs*. The phase has had many different names in the intelligence business. At one time, the top-level problem statements that resulted from the needs phase were called "key intelligence topics" (KITs)—a term that is now used extensively within the business intelligence world.[2] Whatever the name, most intelligence problems come down to answering one or more of the following four questions (and usually all four):

- What is happening?
- Who are the key people involved, what is their intent, and what are their capabilities?

- Where are the key people and things?
- What is inside a facility or a thing?

These questions are broad and need to be referenced to a specific target. When all four are answered, they provide a systems analysis picture (structure, function, process) as discussed in Chapter 1.

First Steps in Problem Definition

Defining a problem begins with answering five questions. This process moves quickly in a collaborative, target-centric environment, but takes much more time in a traditional bureaucratic process.

- *When is the result needed?* Determine when the product must be delivered. (Usually, the customer wants the report yesterday.) In the traditional intelligence process, many reports are delivered too late—long after the decisions have been made that generated the need—in part because the customer is isolated from the intelligence process. Also, tight deadlines are increasingly a problem in all areas of intelligence; the customer values having precise and detailed intelligence in real time. The target-centric approach can dramatically cut the time required to get actionable intelligence to the customer because the customer is part of the process.

- *Who is the customer?* Identify the intelligence customer and try to understand her needs. The traditional process typically involves several intermediaries, and the needs inevitably become distorted as they move through the communications channels. Also, even if the intelligence effort is done for a single customer, the results often go to many other recipients. It helps to keep in mind these second-order customers and their needs, as well.

- *What is the purpose?* Intelligence efforts usually have one main purpose. This purpose should be clear to all participants when the effort begins and also should be clear to the customer in the result. The main purpose, for instance, might be to provide intelligence to support trade negotiations between the United States and the European Union. A number of more specific intelligence purposes support this main purpose—such as identifying likely negotiating tactics and pinpointing issues that might split the opposing negotiators. Again, customer involvement helps to make the purpose clear to the analyst.

- *What form of output, or product, does the customer want?* Written reports (increasingly in electronic form) are standard in the intelligence business because they endure and can be distributed widely. When the result goes to a single customer or is extremely sensitive, a verbal briefing may be the form of output. Briefings have the advantage of customer interaction and feedback, along with a certainty that the intended recipient got the message. Studies have shown that customers never read most written intelligence.[3] Subordinates may read and interpret it, but the message tends to be distorted as a result. So briefings or (ideally) constant customer interaction with the intelligence team during the target-centric process helps to get the message through.

- *What are the real questions?* Obtain as much background knowledge as possible about the problem behind the questions the customer asks, and understand how the answers will affect organizational decisions. The purpose of this step is to narrow the problem definition. A vaguely worded request for information is usually misleading, and the result will almost never be what the requester wanted.

Be particularly wary of a request that has come through several "nodes" in the organization. The layers of an organization, especially those of an intelligence bureaucracy, will sometimes "load" a request as it passes through with additional guidance that may have no relevance to the original customer's interests. A question that travels through several such layers often becomes cumbersome by the time it reaches the analyst. A question about the current Israeli balance of payments, for example, could wind up on the analyst's desk as instructions to prepare a complete assessment of the Israeli economy. The problem of the communications channel is so pervasive in intelligence that it is covered in detail in Chapter 5.

The request should be specific and stripped of unwanted excess. This entails focused (and perhaps repeated) interaction with the customer responsible for the original request—the executive, the policymaker, or the operations officer. Ask the customer if the request is correctly framed. The time spent focusing the request saves time later during collection and analysis. It also makes clear what questions the customer does NOT want answered. When the United States was involved in Lebanon in 1983, U.S. policymakers did not want to hear from U.S. intelligence that there was no reasonable way to force Syrian president Hafez Assad to withdraw from Lebanon.[4] The result of this disconnect between intelligence and the customer was a foreign policy debacle for the United States; on October 23, 1983, terrorists blew up the Marine barracks at Beirut International Airport with a truck bomb that killed 241 Marines. The United States subsequently withdrew from Lebanon. But policymakers sometimes choose not to be informed by intelligence on selected issues, and it is a choice that has to be respected.

After answering these five questions, the analyst will have some form of problem statement. On large (multiweek) intelligence projects, this problem statement will itself be a formal product. The problem definition product helps explain the real questions and related issues. It is then much easier to focus on answering the questions that the customer wants answered.

The Problem Definition Product

When the final intelligence product is to be a written report, the problem definition product is usually in précis (summary, abstract, or terms of reference) form. The précis should include the problem definition or question, notional results or conclusions, and assumptions. For large projects, many intelligence organizations require the creation of a concept paper or outline that provides the stakeholders with agreed terms of reference in précis form.

If the intelligence product is to be a briefing, a set of graphics will become the final briefing slides. If possible, turn these slides into a notional briefing (that is, a briefing with assumptions, notional results, and conclusions) and show it to the customer; it will improve the chances that the final report will address the issues in the customer's mind.

Either exercise will help all participants (customers, collectors, and analysts) understand their assignments or roles in the process. Think of it as a going-in position; no one is tied to the précis or notional presentation if the analysis later uncovers alternative approaches—as it often does.

Whether the précis approach or the notional briefing is used, the problem definition should present a strategies-to-task view of the problem, as the following sections discuss.

Problem Definition: Strategies-to-Task

The basic technique for defining a problem in detail has had many names. Nobel laureate Enrico Fermi championed the technique of taking a seemingly intractable problem and breaking it into a series of manageable subproblems. The classic problem that Fermi posed for his students was, "How many piano tuners are there in Chicago?" The answer could be reached by estimating how many families were in the city, how many families in the city per piano, and how many pianos a tuner can tune a year.[5] Glenn Kent of RAND Corporation uses the name "strategies-to-task" for a similar breakout of U.S. Defense Department problems.[6] The approach has been used in a study of a future U.S. Army and in the U.S. Air Force strategic planning process, for example.

Whatever the name, the process is simple: Deconstruct the highest level abstraction of the problem into its lower-level constituent functions until you arrive at the lowest level of tasks that are to be performed or subproblems to be dealt with. In intelligence, the deconstruction typically details issues to be addressed or questions to be answered. Start from the problem definition statement and provide more specific details about the problem. The process defines intelligence needs from the top level to the specific task level via *taxonomy*—a classification system in which objects are arranged into natural or related groups based on some factor common to each object in the group. At the top level, the taxonomy reflects the policy or decisionmaker view and reflects the priorities of that customer; this top-level problem statement may be a KIT, as noted earlier. At the task level, the taxonomy reflects the view of the collection and analysis team. These subtasks are sometimes called key intelligence questions (KIQs) or essential elements of information (EEIs).

The strategies-to-task approach has an instinctive appeal. Our cognitive structures naturally lead us to form hierarchical social arrangements and to think about problems hierarchically. The strategies-to-task breakdown follows the classic method for problem solving. It results in a requirements or needs hierarchy that is widely used in intelligence organizations. A few examples from different national policy problem sets will help to illustrate the technique.

Figure 6-1 shows part of a strategies-to-task breakdown for political intelligence on a given country or region of the world. For simplicity, only one part of the breakdown is shown down to the lowest level.

Figure 6-1 illustrates the importance of taking the breakdown to the lowest appropriate level. The top-level question: "What is the political situation in Region X?" is difficult to answer without first answering the more specific questions lower down in the hierarchy, such as "What progress is being made toward reform of electoral systems?"

Another advantage of the linear problem breakdown is that it can be used to evaluate how well intelligence has performed against specific problems or how future collection systems might perform. Again referring to Figure 6-1,

Figure 6-1 Strategies-to-Task Problem Breakdown

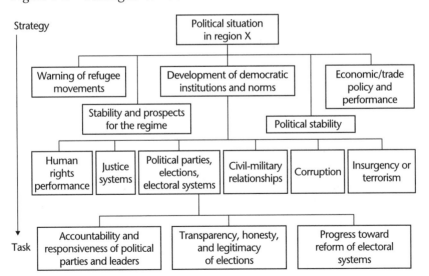

Figure 6-2   Country X Economic Problem Breakdown

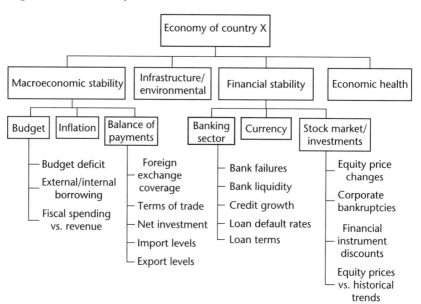

it is difficult to evaluate how well an intelligence organization is answering the question, "What is the political situation in Region X?" It is much easier to evaluate the organization's performance in researching the transparency, honesty, and legitimacy of elections, because these are very specific issues.

There can obviously be several different problems associated with a given intelligence target. If the problem was an overall assessment of a country's economy, rather than its political situation, then the problem breakdown might look very much like that shown in Figure 6-2. Because of space limitations, the figure shows only four of thirteen bottom-level question sets. At the bottom level, issues such as terms of trade and corporate bankruptcies can be addressed with relative ease compared with high-level questions such as "What is country X's financial stability?"

These two strategies-to-task breakdowns are examples of the sorts of problems that intelligence analysts typically encounter about a target, and both are oriented to broad information needs (here, political and economic). But the strategies-to-task breakdown can be much more specific and more oriented to the customer's options for attacking the problem. Figure 6-3 illustrates an example—intelligence support to the design of economic sanctions against a country. An intelligence analyst might have difficulty in directly answering this question from a policymaker: "Tell me what I need to know to develop economic sanctions against country X." So the analyst would

Figure 6-3   Economic Sanctions Problem Breakdown

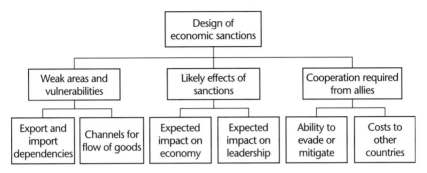

create a strategies-to-task breakdown of the problem and answer more specific questions such as, "What impact will sanctions have on the economy?" and integrate the answers to provide an answer to the top-level question.

No matter how narrow the top-level intelligence task, it still is likely to have an extensive breakout. If the job is to assess the capabilities of an opponent's main battle tank, then an analyst would consider the tank's speed, range, armor, and firepower. Maintenance requirements, quality of crew training, logistics, and command and control supporting the tank should also be examined. Without these less obvious components, the tank is simply an expensive piece of metal and a threat to no one.

Strategies-to-Task and Complex Problems

We have learned that the most important step in the intelligence process is to understand the problem accurately and in detail. Equally true, however, is that intelligence problems today are increasingly complex—often described as nonlinear, or "wicked." They are dynamic and evolving, and thus their solutions are too. This makes them difficult to deal with, and almost impossible within the traditional intelligence cycle framework. A typical example of a complex problem is that of a drug cartel—the cartel itself is dynamic and evolving and so are the questions being posed by intelligence consumers who have an interest in it.

A typical real-world customer's problem today presents an intelligence officer with the following challenges:[7]

- *The problem represents an evolving set of interlocking issues and constraints. There is no definitive statement of the problem. The intelligence officer may not understand the problem until she has finished the analysis—if then. Only by working through the problem to get answers can one understand the ramifications. Often even when the project is complete, an analyst finds out from the* customer that she didn't fully appreciate the issues involved. The narcotics example has an evolving set of interlocking issues and constraints. Take the constraints on possible solutions: Selectively introducing poison into the narcotics supply to frighten consumers and kill demand might reduce drug use, but it is not an acceptable option for the United States.

- *There are many stakeholders—people who care about or have something at stake in how the issue is resolved.* (This makes the problem-solving process fundamentally social, in contrast to the antisocial traditional intelligence cycle.) The contraband narcotics problem has many stakeholders on both sides of the problem. Among the stakeholders trying to eliminate contraband narcotics are the Drug Enforcement Agency, law enforcement, U.S. customs, the military, U.S. banks, and governments in drug-producing countries. The opposing side's stakeholders include the cartel, its supporters in the foreign government, the financial institutions that it uses for funds laundering, farmers, processors, intermediaries, street forces, and drug users. And the stakeholders have different perspectives on the problem. Consider the Pablo Escobar example from Chapter 1. From the U.S. point of view, the problem was to stem the flow of narcotics into the United States. From the Colombian government point of view, the problem was stopping the assassinations and bombings that Escobar ordered.

- *The constraints on the solution, such as limited resources and political ramifications, change over time.* The target is constantly changing, as the Escobar example illustrates, and the customers (stakeholders) change their minds, fail to communicate, or otherwise change the rules of the game. Colombians didn't want high visibility "gringos" involved in the hunt for Escobar, though they relaxed this constraint as they gained confidence in the U.S. operatives.[8] The U.S. government didn't want to be associated with killings of Escobar's relatives, business associates, and lawyers.

- *There is no definitive problem and thus no definitive solution.* The intelligence process usually ends when time runs out, and the customer must act on the most currently available information. Killing Escobar did not solve the problems of the United States or Colombia. Instead the rival Cali Cartel became the dominant narcotics supplier in Colombia—an example of an unintended consequence. Many Colombian officials still live in fear of assassination.

Because complex or "wicked" problems are an evolving set of interlocking issues and constraints, and because the introduction of new constraints cannot be prevented, the strategies-to-task breakdown of a complex problem must be dynamic; it will change with time and circumstances. As the intelligence customer learns more about the target, his needs and interests will shift.

Furthermore, the complex problem breakdown should be created as a network rather than a hierarchy because of the interrelationship among the elements. In Figure 6-1 the "political stability" block is related to all three of the lowest blocks under "political parties, elections, and electoral systems," though they all appear in different parts of the hierarchy; political stability being enhanced, for example, when elections are transparent, honest, and legitimate. In Figure 6-3 "ability to evade or mitigate" sanctions is clearly related to "expected impact on the economy," or "expected impact on leadership," though they also are in different parts of the hierarchy. Iraq's ability to evade or mitigate sanctions during the previous decade was sufficient to minimize the impact on its leadership, but insufficient to keep the Iraqi economy healthy. If lines connected all of the relationships that properly exist within these figures, they would show very elaborate networks. The resulting dynamic network becomes quite intricate and difficult to manage at our present stage of information technology development.

The linear problem breakdown or strategies-to-task approach may be less than ideal for real-world complex problems, but it works well enough. It allows analysts to define the problem in sufficient detail and with sufficient accuracy so that the rest of the process remains relevant. There may be redundancy in a linear hierarchy, but the human mind can usually recognize and deal with the redundancy. To keep the problem breakdown manageable, analysts should continue to use the strategies-to-task hierarchy until information technology comes up with a better way. Complexity can be managed by maintaining a separate model of the target, as discussed in the next chapter.

Summary

Before beginning intelligence analysis, the analyst must understand the customer's problem. This usually involves close interaction with the customer until the important issues are identified. The problem then has to be deconstructed in a strategies-to-task process so that collection, synthesis, and analysis can be effective.

All significant intelligence problems, however, are complex and nonlinear. The complex problem is a dynamic set of interlocking issues and constraints with many stakeholders and no definitive solution. The linear strategies-to-task process is not an optimal way to approach such problems, but it works and is our best option at this point.

The result of problem definition through a strategies-to-task process is that a *model* of the problem has been created in hierarchical form. Chapter 7 discusses how to use this model in conjunction with the target model discussed in earlier chapters.

Notes

1. Stew Magnuson, "Satellite Data Distribution Lagged, Improved in Afghanistan," *Space News,* September 2, 2002, 6.
2. Jan Herring, "KITs Revisited: Their Use and Problems," *SCIP Online,* http:// www.imakenews.com/ scip2/e_article000069099.cfm, November 22, 2002.
3. Jack Davis, "Intelligence Changes in Analytic Tradecraft in CIA's Directorate of Intelligence" (CIAPES ICATCIADI-9504), April 1995, 2.
4. David Kennedy and Leslie Brunetta, "Lebanon and the Intelligence Community," Case Study C15-88-859.0 (Cambridge: Kennedy School of Government, Harvard University, 1988).
5. Hans Christian von Baeyer, *The Fermi Solution,* (Portland, Ore.: Random House, 1993).
6. Glenn Kent and William Simon, *New Challenges for Defense Planning: Rethinking How Much Is Enough* (Santa Monica: RAND, 1994).
7. E. Jeffrey Conklin, "Wicked Problems and Fragmentation," CogNexus Institute, www.cognexus org/ wpf/wickedproblems.pdf, March 24, 2003.
8. Mark Bowden, "Martinez Pushes Ahead with the Hunt," *Philadelphia Inquirer,* December 3, 2000.

7

Interrelating Models

Whereas information enters the intelligence machine by source, it has to leave it by subject; it is this changeover inside the machine that causes all the difficulty.
R. V. Jones, assistant director of Britain's Royal Air Force
Intelligence Section during World War II

At this point we have covered the idea of a target model and a customer problem (strategies-to-task) model. *The target model and the problem model are separate.* Though they often look very similar, it is important to remember which is which and to use them both in crafting intelligence. Using only a target model gives the customer unwanted information and forces her to select what is relevant from a mass of detail; for example, a field commander is usually very interested in the combat forces model of a target country, but does not want to delve into the country's political and economic models. Using only a problem breakdown model results in too narrow a focus; the analyst tends to develop tunnel vision and to miss things that the customer needs to know on important related issues. The field commander might be quite interested, for example, in religious shrines that are located close to opposing military forces.

Although the target model and the problem model are separate concepts, they are related to each other. When the analyst has defined the problem, as discussed in the preceding chapter, she must ask questions such as: How do I pull information out of the target model to address the problem that is before me? Does the target model, in its present form, give me everything I need to answer my customer's questions? If not, where are the gaps in knowledge of the target, and how can I fill those gaps? This chapter describes a formal process that an analyst might go through in considering those questions. Veteran intelligence analysts do follow the process described in this chapter, though they do so intuitively and seldom in such a formal way.

Collateral Models Revisited

Chapter 2 introduced the concept of collateral models, which include different perspectives of the target model. Figure 7-1 illustrates an extension of the

Figure 7-1   Collateral Models Associated with the Target Model

Note: The bidirectional arrows indicate interactions among the models and the knowledge bases.

collateral model concept. In practice, *two* general classes of models are associated with the target model, as the figure shows. Each customer has an associated problem model, typically a strategies-to-task breakdown as discussed in Chapter 6. Each collector has an associated collection problem model. The analyst uses the target model to request collection, to plan analysis, to organize results of the analysis, and to get the results to the right customer. Collectors use the target model along with their collection problem model to plan collection; customers use the target model along with their own problem model to plan actions against the target. An example of a customer model would be a military operations plan against the target or a battlefield scenario that includes the target.

The process of using target models and problem models is easy to explain, though doing it with typical targets and problems can take a great deal of time. The analyst takes the problem definition breakout (described in Chapter 6) and a graphic or text depiction of the target model (described in Chapters 2 and 3), lays them side by side on a desk or on a computer display, and connects related parts of the problem and target models.

Let's illustrate collateral models with a simple example. Take the problem of money laundering—the movement of illicit proceeds into mainstream commerce and other funds transactions designed to conceal the source, ownership, or use of the funds. Criminal organizations, terrorist groups, and pariah states use money laundering to evade international sanctions. Money laundering can be thought of as a process having three distinct stages—placement, layering, and integration—as shown in the simple process model of Figure 7-2.[1]

The Abacha family's laundering of stolen Nigerian government funds, discussed in Chapter 3, is an example of the process shown in Figure 7-2. The Abachas placed money in a Citibank London account; "layered" the funds by moving them among different Citibank London and Citibank New York accounts, shown in Figure 3-10, as well as through Citibank AG Frankfurt and Swiss banks; and integrated the funds using shell (dummy) companies Morgan Procurement and Selcon Airlines.[2]

The problem of constraining money laundering naturally divides into dealing with the three stages shown in Figure 7-2. But different customers of intelligence will be interested in different stages. Countermeasures, it turns out, have been most effective when aimed at the placement stage. It is easier to detect money laundering in this first stage, and most law enforcement and regulatory work has concentrated on detecting the placement of illicit funds.[3]

Figure 7-2   Model of a Money
Laundering Process

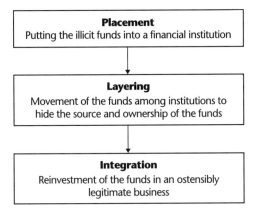

Therefore, law enforcement organizations such as Interpol or the U.S. Financial Crimes Enforcement Network might focus on the placement stage, though law enforcement would want intelligence from all three stages, and financial regulatory customers such as the United Kingdom's Financial Services Authority focus on both placement and layering in this simplistic model. Business regulatory customers such as the U.S. Securities and Exchange Commission or state regulatory agencies might focus on the integration stage. As indicated in Figure 7-3, the problem breakdown models for each of these customers would be closely tied to specific elements of the target model.

Figure 7-3   Interaction of Customers with the
Target Model of a Money Laundering Process

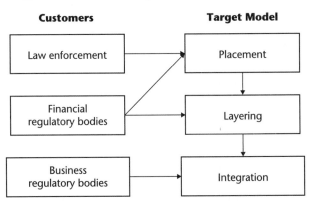

Note: The horizontal and diagonal arrows indicate interaction between the customers and specific parts of the target model. The vertical arrows show movement from the placement stage to the integration stage in the money laundering process.

Figure 7-4   Interaction of Collectors
with the Target Model of a Money
Laundering Process

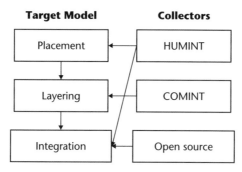

Note: The horizontal and diagonal arrows indicate interaction between the collectors and specific parts of
the target model. The vertical arrows show movement
from the placement stage to the integration stage in
the money laundering process.

Collectors also interact selectively with the target model, as Figure 7-4
shows. HUMINT collection is likely to be most useful against the placement
and integration stages, where well-placed human sources can monitor and report on unusual transactions. COMINT collection is well positioned to help in
tracking the financial transactions associated with layering, because such
transactions are typically made via international data transmission; and open
source intelligence can be useful in analyzing the business activities involving
integration.

In summary, two problem models—the customer's problem model of
Chapter 6 and the collection problem model—interact with the target model
(see Figure 7-5). The analyst wants to interrelate the target model and the
problem model so that she can assemble information that will be part of the
intelligence report and organize it logically to answer the customer's questions.
She wants to interrelate the target model with collection sources so that she
can plan collection to fill gaps in knowledge, making use of the best available
sources.

The Abacha case illustrates how the collection-target interaction could
have worked. A HUMINT source connected to any of the banks involved with
the Abachas could have identified the suspicious transactions that indicated
placement and integration. Indeed, bank personnel were aware of and concerned about a sudden influx of more than $20 million into the New York ac-
counts, a transfer of $5 million to an unfamiliar person, and a discovery that
the Abacha sons were conducting business in Libya, which had no apparent
connection to the supposed source of funds in the accounts. These transactions

Figure 7-5 Ongoing Interactions with the Target Model of a
Money Laundering Process

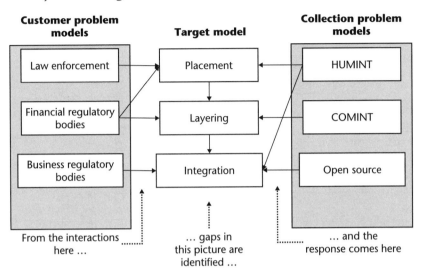

Note: The horizontal and diagonal arrows indicate interactions among the models. The vertical arrows show movement from the placement stage to the integration stage in the money laundering process.

were out of line with the account history. COMINT could have identified the patterns of funds movements among banks that were a sign of layering activity. U.S. Department of Transportation records and other open sources could have provided the indications that Selcon Airlines was a shell company being used for the funds integration stage.

Now let's go into some more detail on the nature of these interrelationships to illustrate how an analyst goes through the process shown in Figure 7-5.

Interrelating the Customer Problem
Model and the Target Model

The first step an analyst takes is to interrelate the customer's problem model and the target model for both information-gathering and analysis purposes. Veteran analysts do this naturally, seldom making the interrelationships of Figure 7-5 explicit. For simple problems, explicit definition may be unnecessary. However, when we deal with complex (nonlinear) problems, the target model or scenario should be made explicit. Even when dealing with simple problems, it is easy for an analyst to omit important points or fail to take full advantage of the information sources without an explicit interrelationship diagram. An explicit representation of the interrelationship, following the examples given in this chapter, is useful for the veteran analyst and essential for the novice.

Figure 7-6   Interrelationship of a Problem Model and a Target
Model of the Political Situation in the Democratic Republic
of the Congo

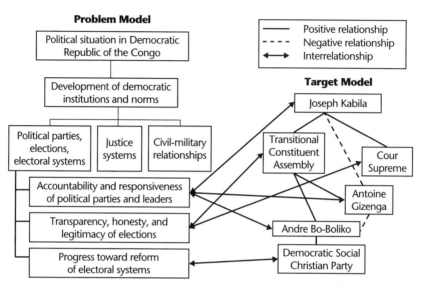

A more detailed example may help to illustrate the process of tying the
problem breakdown to the target model. If, for instance, the problem is to assess
the political situation in Democratic Republic of the Congo (DRC), one part of
the problem is to assess the country's political parties, elections, and electoral
systems. The left side of Figure 7-6 shows the relevant strategies-to-task problem breakout. The right side is a relationship diagram of the target, showing hypothetical relationships among some entities (people and organizations) in the
DRC. The solid lines that interconnect the target network on the right show positive (friendly) relationships among entities; the dotted lines show negative (hostile) relationships. The arrows interconnecting the problem breakdown on the
left with the target on the right are intended to identify the key interrelationships
between the problem and the target for planning the analysis effort.

Generally, the target model will be a network of the sort shown on the
right in Figure 7-6. A network model is one type of *pattern* model, as discussed
in Chapter 4.

The reason for this structured approach to dealing with the problem
(strategies-to-task) model on the left and the target model on the right is to facilitate managing a complex problem. Almost all intelligence issues involve
multiple relationships among elements of the target model and the problem or
needs hierarchy. Managing the synthesis/analysis problem requires that these
relationships be made explicit. Managing collection requires a similar definition of explicit relationships, as discussed in the next section.

Interrelating the Collection Model and the Target Model

A target model is never complete enough to satisfy the intelligence customers. After a problem hierarchy is defined and interrelated with the target model as described above, it will become obvious that there are gaps in knowledge of the target. These gaps have to be made explicit, and intelligence collection has to fill in the missing pieces of the model to answer the customers' questions.

Identifying Knowledge Gaps

After reviewing existing data and incorporating it into the target model, the next step is to identify the gaps in data, information, or knowledge. A gap is a missing element that, if found, allows one to choose among alternatives with greater confidence. These gaps always exist in the intelligence business. The skill we have in organizing thoughts and evidence influences how well we are able to generate or discover new thoughts and evidence.

Analysts have a natural tendency to draw conclusions based on the available information rather than determine what policy questions must be answered and go after the needed information. Some veteran (or lazy) analysts, faced with a new project, will simply sift through their carefully kept files, add a few items that are within easy reach, and write a report. They never get to gap analysis. The opposite, and equally poor approach, is to keep looking for the one last scrap of information that makes the other pieces fall into place. An analyst almost never gets that last piece of the puzzle. So gap analysis (and filling gaps) has to be done, but not overdone; the analyst needs to know when to stop.

Identifying data gaps is a continuous and iterative process—as new data comes in and is fitted into the model, new gaps can be identified. Gap analysis is the process of:

- Identifying and prioritizing gaps based on the importance of the underlying need and size of the gap.
- Classifying gaps as to their nature: do they occur in collection, processing, analysis, or dissemination?
- Sorting gaps as either short term, for current collection systems "tuning," or long term, for new capabilities development.

Suppose that a Japanese company is considering the acquisition of a French firm (called "Target Company"). Figure 7-7 shows a simple mergers and acquisitions model that we have constructed as a result of a problem breakdown exercise of the sort discussed in Chapter 6. We are concerned about how the French government and European regulatory bodies will react to the acquisition. In addition to assessing the relationship between these bodies and Target Company, we have to assess their ties to Competitor

Figure 7-7   Gaps in the Target Network

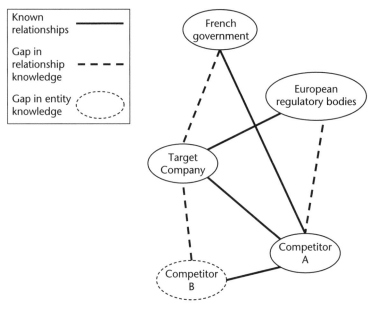

A (a European company) to assess the likelihood that Competitor A will influence the French government or European regulatory bodies to delay or block the acquisition. We also would like to know the reaction of Target Company's major competitors (Competitor A and Competitor B) to the acquisition in order to predict the Japanese company's countermoves. We already know some of these relationships and have included them in the model, as Figure 7-7 indicates. Some of the relationships are not well known, and are therefore gaps that need to be filled (shown as dashed lines in the figure); and we lack important knowledge about one of the entities, Competitor B (shown as a dashed oval).

After constructing the relationship model of Figure 7-7 from available data, we find four major gaps in our knowledge, shown in Figure 7-7 as dashed lines and a dashed oval:

- The relationship between the French government and Target Company.
- The relationship between Competitor B and Target Company.
- The level of influence that Competitor A has on European regulatory bodies.
- The likely reaction of Competitor B to news of the potential merger.

The customer's information needs are almost always being partially filled, as Figure 7-7 illustrates. The analyst needs to determine how much is already known about the target and how much more needs to be learned. Specifically, the analyst needs to know the customer's current level of satisfaction and the remaining gaps. In the example of Figure 7-7, first priority for collection would go to two critical gaps—the relationship between Competitor A and the European regulatory bodies and the likely reaction of Competitor B to news of the impending merger. Second priority would be on closing the two remaining gaps between the French government and Target Company and between Target Company and Competitor B.

Measures of user satisfaction can be used after collection to evaluate how well the intelligence process performed against that need or closed that gap. Expressed another way, the measurement is a quantification of how well a particular requirement or condition has been satisfied. Meaningful measures of user satisfaction could include: What percent of all Iranian mobile missiles were located? Where are the petroleum industry's planned oil exploration regions? What is the expected size of the 2002 opium crop in Pakistan, Laos, Mexico, Thailand, Afghanistan, and Burma? Where are the opium processing centers in these countries and how much can they process? Where are the concealed weapons of mass destruction production centers in Iraq? All of these questions call for analytic conclusions, but all lead to more specific definitions of measures of user satisfaction. A poor example of a measure of user satisfaction is: How much of the target area was searched in imagery at a given resolution? One hundred percent of the target area could be searched without turning up a single item of useful intelligence. Collectors are fond of using such quantitative measures because they provide a firm and technically computable measure.

Before designing a collection strategy to fill a gap, it is important to understand the nature of the gap. Some intelligence gaps exist because of nonexistent or inadequate analysis of the problem, not because of lack of collection. Other gaps need research to determine what part collection can play. An analyst should not treat all gaps as collection gaps; the collector will simply collect again without solving the problem, and in some cases compounding the problem by adding more unneeded data to be analyzed.

An example of a useful gap-filling approach is illustrated in Figure 7-8 using the earlier example from Figure 7-7 of a Japanese company that is considering the acquisition of a French firm. An industry expert was able to provide much of the information that was needed to fill two of the gaps. An Internet search was used to provide information on Competitor B. A French search firm and a French consultant were asked to research the relationship between the French government and Target Company, and their collection provided large volumes of material in French; as a result, the language processor (a French language translator) was swamped with material to translate. The French consultant was subsequently given the same task. After all the

Figure 7-8   The Collection Network Fills Gaps in the Target
Network

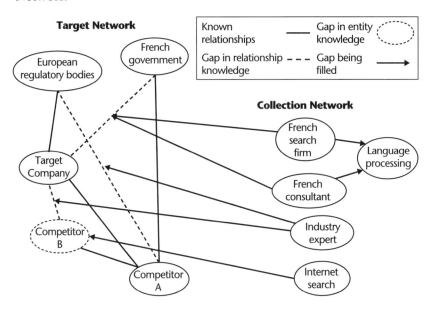

material was translated, it turned out that the French search firm and the
French consultant both provided basically the same information about the
connection between the French government and the Target Company. The gap
was not in collection; it was in processing (language translation).

Enigmas

While identifying knowledge gaps in the target model, an analyst will occasionally encounter a type of gap that is common in the intelligence business:
the unidentified entity, or enigma.

An enigma is a different type of thing for the analyst than for the collector.
For analysts, the enigma is something that the analyst knows exists but of which
he has no physical evidence. Examples include a communications link that has
to exist from narcotics suppliers to distributors, a fabrication facility that must
exist somewhere if cell phones are being produced, or an unnamed terrorist
organization that must be responsible for recent acts of violence. The gap may
be in identifying the communications link, in finding evidence that the facility
exists, or in naming the terrorist organization and identifying its leader.

For collectors, the enigma is a physical object that cannot be fit into
existing models. Among IMINT collectors, it occurs as the mysterious facility
observed in imagery whose purpose cannot be determined. Among ELINT
collectors, it is the strange new radar signal. Among COMINT collectors, it is
the encrypted communications link between two unidentified organizations.

The gaps here may be in identifying the function of the radar or in establishing the identity of the organizations.

Dealing with enigmas requires analyst-collector teamwork in using the target model. The target model must identify entities that, in the analyst's view, have to exist. The collector's input to the model must call out potentially relevant unidentified facilities and signals and communications links, and analysts must respond by helping the collectors—typically by finding a model into which the collector's unidentified entities fit.

Acquiring New Information

At this point in the analysis process, the problem has been defined and the gaps in information identified. It is time for the analyst to plan a collection activity to fill the gaps and to follow up by offering guidance to collection sources and organizations.

As Chapter 4 indicates, a rich set of collection "INTs" is available to help an analyst acquire information. Two distinct questions arise in planning for collection:

- In the near term, how can the analyst best use existing assets to answer the questions that are important right now to the analysis effort?
- What collection assets should be developed to answer the questions that are expected to arise about the target in the future?

Using Existing Collection Assets

Acquiring new data to fill gaps is a matter of making good use of existing collection assets. These assets are the agents already in place, the open literature that is coming in and being translated, the collection satellites or aircraft currently flying, and so on. The process of asking for use of these assets to fill gaps is called tasking.

Analysts rely on their judgment in putting together the best collection strategy to fill gaps. Analysts traditionally initiate the tasking and must pull together the incoming information to form a coherent picture. In the collaborative environment envisioned in Chapter 1, formulating a collection strategy would be a team effort, with input from collectors and processors.

For straightforward collection problems, collection planning can be done quickly and efficiently using the approach described in this chapter and summarized in Figure 7-5. Starting with a given target model, an analyst invokes the strategies-to-task methodology to define requirements and identify gaps. After the analyst reviews his collection assets and their capabilities, he defines a collection strategy for using the various "INTs" and tasks them against specific elements of the target, as indicated in Figures 7-5 and 7-8, to fill the gaps.

On more complex collection problems, the general approach is the same but a formal process may be needed to develop and compare alternative collection strategy "packages." This is a resource allocation step—an effort to fill short-term gaps (immediate needs) by identifying possible collection mechanisms and selecting the most promising combination of collection assets. Consider the collection network illustrated in Figure 7-8, for example. It represents one possible combination of collection assets, or one strategy, to fill the identified gaps. An analyst could also have chosen a combination of a clandestine HUMINT source in the European Union staff in Brussels and a COMINT source of the target company's communications.

Most collection strategies are developed as a result of past experience. Making use of existing methods is a good way to save effort, time, and cost. Stated another way, most collection problems are old ones; only the specific questions to be answered are new. It is prudent to avoid recreating solutions that already have been tried at least once before. Begin by looking at what has succeeded in the past.

Start with a review of the previously used collection strategies and their results. Each specialized substantive area of intelligence has its own collection techniques that have been tested over the years. Political intelligence traditionally has relied on a combination of open source and HUMINT, with some COMINT thrown in. Military intelligence relies heavily on COMINT and IMINT, along with some specialized technical collection. Analyzing previous strategies and their results will foreshadow the prospects for future strategies.

An analyst cannot rely only on previous strategies, however. As noted in the section in Chapter 5 on denial and deception, a predictable collection strategy can be defeated. Also, simply shifting tasking from one target to another usually opens gaps in other areas.[4] If possible, develop innovative approaches to using existing assets. Collectors must be encouraged not to repeat collection that does not obtain the needed information but to try new ideas. Techniques that work in economic or political intelligence problems may be applied to problems in other areas, such as military or scientific and technical intelligence.

In identifying collection strategies, be sure to distinguish collectors' actual contributions from their potential contribution. In some cases, gaps can be closed by applying collection resources where they now contribute very little. A HUMINT source that reports on political affairs may also be able to obtain economic information. A COMINT source that provides order of battle information may also have insights into the personalities of enemy field commanders.[5] However, major reorientation of collection assets often requires considerable planning and may have to be considered a long-term solution.

In developing strategies, look ahead to the processing and exploitation steps. An analyst can get synergistic benefits by more intelligently timing collection by different resources. Time collection so that it occurs when the highest probability of getting desirable content will occur. For example:

- Missile range testing has consistent patterns; when a pattern of vehicle deployments indicates that a missile test is about to take place, it is the right time to task collection assets.

- People consistently use the telephone heavily at certain times of day; ask for COMINT collection during those times.
- Questioning technical staff at professional conferences elicits more useful information than questioning at other times.
- Coordinated collection by different "INTs" at the same time can provide insights that those INTs could not provide individually.

The result of this effort should be a strategy "package"—a combination of strategies for closing the gaps. Once alternative strategies have been developed, they can be compared and the best alternative selected. The most straightforward and accepted method of comparison is cost/benefit or cost/utility analysis:

- Estimate the benefit or utility of each strategy (option) and combination of options.
- Estimate the costs or risks of each strategy and combination.
- Select a package that has a high ratio of benefits (or utility) to costs (or risks).

The first step is to estimate the benefit or utility of each collection option. At this point we have determined the importance of the requirement and the value if the gap is filled. Now focus on the probability of success. Which asset has the best chance to get the needed information? Determine the value of the information that could be provided. Also examine ways to increase the probability of success and to maximize the value of the information collected.

Establish the probability of success for each category of collection or for fusion of sources, if appropriate. Denial and deception is a critical factor here; the probability of success drops significantly if it is likely that denial and deception will be used successfully against collection.

Distinguish contingent collection from certain collection. A broad area search for mobile missile sites has high payoff if a successful hit occurs, but success is stochastic (controlled by probabilities) and the probabilities are low. A fixed intercontinental ballistic missile site is an almost certain hit for IMINT collection (assuming no cloud cover), since its location is known, but the value of the intelligence gathered may be low. The evaluation ought to incorporate the probability of obtaining the desired *content* (a relevance issue) and the ability to beat denial and deception.

In summary, the short-term gap problem involves efficiently allocating existing collection resources based on the:

- Importance of the requirement or specific task.
- Value of the information collected if successful.
- Probability of success.

Next, determine the resource cost or risks of the options. One method is to produce a resource cost estimate that identifies the opportunity costs associated with using collection assets as proposed. Actual costs of collection may be difficult to come by; collection organizations guard such information zealously.

Risks may be more important than costs as a factor against which to measure benefit. In making the decision to conduct aerial reconnaissance over the USSR during the 1950s, the costs of the U-2 program were a relatively minor factor in the Eisenhower administration's decisionmaking process. A much larger factor was the risk of a shoot down and of consequent damage to the U.S. image and to U.S.–USSR relations. A U-2 was indeed shot down, and the subsequent political fallout might suggest that risk was in fact a better measure than program cost, though the benefits gained by the U-2 program were sufficiently great that the decision to overfly was a good one.[6]

If an analyst cares about performance metrics of the intelligence network, it is essential to use the target model/intelligence system process of the sort illustrated in Figure 7-8. A target-centric process allows analysts to measure the incremental value of collection, processing, and analysis, because it is tied to the questions that must be answered. It therefore measures outputs, which a performance measurement system should do, instead of measuring inputs.

Filling the Long-Term Gaps

A distinctly separate problem arises when the need is not to task existing collectors but to fill gaps that no existing collector is able to fill. Then the requirement is either to develop new capabilities—to recruit a new agent with the necessary access, to acquire new open source publications, to develop a new SIGINT or IMINT collection system—or to find a new way to use existing systems.

Developing new capabilities is a long-term process that requires time and means that analysts may not have. Thus the analyst must either have exceptional prescience or (as is usually the case) depend on the collectors to do the long-range planning. In developing new HUMINT sources, the lead time can be one to five years or more. New satellite SIGINT or IMINT collection systems take ten years to develop and deploy during peacetime, though experience indicates that they can be deployed much faster in crisis or wartime.

One problem with filling long-term gaps is that a formal requirements system tends to focus on today's needs and gaps. Major intelligence problems such as proliferation of weapons of mass destruction, terrorism, and international criminal activity tend to endure. But they change in relative importance, and new problems arise. In 2020 environmental problems, mass migration, and basic resource (food and water) shortages might be more important than today's problems. The existing U.S. collection requirements structure is not well suited to dealing with the future, and it has other problems as well, as the next section discusses.

The U.S. Collection Requirements Problem

Management of information acquisition is a major effort in large intelligence communities. Here, high volume collection is based on a formalized process of defining requirements, needs, or information gaps. The U.S. intelligence community has for decades attempted to create structures for handling requirements.

Collection requirements form a hierarchy. Chapter 6 illustrated some requirements hierarchies that result from the strategies-to-task problem breakdown. Lower elements in the hierarchy are more specific and, in a well-drafted requirements hierarchy, are linked to the higher elements by some measures that indicate their relative value in the overall scheme of things. The number of specific, lower-level targets will be in the dozens for a specific company, in the hundreds for even a small country or a consortium, and in the thousands for an illicit network target such as international narcotics. A typical requirement at the lower levels might read: "Geolocate all armored vehicles in the battlefield area"; "Obtain a copy of Ambassador Smythe's negotiating notes for tomorrow's trade negotiations"; or "Determine the intentions of the Cuban leadership on seaborne migration."

The collection requirements problem stems in part from the success that the United States has had in developing collection assets. The intelligence literature often makes a point of criticizing U.S. intelligence collection capabilities as being cumbersome and inefficient.[7] It is true that some small government intelligence services, such as Israel's Mossad, and a number of multinational corporations can be successful within the areas where they have concentrated their intelligence expertise. They also have all of the advantages that accrue to a small, tightly knit organization. However, U.S. government collection capabilities are unquestionably the best in the world. The U.S. intelligence community has the most resources and does the best systems planning. It innovates constantly and attempts things few other services would try. In breadth and depth of coverage, the United States remains the best; and therein lies its problem. Because U.S. intelligence can do so much, it is asked to do too much. Expensive collection assets are used too often where cheaper ones might suffice.

As a result, the U.S. intelligence requirements structure has received considerable criticism, and repeated attempts to define such a structure over decades suggest that something may be fundamentally wrong with the concept. One critic of the requirements process, as it has been practiced in recent years, notes:

> Analysts themselves often thought that too many people were employed and too much activity was oriented solely to generating "intelligence requirements"; a better job could probably have been done by a few experienced people, working with the available data, and therefore aware of what was missing. Instead intelligence requirements were the object of repeated studies and reorganization efforts.[8]

This commentary on the requirements structure bears a striking resemblance to R. V. Jones's observation that "Intelligence is best done by a minimum number of men and women of the greatest possible ability." Analysts believe that the existing requirements process is a bureaucratic beast that consumes resources but adds little value.

In spite of the analyst view, formal requirements structures are necessary in dealing with high-volume satellite IMINT and COMINT and with open source material, where a large volume of potential targets exist, and where a large customer suite with competing priorities wants more collection than could be accomplished with the entire national budget. This requirements structure has several problems, however. First, as one senior U.S. intelligence official noted, everyone tasks the system, but no one prioritizes.[9] No one is willing to fight the special interests and say "we don't need this badly enough to spend resources on it." In contrast, businesses tend to watch their overhead costs closely and are willing to cut low-payoff functions. Second, if information is available from unclassified sources, intelligence collection assets should not be used to get it, except where cross-checking is essential—for example, in countering suspected deception. Increasingly, commercial sources such as commercial imaging satellites can do collection that once required national intelligence assets, and can do it more cheaply. Third, formal requirements structures tend to focus on bean counting. Content, not quantity, is the critical measure, and formal requirements structures do not handle content evaluation well. Only analysts and customers can evaluate content and thereby place a value on collection.

When these problems are not addressed, then the bulk of raw data collected by the INTs is irrelevant. For example, most new overhead imagery contains information that is already known; natural terrain features and fixed structures change little, if at all, in the course of a year. Most COMINT traffic, which consists of personal telephone conversations and unusable (encrypted) traffic, must be discarded as irrelevant. And most open source information winds up in the wastebasket.

However, all of the data that is collected must be processed to some extent, and the handling of this volume of irrelevant data chokes the processing and exploitation systems and often chokes the analyst as well. The problem derives from trying to force a process based on the idea of an intelligence cycle instead of using the shared target process of Chapter 1. To come closer to the effectiveness of the target-centric paradigm, it is essential to make the hierarchical requirements structure efficient and responsive, and this is a continuing challenge for U.S. intelligence.

Summary

In addition to the target model, we encounter a number of collateral models in target-centric intelligence analysis. One commonly used collateral model is the problem definition breakout, discussed in Chapter 6. These two models—the target model and the problem definition model—are interrelated to identify gaps in knowledge and to plan for the intelligence response to the customer.

Once gaps in knowledge are identified, they are filled by interrelating another collateral model—the collection model—with the target model. From the collection model interrelationship with the target model, the analyst and collector collaboratively form a collection plan to fill the gaps in knowledge. They develop a collection strategy based on previous successful strategies plus new approaches in using existing assets, keeping in mind the requirements for processing and exploiting the collection result. For complex problems, it may be necessary to develop alternative strategies and to balance costs and risks against the potential payoff (utility) of the strategy.

Formal collection requirements systems are used for filling intelligence gaps in large intelligence communities such as that of the United States. These formal systems are structured around the traditional intelligence cycle. As a result, they are less effective and less responsive than they would be if structured to support a target-centric process.

Notes

1. Joseph M. Myers, "International Strategies to Combat Money Laundering," speech to the International Symposium on the Prevention and Control of Financial Fraud, Beijing, October 19–22, 1998.
2. "Minority Staff Report for Permanent Subcommittee on Investigations—Hearing on Private Banking and Money Laundering: A Case Study of Opportunities and Vulnerabilities," November 9, 1999, http://levin.senate.gov/issues/psireport2.htm.
3. Ibid.
4. At the time this book was written (November 2001), the United States had just shifted a large segment of its intelligence collection and analysis capability onto the terrorism target in response to the attacks of September 11, 2001. The knowledge gaps that are being opened in other areas will take years to close. Unfortunately, it is doubtful that the shifted resources can be used efficiently, as explained by the Brooks curves (see Chapter 12).
5. The Department of Defense defines order of battle as "the identification, strength, command structure, and disposition of the personnel, units, and equipment of any military force." See "DOD Dictionary of Military Terms," http://www.dtic.mil/doctrine/jel/doddict/, April 10, 2003.
6. John Prados, *The Soviet Estimate* (Princeton: Princeton University Press, 1987), 96–102.
7. See, for example, Roy Godson, *Intelligence Requirements for the 1990s* (Lanham, Md.: Lexington Books, 1989).
8. Prados, *The Soviet Estimate,* 181.
9. Godson, *Intelligence Requirements,* 68.

8

The Analytic Spectrum

CAPTAIN MATTHEW GARTH (Charleton Heston): "Joe, you're guessing!"
INTELLIGENCE OFFICER JOSEPH ROCHEFORT (Hal Holbrooke): "Sir, we like to call it analysis."

Midway, the movie, 1976

Having populated the model with intelligence information (synthesis), the next step is analysis, which entails drawing conclusions from the target model. The type of intelligence that must be extracted from the model changes depending on the customer and on the time allowed for action on the resulting intelligence. No intelligence categorization scheme works perfectly. The categorizations shown in this chapter have their own problems and overlaps, but they encourage more effective collection and synthesis/analysis than do disciplinary categorizations such as political, economic, and military. They are equally applicable to government and business intelligence.

The Conflict Spectrum

As we learned in Chapter 1, intelligence is about conflict. Against any opponent in a conflict, three successive levels of action can be taken: *prevention, deterrence,* or *defeat.* Figure 8-1 shows the operations spectrum that includes these levels of action. Preventive operations tend to be strategic and to focus on planning. Operations intended to deter or defeat are mostly tactical; they transition from planning to managing the developing crisis and executing the plans. The costs of the action tend to increase as one goes from prevention to deterrence to defeat.

- *Prevention.* Operations organizations first try to prevent a disadvantageous situation from developing. Examples include preventing the opponent from acquiring or developing a capability, a strategy, or a new weapons system; preventing an unfavorable decision from being made; preventing the opposing negotiations team from taking a certain position; reversing an unfavorable decision that has been made; rolling back a capability; or inducing the opponent to abandon a development or pull out of a contested area.

Figure 8-1   The Operations Spectrum

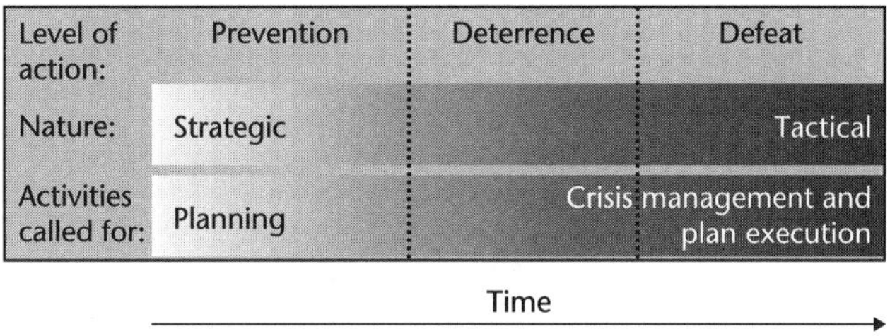

Level of action:	Prevention	Deterrence	Defeat
Nature:	Strategic		Tactical
Activities called for:	Planning	Crisis management and plan execution	

Time →

- *Deterrence.* Deterrence is used when it is too late for prevention. Examples include deterring an attack, deterring the use of a capability or weapons system; deterring the opponent from escalating or aggravating a crisis; or creating uncertainty that induces the opponent to be cautious. Prevention keeps a situation from becoming unfavorable; deterrence focuses on an opponent's potential actions to resolve an already unfavorable situation.

- *Defeat.* When all else fails, resolve the conflict on favorable terms. Examples include defeating the opponent in armed combat, destroying the opponent's weapons of mass destruction, or taking market share away from the opponent in commerce.

Until September 11, 2001, when terrorists attacked the World Trade Center and the Pentagon, the U.S. Department of Defense's Central Command (CENTCOM) was primarily focused on prevention in affairs regarding Afghanistan. After September 11, CENTCOM moved quickly to tactics for defeat.

The Temporal Synthesis/Analysis Spectrum

Figure 8-2 shows how intelligence synthesis and analysis proceed on a particular problem or issue over time. As the operations focus on strategic issues and planning, intelligence concentrates on creating the target model via

Figure 8-2   The Temporal Synthesis/Analysis Spectrum

Type of intelligence:	In-depth research		Current intelligence
Specific target:	Capabilities Plans	Intentions	Indications and warning
Nature of product:	What-if (scenarios)		Specific situation

Time →

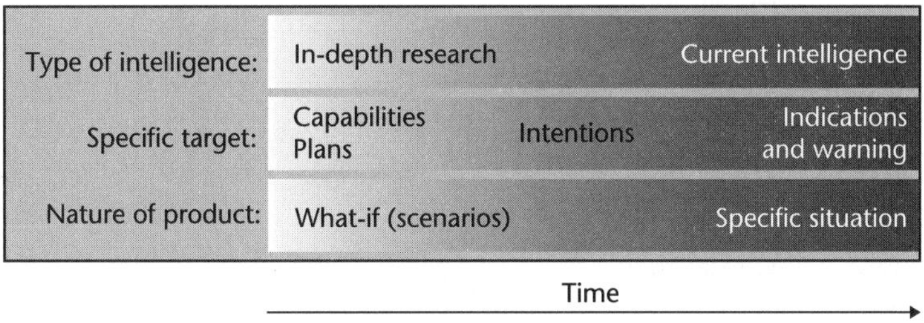

in-depth research, and the focus is on an opponent's capabilities and plans or intentions. The intelligence customer's focus is strategic, and so is the intelligence effort. Alternative target scenarios, as discussed in Chapter 9, are created. On the right side of Figure 8-2, the problem is tactical. The scenario or situation is known. The intelligence focus is not on building target models but on updating and exploiting them to determine current intentions and to provide indications and warning. Intelligence is about current developments, and it reacts quickly to new information. The intelligence customers must make and execute decisions, and intelligence must help them.

We said in an earlier chapter that intelligence supports operations. Figure 8-2 illustrates the relationship. As an example, consider operations in a diplomatic or a business negotiation context—in either type of negotiation, one plans strategy first, then develops tactics, then modifies the tactics in response to the opponent's moves. On the left side of Figure 8-2, the process is one of data gathering and evaluation, followed by cool, reasoned, analytical research. On the right side it is a fast-paced, frenetic, newsgathering atmosphere in which all of the carefully laid plans tend to go out the window if the process is poorly managed. (Sometimes they go out the window regardless of the management.) The tempo of intelligence varies accordingly, from the normal maintenance of the target model and assembling of information as it comes in, to the surge of activity in the late operational phase. This increased tempo is well suited to support "swarm" operations against a target network as discussed in the netwar strategy developed by John Arquilla and David Ronfeldt of RAND Corporation (see Chapter 1).[1] In short, intelligence, like operations, can be broadly defined at the top level as being either *strategic* or *tactical.*

Strategic Intelligence

Strategic intelligence deals with long-range issues. Monitoring arms limitation treaties, supporting strategic planning in companies, and national industrial policymaking are examples. Here, an analyst must spend much time in building the model from scratch or populating a model template. There are lots of options. One can consider many possible target models (scenarios), and the situation can evolve many different ways. Intelligence takes a long-term, analytical view.

Strategic intelligence is much tougher than tactical intelligence. For one thing, the intelligence analyst is seldom able to drop the short term tactical support to customers while developing a clientele having the long-term view.[2] The analyst needs a champion in the customer suite to support her in strategic intelligence, because tactical intelligence—dealing with current issues— usually consumes all available resources. The analyst will need to add more sophisticated and difficult analytic techniques to her repertoire. The models will be similar or identical to those used for tactical intelligence, but usually more complex because of the long-term view.

Strategic intelligence involves creating much the same target models in business and government. Both business and government look at the political structure and alliances of opponents, both create biographical or leadership profiles, both do assessments of the opponent's technology.

Tactical Intelligence

Tactical intelligence deals with issues that require immediate action. Supporting trade negotiations, providing relief to flood or famine victims, enforcing laws, and stopping narcotics or clandestine arms shipments are examples. At the tactical level the intelligence process is very fast. The model must already exist—it was created in the strategic intelligence phase in the normal course of things. Incoming intelligence is simply added to refine the model, and an analysis of changes is extracted and reported quickly.

On the right side of Figure 8-2, the scenario is *here,* and mostly it is known. Now the customer wants details. Intelligence has to be fast and highly reactive. A military commander doesn't care, for example, what the tank can do; he already knows that. What he needs to know is where it is and where it is going. At the tactical level in diplomacy, the diplomat worries less about negotiating strategy and more about an opponent's likely reaction to the diplomat's initiatives.

A type of "fast synthesis" of data is necessary to support ongoing tactical operations and to allow additional collection to be done intelligently in a short period of time. This short-fuse synthesis is often called *fusion.* It differs from normal synthesis/analysis only in the emphasis: time is of the essence. Fusion is aimed at using all available data sources to develop a more complete picture of a complex event, usually with a short deadline. The target model exists, and the analyst's job is to fit in any new data. The analyst works only with the incoming data plus anything that he has in an immediately accessible database or in his memory. Fusion is common in intelligence support to military operations, crisis management, law enforcement, and similar direct operations support where time is the critical element.

Which area to stress in Figure 8-2 depends on the customers and where they are in operations. Almost all national leaders want current intelligence or indications and warning intelligence that is specific.[3] But as former CIA deputy director for intelligence Bruce Clarke once noted, "Intelligence research is putting money in the bank; current intelligence is making a withdrawal." The problem with abandoning strategic intelligence is that eventually the intelligence models become irrelevant to the problem. Without a clear picture of long-term trends, analysts cannot make short-term predictions. The intelligence outfit becomes bankrupt. It not only cannot provide strategic intelligence, it can't even do decent tactical intelligence.

The specific targets of intelligence shown in Figure 8-2 can be tactical, strategic, or both, but the categories tend naturally to be one or the other. Indications and warning tend to be more tactical; capabilities, plans, and intentions tend to be more strategic. The division is based on the timeliness and quality of intelligence required. Collection tends to be handled differently, and use different sources, for each category of target.

Another way to make this division is to contrast current intelligence with intelligence research or in-depth synthesis/analysis. Current intelligence follows principles that are common to news reporting, whether in newspaper or television form. Intelligence research much more resembles the world of a university or a research laboratory. It looks to the long term, or it looks in depth at a specific issue.

Both types of intelligence have their proponents in intelligence organizations and among policymakers. It is not useful to think of them in "either/or" terms when allocating time and resources, because both are needed. Current intelligence allows analysts to be in close touch with policymakers and facilitates better understanding between the two. In-depth research provides the background that allows an analyst to make credible judgments in current reporting.

Capabilities, Plans, and Intentions

The strategic intelligence target tends to divide into two major areas: capabilities and plans. This view of strategic intelligence is closely tied to the strategic planning process as it is done in government and industry. Such strategic planning proceeds from analysis of what is known as the "SWOT":

Strengths.
Weaknesses.
Opportunities.
Threats.

Strengths and weaknesses define *capabilities* and are determined by looking internally within the opposing organization. Opportunities and threats shape *plans* and are determined by looking externally. The job of strategic intelligence, in this view, is to assess the opposing organization's capabilities (strengths and weaknesses) and its consequent plans (shaped by opportunities and threats). In tactical intelligence, the use of capabilities to execute plans—specifically, intentions—becomes important. Intent to launch a military attack, intent to impose an embargo, or intent to break off negotiations are all tactical. Plans and intentions tend to be lumped together in traditional intelligence definitions, but they are in fact two different targets separated by their time scale; plans are longer term, intentions more immediate.

Indications and Warning

Indications and warning (commonly referred to as "I&W") for governments involve detecting and reporting time-sensitive information on foreign developments that threaten the country's military, political, or economic interests. Providing indications and warning on threats to national security is traditionally an intelligence organization's highest priority.

The purpose of indications and warning is to avoid surprise that would damage the organization's or country's interests. Tactical indications and warning can include warning of enemy actions or intentions, imminent hostilities, insurgency, and terrorist attacks. Indirect and direct threats are targets of indications and warning, including warnings of coups or civil disorder, third-party wars, and refugee surges, though these examples may not immediately and directly affect the country making the assessment.

Strategic indications and warning involve identifying and forecasting emerging threats. Warnings about instability or new defense technologies or breakthroughs that could significantly alter the relative advantages of opposing military forces are examples.

For the forty years from 1950 to 1990, U.S. national indications and warning were dominated by a concern about Soviet strategic attack. A secondary focus was persistent world "hot spots": the likelihood of Arab-Israeli, Indo-Pakistani, or Korean conflict. National indications and warning for many Middle Eastern countries was dominated by the Arab-Israeli situation. Today indications and warning are much more complex—many countries are focusing on the threat of terrorist attack, particularly an attack using weapons of mass destruction. Indications and warning also are closely related to (and overlap with) two other categories of intelligence—capabilities, plans, and intentions and crisis management and operations support.

The traditional approach to indications and warning has been to develop indicators, or norms, for military force deployments and activity. If a U.S. indications and warning organization had existed in December 1941, it would have had the following indicators, among others, about Japanese plans and intentions that year:[4]

- In January a HUMINT report from Peru's minister in Tokyo stated that in the event of trouble between the United States and Japan, the Japanese intended to begin with a surprise attack on Pearl Harbor.

- Intercepts of Japanese Foreign Ministry traffic on November 19 contained the message "East wind rain," which some U.S. intelligence officers interpreted as indicating a decision for war in the near future.

- On November 22 Foreign Minister Togo Shigenori notified Ambassador Nomura Kichisaburo in Washington, D.C., that negotiations had to be settled by November 29, stating "after that things are going automatically to happen."

- In late November the Japanese began padding their radio traffic with garbled or redundant messages—a classic tactic to defeat COMINT operations.

- At the beginning of December the Japanese navy changed its ship call signs, deviating from their normal pattern of changing call signs every six months.
- On December 2 the Japanese Foreign Ministry ordered its embassies and consulates in London, Manila, Batavia, Singapore, Hong Kong, and Washington, D.C., to destroy most codes, ciphers, and classified documents.
- In early December the locations of Japan's aircraft carriers and submarines were "lost" by U.S. naval intelligence.
- Scattered reports came in of recent Japanese naval air practice torpedo runs against ships anchored in a southern Japanese harbor.

In hindsight these bits of intelligence together clearly indicate an impending Japanese attack on Pearl Harbor. In practice, these bits would have formed a partial picture within a mass of conflicting and contradictory evidence, as Roberta Wohlstetter pointed out so well in her book, *Pearl Harbor: Warning and Decision.*[5] At best, a cautiously worded warning could have been issued as to the likelihood and nature of an attack within days. In 1941, however, no national indications and warning organization existed. Today, most countries of any size have such organizations to warn of pending military action and against other types of surprise.

Before the 1990 Gulf War, the U.S. did a better job of predicting an attack. Charlie Allen, CIA national intelligence officer for warning, issued a warning estimating a 60 percent chance of an Iraqi attack against Kuwait on July 25, 1990, more than a week before the war began.[6] Nevertheless, the problem of pulling a coherent picture out of the mass of available information has not gotten easier since 1941. Similar lists of the evidence of an impending terrorist attack on the United States using airplanes have been compiled. They are no more a fair judgment of the U.S. intelligence community's performance before the September 11, 2001, terrorist attacks than was the Pearl Harbor evidence.

Collection of indications and warning intelligence for nontraditional problems is likely to be much less structured and subject to change when compared with the traditional indications and warning that focus on the breakout of armed conflict. The indicators of an impending Iraqi attack on Kuwait in 1990 were well established and were sufficient to allow a warning to be given. Warning norms for terrorism, instability, low-intensity conflict, and technological breakthroughs are much more difficult to deal with.

For commercial organizations, the highest indications and warning priority is on significant threats to the organization's survival—impending alliances among competitors or a competitor's impending product breakthrough, for example. But indications and warning have a broader role in business intelligence.

Competitors often send out deliberate signals of their intentions. The business intelligence analyst must be attuned to these indicators and ensure that the customer is aware of the signals.[7] Analysis of the meaning of deliberate signals is a special skill that all analysts should possess, because governments send out deliberate signals, too.

Indications and warning intelligence always has had a tradeoff problem. Analysts don't want to miss the indicators and fail to give a warning. This problem is complicated by the opponent's increasing use of denial and deception. On the other hand, if the analyst sets the warning threshold too low, he gets lots of false alarms and becomes vulnerable to the "cry wolf" problem; customers become desensitized, and the real alarm is ignored.[8] The trick is to have a set of indicators that are both necessary and sufficient, so that one can successfully navigate between the unfortunate outcomes of false alarms and missed events. Such sets of indicators are pulled together through experience and through accumulated knowledge of common indicators. Some standard indicators of impending military attack, for example, are a stockpiling of whole blood, recall of diplomatic personnel, recall of military personnel on leave and canceling leave, threats made in the press, and movement of warheads out of storage.

Crisis Management and Operations Support

This area includes primarily support to military operations, though most law enforcement intelligence tends to be of this nature. It is strongly tactical in orientation. In military support it includes provision of planning data for development of operational, contingency, and capabilities plans and for targeting. The trend to highly precise weaponry and operations places a premium on highly accurate data. Intelligence systems that can geolocate enemy units to within a few meters become more important. The rapidly expanding field of geospatial intelligence supports such surgical operations with mapping, charting, and geodesy data, which can be used for the guidance of smart weapons and detailed planning for tactical responses.[9]

Summary

Intelligence analysis must support operations and policy across the spectrum of conflict. The type of analysis and the speed with which it must be prepared and delivered to the customer vary accordingly. Analysis to support strategic intelligence tends to be in-depth research focused on capabilities and plans and to consider many possible scenarios. Tactical intelligence support tends to be rapid response, or current intelligence, to support crisis management and plan execution; it is focused on the current situation and on indications and warning. Whether strategic or tactical, intelligence that predicts important events is of most value to the customer, as discussed in the next chapter.

Notes

1. John Arquilla and David Ronfeldt, "Looking Ahead: Preparing for Information-Age Conflict," in *In Athena's Camp: Preparing for Conflict in the Information Age,* ed. John Arquilla and David Ronfeldt (Santa Monica: RAND Corporation, 1997), 468. "Swarm" operations are a modern extension of the blitzkrieg concept—the application of coordinated and overwhelming force against an opponent using all available instruments of power: political, economic, military, and psychosocial, as appropriate.

2. Bill Fiora, "Moving from Tactical to Strategic Intelligence," *Competitive Intelligence Magazine,* 4 (November–December 2001): 44.

3. Competent national leaders do think about long-term strategy, but they seldom want the help of strategic intelligence. In contrast, they are usually avid consumers of tactical intelligence.

4. Harold P. Ford, *Estimative Intelligence* (Lanham, Md.: University Press of America, 1993), 3–5.

5. Roberta Wohlstetter, *Pearl Harbor: Warning and Decision,* (Stanford: Stanford University Press, 1962). The difference between conflicting and contradictory evidence was discussed in Chapter 5.

6. Michael R. Gordon and Bernard E. Trainor, *The General's War: The Inside Story of the Conflict in the Gulf* (London: Little, Brown, 1996).

7. Liam Fahey, *Competitors* (New York: John Wiley and Sons, 1999), 78.

8. Mark M. Lowenthal, *Intelligence: From Secrets to Policy,* 2d ed. (Washington, D.C.: CQ Press, 2002), 87.

9. Geodesy is concerned with the size, shape, and gravitational field of the earth, its coordinate systems and reference frames.

9

Prediction

Your problem is that you are not able to see things before they happen.

Wotan to Fricka, in Wagner's opera *Die Walküre*

Describing a past event is not intelligence analysis, it is history. The highest form of intelligence analysis—the form most desired by policymakers and executives—requires structured thinking that results in a prediction of what is likely to happen. True intelligence analysis is always predictive.

To go beyond description to prediction, an analyst must be able to apply a proven prediction methodology and to bring multidisciplinary understanding to the problem. Understanding a narrow technical specialty may be useful for synthesis, but it is insufficient beyond that.

Extrapolation—the act of making predictions based solely on past observations—serves us reasonably well in the short term for events that involve established trends and organizational actions. Long-term prediction is considerably more challenging because it is constrained by the second law of thermodynamics introduced in Chapter 5: Entropy (chaos, randomness) always increases with time.

Convergent and Divergent Phenomena

In Chapter 5 we discussed convergent and divergent evidence. Items of evidence were convergent if they tended to reinforce the same conclusion and divergent if they pointed to different conclusions. In considering trends and events for predictive purposes, we use the same terminology: convergent phenomena make prediction possible; divergent phenomena frustrate prediction.

A basic question to ask at the outset of any prediction attempt is: Does the principle of causation apply? That is, are the phenomena we are to examine and make predictions about governed by the laws of cause and effect? One of the basic principles of classical physics was that of causation. The behavior of any system could be predicted from the average behavior of its component parts. Scientist Irving Langmuir defined such behavior as *convergent* phenomena.

The events leading up to World War I, which Barbara Tuchman superbly outlines in *The Guns of August,* had an inevitable quality about them, as befits convergent phenomena. World War I was predictable—it had been predicted, in fact, by many astute observers at the time. No one person or event actually "started" World War I; the assassination of Archduke Francis Ferdinand and his wife Sophie in Sarajevo merely triggered a process for which groundwork had been laid over many years. Likewise, a war between the United States and Japan was predictable (and both sides had predicted it) throughout most of 1941. Also, a pattern of continued al Qaeda terrorist attacks on U.S. interests worldwide were predictable and had been predicted before September 11, 2001, when terrorists flew airplanes into the Pentagon and the World Trade Center. In the 1940s and 1950s Ambassador George Kennan identified perhaps the most significant convergent phenomenon of the last century in defining his "containment" policy for the United States to pursue against the USSR. He argued that if contained, the Soviet Union would eventually collapse due to its overdeveloped military and underdeveloped economic system.

In contrast, many phenomena are not governed by the laws of cause and effect. Quantum physics deals with the individual atom or basic particles, and has found that their behavior is as unpredictable as the toss of a coin; they can be dealt with only by the laws of probability.[1] Such behavior can, from a small beginning, produce increasingly large effects—a nuclear chain reaction, for example. Irving Langmuir defined such phenomena as *divergent*. In the terms of chaos theory, such phenomena are the result of *strange attractors*—those creators of unpredictable patterns that emerge out of the behavior of purposeful actors.[2] When dealing with divergent phenomena, we have an almost insurmountable difficulty making predictions.

A good example of a divergent phenomenon in intelligence is the coup d'etat. Policymakers often complain that their intelligence organizations have failed to predict coups. But a coup event is conspiratorial in nature, limited to a handful of people, and depends on preservation of secrecy for its success. If a foreign intelligence service knows of the event, then secrecy has been compromised and the coup is almost certain to fail—the country's internal security services will probably forestall it. The conditions that encourage a coup attempt can be assessed and the coup likelihood estimated using probability theory, but the timing and likelihood of success are not "predictable."

The failed attempt to assassinate Hitler in 1944, for example, had more of the "what if?" hypothetical quality that characterizes a divergent phenomenon. Specific terrorist acts, such as those on September 11, 2001, similarly are not predictable in detail. In all such divergent cases, from the Sarajevo assassination to the World Trade Center bombing, some tactical warning might have been possible. An agent within the Serbian terrorist organization, the Black Hand, could have warned of the Sarajevo assassination plan. An agent within al Qaeda might have warned of the planned World Trade Center attack. But tactical warning is not the same as prediction. All such specific events can be described by probabilities, but not predicted in the same fashion as the larger events they were immersed in—World War I, the collapse of Nazi Germany, and increasing conflict between the United States and al Qaeda.

One of the watershed moments in personal computing was clearly a divergent phenomenon. In 1980 IBM was searching for software to run on its planned Personal Computer (PC) and had zeroed in on a small startup company named Microsoft Corporation, located in Bellevue, Washington. Microsoft could provide the languages that programmers would use to write software for the PC, but IBM wanted more; it needed an operating system. Microsoft did not have an operating system and was not positioned to write one, so Bill Gates, Microsoft's president, steered IBM to Digital Research Intergalactic (DRI).

An intelligence analyst assessing the likely future of personal computing in 1980 would have placed his bets on DRI. DRI built the CP/M operating system, at that time the most popular operating system for computers using the Intel processor. It had the basic features IBM needed. Gates arranged an appointment between the IBM team and Gary Kildall, DRI's president, in Pacific Grove, California.

Instead of meeting with the IBM team, however, Kildall chose to take a flight in his new airplane. Miffed, the IBM team told Gates to find or write an operating system himself. Gates found one, and called it the Disk Operating System (DOS), which later became the most widely used personal computer operating system and a major contributor to Microsoft's dominance of the personal computer business. A single event, a decision by one man not to keep an appointment, shaped the future of personal computing worldwide.[3]

In summary, the principles of causation apply well to convergent phenomena, and prediction is possible. Divergent phenomena, such as the actions of an individual person, are not truly predictable and must be handled by different techniques, such as those of probability theory. Where prediction is possible, analysts typically use force synthesis/analysis as discussed later in this chapter.

The Predictive Approach

The target-centric analytic approach to prediction follows a pattern long established in the sciences, in organizational planning, and in systems synthesis/analysis. In intelligence analysis, we are concerned with describing the past and current state of the target in order to make a prediction about its future state.

Prediction is as old as engineering. No large projects—temples, aqueducts, pyramids—were undertaken without some type of predictive process. Many prediction techniques have evolved over the past five centuries as mathematics and science have evolved.[4] They frequently reappear with new names, even though their underlying principles are centuries old.

The predictive synthesis/analysis process discussed in this chapter and the next has been formalized in several professional disciplines. In management theory, the approach has several names, one of which is the Kempner Tregoe Rational Management Process.[5] In engineering, the formalization is called the Kalman Filter. In the social sciences, it is called the Box-Jenkins method. Though there are differences among them, all are techniques for combining complex data and incorporating new data to estimate the present state, or predict the future state, of an entity.

The Kalman Filter is a method of combining data to estimate an entity's present state and evaluating the forces acting on the entity to predict its future state. The concept of the filter—to identify the forces acting on an entity, to identify likely future forces, and to predict the likely changes in old and new forces over time, along with some indicator of confidence in these judgments—is the key to successful prediction. The Kalman Filter's strength is that is takes into account redundant and conflicting data as well as the analyst's confidence in these data. The Kalman Filter is a quantitative approach, using advanced algebra to solve engineering problems. But the concept can be applied qualitatively by subjectively assessing the forces acting on the entity. Figure 9-1 shows an overview of this predictive methodology. The key is to start from the present target model (and preferably, also with a past target model) and move to one of the future models based on an analysis of the forces involved. Other texts on predictive analysis describe these "forces" as issues, trends, factors, or drivers.[6] All of them have the same meaning: They are the entities that shape the future.[7] In most cases, the future target models will be in the form of scenarios, as Figure 9-1 indicates.

The Kalman Filter methodology uses three predictive mechanisms that will be discussed in detail in Chapter 10: extrapolation, projection, and forecasting. All three predictive mechanisms follow the approach of assessing

Figure 9-1   The Kalman Filter Methodology for Prediction

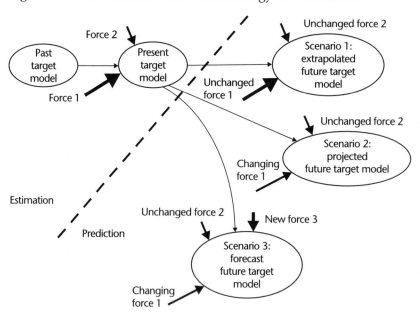

Note: Arrows vary in thickness to indicate the strength of their respective forces. Thicker arrows represent stronger forces; thinner arrows, weaker ones.

forces that act on the entity. An extrapolation assumes that these forces do not change between the present and future states; a projection assumes they do change, and a forecast assumes they change and that new forces are added. The Kalman Filter methodology follows these steps:

- First, estimate at least one past state and the present state of the entity. In intelligence, this entity is the target model, and it can be a model of almost anything—a terrorist organization, a country, a clandestine trade network, an industry, a technology, or a ballistic missile.

- Determine the forces that acted on the entity to bring it to its present state. In the figure, these forces (forces 1 and 2) are shown graphically, with the thickness of the arrow indicating strength. These same forces, acting unchanged, would result in the future state shown as an extrapolation (scenario 1).

- In making a projection, estimate the changes in existing forces that are likely to occur. In the figure, a decrease in one of the existing forces (force 1) is shown as causing a projected future state that is different from the extrapolation (scenario 2).

- In making a forecast, start from the projection and then identify the new forces that may act on the entity, and incorporate their effect. In the figure, one new force is shown as coming to bear, resulting in the forecast future state that differs from the projected future state (scenario 3).

- Determine the likely future state of the entity based on an assessment of the forces. Strong and certain forces are weighed most heavily in this prediction. Weak forces, and those in which the analyst lacks confidence (high uncertainty about the nature or effect of the force), are weighed least.

Figure 9-2 is a variant of Figure 9-1. In this figure we are concerned with some target (technology, system, person, organization, industry, country, or some combination) that changes over time. We want to describe or characterize the entity at some future point. We might want to establish the future performance of an aircraft or missile, the future state of a country's economy, the future morale and effectiveness of a terrorist organization, or the future economic health of an industry. The models are created in an iterative process, each one building on the results of the previous ones. They become more difficult to create as you move upward in the figure.

Designing good predictive scenarios requires such an iterative process, as Figure 9-2 indicates. Iteration is the key to dealing with complex patterns and complex models.[8] The basic analytic paradigm is to create a model of the past and present state of the target, followed by predictive models of its possible future states, usually created in scenario form.

Figure 9-2   The Iterative Approach to
Prediction

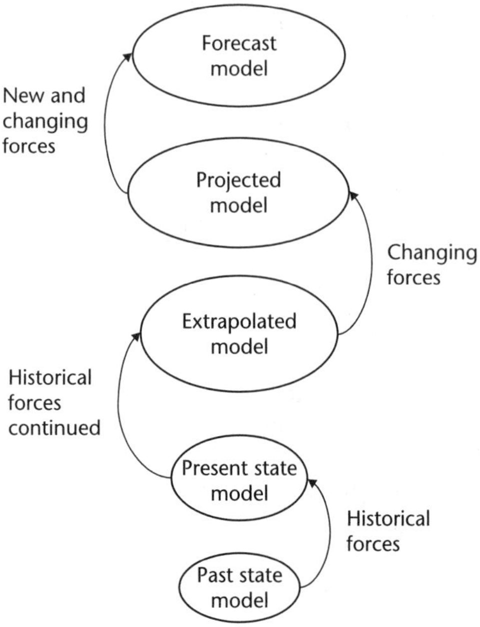

Introduction to Force Synthesis/Analysis

Force synthesis/analysis has many names—*force field analysis* and *system dynamics* are two.[9] It is a technique for prediction that involves finding out what the existing forces are, how they are changing, in what direction, and how rapidly (see Box 9-1). Then, for forecasting, the analyst must identify new forces that are likely to come into play. Most of the following chapters focus on identifying and measuring these forces. One of the most important comes from the feedback mechanism, which is discussed in Chapter 11. An analyst can shape the outcome (wrongly) by concentrating on some forces and ignoring or downplaying the significance of others.

Four factors, or instruments of national power, are usually cited as the "levers" a policymaker can pull in international relations. Three are well established: political (or diplomatic), economic, and military instruments. The fourth was once called psychosocial, and more commonly is called a social instrument. Some authors divide "social" into psychological and informational.[10] Others, reflecting the current stress on information, call the four instruments diplomatic, economic, military, and information. In the business world, they are almost the same: political, economic, environmental, and social. The argument can be made that technology is a fifth major instrument of national power, or of business power, on the same level as the other four. Science and technology certainly are a factor in, and often dominate, intelligence assessments.

Analysis Principle ●——————————————————————

Box 9-1   Force Analysis according to Sun Tzu

Factor or force synthesis/analysis is an ancient predictive technique. Successful generals have practiced it in warfare for thousands of years, and one of its earliest known proponents was a Chinese general named Sun Tzu. He described the art of war as being controlled by five factors, or forces, all of which must be taken into account in predicting the outcome of an engagement. The five forces he called Moral Law, Heaven, Earth, the Commander, and Method and Discipline. The following is an extract from *The Art of War*:

- The *Moral Law* causes the people to be in complete accord with their ruler, so that they will follow him regardless of their lives, undismayed by any danger.
- The *Commander* stands for the virtues of wisdom, sincerity, benevolence, courage, and strictness.
- *Heaven* signifies night and day, cold and heat, times and seasons.
- *Earth* comprises distances great and small; danger and security; open ground and narrow passes; the chances of life and death.
- *Method and Discipline* are to be understood as the marshaling of the army in its proper subdivisions, the gradations of rank among the officers, the maintenance of roads by which supplies may reach the army, and the control of military expenditure.

Sun Tzu concluded that, "These five factors should be familiar to every general. He who knows them will be victorious; he who knows them not will fail."

Source: James Clavell, ed., *The Art of War*, (New York: Dell Publishing, 1983), 9.

Note that these factors of national power or industrial power can be external, internal, or feedback forces. For instance, regulatory forces, discussed in Chapter 11, are a political feedback force—that is, they result from monitoring the state of an economy or an industry, for example, and taking regulatory actions to change that state. Contamination, also in Chapter 11, is an internal force that can be social, environmental, or both.

Qualitative Force Synthesis/Analysis

Qualitative force synthesis/analysis is the simplest approach to both projection and forecasting and the easiest to do. It usually is done by an analyst who is an expert in the subject area and who answers the following questions.

- What forces have affected this entity (organization, situation, industry, technical area) over the past several years?[11]
- Which five or six forces had more impact than others?
- What forces are expected to affect this entity over the next several years?

- Which five or six forces are likely to have more impact than others?
- What are the fundamental differences between the answers to questions two and four?
- What are the implications of these differences for the entity being analyzed?

The answers give the changes in direction of the projection shown in Figure 9-1. At more sophisticated levels of qualitative synthesis/analysis, the analyst examines adaptive forces (feedback forces) and their changes over time.

This section has introduced some fairly advanced prediction concepts. An example may help to clarify how the predictive methodology works in practice.

Predicting Organizations' Behavior and Future

Intelligence is often called upon to predict the future of a target organization. Table 9-1 summarizes the steps in such predictive synthesis/analysis. The steps are to:

- Create a *present state* model of the target. The quality of synthesis in this task hinges on the quality of data available and on how well it is sifted and evaluated. Typically, a past state also needs to be determined to help assess the forces that are acting on the target organization.
- Determine the *transition process* by which the target organization is likely to get from its present state to a future state. The quality of predictive analysis hinges on how well the analyst can identify and assess the forces acting on the entity.
- Determine the expected *future state* of the target (the prediction). The quality of analysis here is determined in part by the accuracy of the present state estimate, but more by the force analysis used to make the prediction.

Table 9-1   Predictive Analysis Approach for an Organization

State of the target	Analysis	Product
Past and present	Where is the organization now and how did it get there?	Estimate
Transition from present to future	What forces are acting on the organization to move it to a future state?	Forces and probability analysis
Future	Where is the organization expected to be in the future?	Prediction (extrapolation, projection, or forecast)

It is critical that this approach be conducted in a target-centric way, with full participation by the customers of intelligence, since the actions by one organization will affect decisions of an opposing organization. An organization's planners and its intelligence analysts are natural partners in what becomes a game to outwit their opponents. Companies must think ahead to develop a strategy based on competitors' expected countermoves. Game theory (where all participants strive to obtain maximum gains by choosing particular courses of action) may provide better insights into corporate actions and market performance than more traditional economic theories.

To illustrate the prediction process for organizations, let's attempt a predictive assessment of the al Qaeda terrorist organization, starting from the organization's historical states and going forward in time to alternative predictive states. The example is highly simplified; it considers only a few of the forces involved, for illustrative purposes, and does not represent all of the possible future scenarios. Figure 9-3 shows the rise of al Qaeda and some possible future directions; movement upward indicates increasing power and ability of al Qaeda to achieve its goals; movement downward indicates the opposite.

The figure illustrates two past states of al Qaeda. Past state 1 is the earlier of the two. In the mid-1980s Osama bin Laden and Palestinian Muslim Brotherhood leader Abdallah Azzam cofounded the Maktab al-Khidamat (MAK) to fight against the Soviet occupation of Afghanistan. The effort funneled fighters and money (military and economic forces) into the fight. In the late 1980s Bin Laden split from MAK to form al Qaeda, and the organizational focus turned from Afghanistan to global promotion of Islamic fundamentalist goals.

Figure 9-3   Predictive Model of Possible Future States of al Qaeda

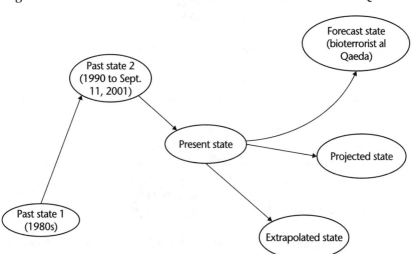

Note: Nodes are elevated to indicate strength and lowered to indicate weakness.

Past state 2 covers the period when the organization grew stronger due to continuing positive military, economic, and social forces. Funding came in from large parts of the Islamic world, more terrorist "cells" were formed, military training was expanded and improved, and recruits were attracted to the increasingly extreme fundamentalist Islamic message of bin Laden. Political forces constrained the growth of the organization as Middle Eastern governments and United Nations pressure drove bin Laden out of Saudi Arabia to the Sudan and then to Afghanistan. The political pressure and opposing military forces (continuing U.S. military presence in the Gulf region and attempts to attack bin Laden in Afghanistan) drove al Qaeda to more aggressive terrorist attacks, culminating in the attack on the United States on September 11, 2001.

The figure then moves to the present state of al Qaeda, which we define as the state since September 11, 2001. Al Qaeda fortunes have taken a turn for the worse as a combination of powerful new military, political, and economic forces worldwide degrade the organization's capabilities by closing cells, hunting down leaders, and shutting down sources of al Qaeda funding. The result is an organization in disarray and much weaker compared with its powerful position before September 11. It is under pressure in the military, economic, and political arenas, and no government wants to be identified as a safe harbor for al Qaeda cells. Social forces are both positive and negative; al Qaeda continues to have strong popular support in the Islamic world because it continues to fight the United States, but it is viewed negatively in much of the rest of the world and in parts of the Arab world as well.

From the present state the analyst devises three future states: extrapolated, projected, and forecast. In the extrapolated state, al Qaeda continues to decline under the combination of unchanging military, economic, and political pressures. Remaining cells are hunted down, but followers continue to be recruited (social force continues unchanged). Funding to the group decreases as governments continue to close down the sources of funding, and the organization eventually cannot train or equip its cells to carry out significant terrorist activity. (Eventually, this extrapolation has to become invalid, as extrapolations do in time; the continued decline of al Qaeda would eventually cause the social force to weaken as a "lost cause" mentality takes hold among potential recruits.)

In the projected state, changes occur in the political and economic forces that allow al Qaeda to arrest its decline. Most governments turn to other concerns or perceive that they have done enough to deal with the terrorism threat, and funding and recruitment resume. Al Qaeda continues to lose cells due to U.S. and British efforts, but new cells are created as new followers, attracted to the cause by admiration of the group's willingness to fight the United States (a progrowth social force), join.

The forecast state is much the same as the projected state, except that new technology forces are added to the target model, and the result affects the other forces. Specifically, new methods of terrorism are developed and employed as al Qaeda employs its new funding to develop a genetic engineering capability; with that capability it creates a series of virulent and deadly bioorganisms and employs them in attacks on the United States and allied countries. Political and military forces against al Qaeda weaken as public sentiment in the United States and allied countries changes from a desire to battle al Qaeda to a wish for an accommodation that would end the bioterrorist attacks. The resulting negotiations with al Qaeda strengthen its position as the defender of Islam against the infidels worldwide.

Note that all three outcomes presented above—extrapolated, projected, and forecast—represent alternative scenarios, and the fact that the forecast state incorporates both new and changing forces does not make it the most likely outcome. None of the three scenarios could happen, or all three could happen in turn. Because most intelligence predictions, like this example, are in scenario form, the next section discusses how to develop scenarios.

Scenarios

Intelligence scenarios are descriptions in story form of a future target model. Scenarios are used primarily for planning and decisionmaking. Scenario planning is normally used to explore possible future conditions given a set of assumptions. Each scenario represents a distinct, plausible picture of a segment of the future.

Because it is impossible to know the future precisely, the solution is to create several scenarios. These scenarios are, essentially, specially constructed stories about the future, each one modeling a distinct, plausible outcome. The scenarios establish the boundaries of our uncertainty and the limits to plausible futures.

Why Use Scenarios?

The purpose of scenario planning is to highlight large forces that shape the future. Scenario planning makes these forces visible, so that if they do happen, the intelligence officer will at least recognize them.[12] Scenario planning helps the intelligence officer and the customer anticipate the future and better respond to events.

Scenarios have great power to communicate the sense or feel of situations that do not and may never exist, a power that is at once an asset and a danger. They give the user a feel for what might happen if he or she pursues a certain course of action in a complex situation that cannot be quantified. An example scenario would be one that describes the likely pattern of daily life in the future under specified assumptions about nuclear power plant regulation. Depending on the views of the scenario planner, the scenario could be used to support or oppose increased regulation. A supporter of regulation would likely develop scenarios that included a series of Three Mile Island or Chernobyl disasters absent regulation. An opponent of regulation would be more likely to devise scenarios that showed a world of high electric power costs, atmospheric pollution due to smokestack power plants, and declining economies due to the increasing energy costs of regulation. An intelligence analyst must have the objectivity to avoid such slanted scenarios.

Scenarios are used in strategic planning—for instance, in business—to examine merger candidates or consider a new product line. Such scenarios are often global scenarios. Scenarios are used also in tactical or operational planning—for example, for interdicting illicit traffic such as narcotics. In narcotics interdiction, the scenario would include a geospatial target model of narcotics growing and processing areas and drug transshipment routes, possibly with timeline models showing when transshipments take place. The scenario would also include relationship models (link or network diagrams) showing the pattern of funds laundering. For operational planning, the scenario would then be modified to show the effect of specific narcotics interdiction actions—for example, deployment of radar surveillance aircraft into the Caribbean or a program to pay farmers not to grow the crop. Because of the analyst's knowledge of the target, she is a key player in incorporating such effects into the scenario.

Once scenarios are created, the job of the intelligence analyst is to track indicators that point toward a specific scenario (for example, favorable consumer reaction to the new product line or the increased flow of narcotics through a specific location). How the analyst does this is discussed later.

In an alternative future as depicted by a scenario, a decisionmaker can identify relationships among forces, the probable impacts of these forces on an organization or situation, the key decision points for taking action, and foundations for decisions and strategies. By providing a realistic range of possibilities, the set of alternative scenarios helps the decisionmaker to identify common features likely to have an impact on the organization no matter which alternative occurs.

Predicting the future in detail is no more possible than predicting the weather in detail. The details tend to be controlled by divergent phenomena, such as an assassination in Sarajevo. But the dominant forces and trends tend to be convergent phenomena that allow the creation of a few "most likely" outcome scenarios, with indicators that can tell which outcome is more likely. Scenario synthesis/analysis is used to create these scenarios.

Types of Scenarios

Analysts use four basic types of scenarios.[13] Demonstration scenarios, driving-force scenarios, and system-change scenarios move through time so that the user can understand the forces and decision points that lead to the final "scene" of the scenario. The slice-of-time scenario is a snapshot; it dwells on the final "scene." All four types are used by science fiction writers (who, after all, write scenarios about alternative futures). Some science fiction writers simply drop the reader into the final scene, others explain the history and developments that led to the final scene.

Demonstration Scenario. The demonstration scenario was pioneered by Herman Kahn, Harvey DeVeerd, and others at RAND in the early days of systems analysis. In this scenario, the writer first imagines a particular end-state in the future and then describes a plausible path of events that could lead to that state. The *branch-point* version of this type of scenario identifies decisive events along the path (events that represent points at which key choices determine the outcome). The branch points serve as indicators that a particular scenario is happening. The idea is to focus attention on the branch points, rather than the final outcome. As Kahn and Anthony Wiener of the Hudson Institute think tank, point out, this kind of scenario answers two questions: How might some hypothetical situation come about, step by step? What alternatives exist at each step for preventing, diverting, or facilitating the process?[14] The major weakness of the demonstration scenario is that it depends on the idiosyncrasies and experiences of the scenario creators.

Driving-Force Scenario. This scenario is most commonly used in governmental and business planning and is most useful in predictive intelligence. It is basically an implementation of the Kalman Filter or force synthesis/analysis approach: examine the major forces acting on the target, determine how they are changing and what new forces are expected to come into play, and assess the resulting state of the target over time.

In creating multiple driving-force scenarios, one approach is to identify a set of key factors or forces, specifying at least two distinctly different levels of each factor or force and developing a matrix that interrelates each factor at each level with each other. For example, two commonly used driving forces in economic scenarios are growth in gross national product and growth in population. If each is set to "high," "medium," and "low," there are nine possible combinations, each of which defines the context of a possible future. The scenario planner's task is to describe each of these futures, assuming that the driving forces remain constant. Another alternative, taken in the U.S. National Reconnaissance Office book of possible future scenarios, *Proteus,* is to select different dominant forces for each scenario. In *Proteus,* for example, the scenario *Amazon.plague* has a single dominant force: a series of highly contagious, deadly viruses that sweep the globe.[15]

The purpose of the driving-force scenario is to clarify the nature of the future by contrasting alternative futures with others in the same scenario space. It might be that certain policies would fare equally well in most of the futures, or that certain futures might pose problems for the organization. In the latter case, decisionmakers will know where to direct their monitoring.

A flaw in driving-force scenarios is that they assume that the forces, once specified, are fixed. This assumption is made to simplify the problem, but it ignores potential events that would affect the strength of forces or introduce new forces.

System-Change Scenario. The system-change scenario addresses the flaw in driving-force scenarios. It is designed to explore systematically, comprehensively, and consistently the interrelationships and implications of a set of trend and event forecasts, including significant social, technological, economic, and political forces. Thus this scenario type varies both from the demonstration scenario (which leads to a single outcome and ignores most or all the forces that might lead to other outcomes) and from the driving-force scenario (which takes account of a full range of future developments but assumes that the driving forces do not change). Typically, there is no single event that caps the scenario, and there are no dominant driving forces.

The system-change scenario depends on cross-impact analysis (discussed later in this chapter) to identify interactions among events or developments and from these interactions to develop the outline of alternative futures. This is a very difficult scenario to develop because it includes changing forces and their interrelationships.

Slice-of-Time Scenario. The slice-of-time scenario jumps to a future period in which a synthesis of explicit or assumed forces shapes the environment, and then describes how stakeholders think, feel, and behave in that environment. Science fiction provides such scenarios in George Orwell's *1984* and Aldous Huxley's *Brave New World.* The objective is to show that the future may be more (or less) desirable, fearful, or attainable than is now generally thought. A slice-of-time scenario is the same as the "environmental assumptions" found in many business plans; environmental assumptions describe a specific future environment—a world of reduced tariffs or of combined high unemployment and inflation—without explaining how the environment came to be. Slice-of-time scenarios are not generally useful in intelligence because they give short shrift to the driving forces that lead to the scenario. They therefore provide few indicators for intelligence analysts or their customers to monitor.

Scenario Perspectives

Scenarios are models, and like the models discussed in Chapter 2, can be either descriptive or normative. Descriptive scenarios are usually described as *exploratory.* Scenario planners using this exploratory perspective adopt a neutral stance toward the future, attempting to be objective, scientific, and impartial. The scenario usually begins in the present and then unfolds from there to some future time. A simple exploratory scenario is the straight-line extrapolation; it assumes that only current forces and policy choices are allowed to be felt in the future (no technological discoveries or revolutions, for example, are permitted). These extrapolation scenarios are *momentum* scenarios—they are dominated by inertia, and no countervailing forces arise to slow the observed trend.[16] Inertia is the tendency for organizations and other bodies to stay their course and resist change. Most China scenarios tend to be momentum scenarios based on the country's recent spectacular growth. They don't contemplate a weak divided China of the future (for example, a China ruled by economic or military "warlords") in spite of the Soviet example and of Chinese history. Scenarios about Japan created in the early 1980s had a similar momentum pattern and proved to be inaccurate. Because momentum scenarios are straight-line extrapolations, it is prudent not to use them for long-term assessments. An analyst can start with extrapolation but should then look at new and changing forces that create projection and forecast scenarios.

Scenario planners using the *normative* perspective focus on the question, "What kind of future might we have?" As with a normative model, the purpose is to indicate a preferred course of action. The scenario planner therefore describes a "favored and attainable" end state, such as a stable international political environment, and the sequence of events by which this could be achieved. An alternative normative approach is to define a "feared but possible" end state (for example, increasing international terrorism and governmental instability) and show the sequence of events that lead to this end state.

How to Construct Scenarios

Scenario planning is really a variant of the well-known modeling, simulation, and gaming methods. It is an art, not a standardized or systematic methodology. The assumptions on which the scenario is based must be made explicit because of its great potential for misuse.

Numerous approaches can be taken in writing the scenarios, ranging from a single person writing a description of a future situation to the use of an interactive computer model. A common technique is to create three scenarios: a "most likely" future (exploratory, driving-force), a "worst case" future (normative-feared but possible, driving-force), and a "best case" future (normative-desired and attainable, driving-force).

Peter Schwartz, former head of global planning for Royal Dutch Shell, has described a four-step process of scenario construction: Define the problem, identify factors bearing on the problem, identify possible solutions, and find the best (most likely) solutions.[17]

Define the Problem. Scenario planning begins by identifying the focal issue or decision. Rather than trying to explore the entire future, ask yourself, "What question am I trying to answer?" There are an infinite number of stories that we could tell about the future; our purpose is to tell those that matter, that lead to better decisions. So we begin by agreeing on the issue that we want to address. Sometimes the question is broad (What are the future prospects in the Middle East?); sometimes it's specific (Is a terrorist attack on the U.S. railroad industry likely in the next year?). Either way, the point is to agree on the issues that will be used as a test of relevance as we go through the rest of the scenario planning.[18]

Identify Factors Bearing on the Problem. This step is basically an extension of the strategies-to-task approach to a problem breakout that was discussed in earlier chapters. In this step, the analyst identifies the key forces in the local environment. Because scenarios are a way of understanding the dynamics shaping the future, we attempt to identify the primary driving forces at work in the present. These fall roughly into four categories:[19]

- Social dynamics—quantitative, demographic issues (What will be the ethnic mix of Country X in 2010? Will immigration increase or decrease?); softer issues of values, lifestyle, demand, or political activism (How is the United States likely to be regarded in Western Europe if it builds a missile defense shield? What is the political and economic impact of a large retiree population?).

- Economic issues—macroeconomic trends and forces shaping the economy as a whole (What are the effects of international trade barriers and exchange rates on raw material costs? What are economic sanctions likely to do to our markets?); microeconomics (What might industrial competitors do? How will the defense industry's fundamental structure change?); and forces at work on or within an organization (level of debt, and that of potential partners; Is the organization facing a loss of skilled employees? Does it have an up-to-date computer network?).

- Political issues—electoral (Will the prime minister be reelected?); legislative (Will further safety restrictions be imposed on handguns?); regulatory (How will U.S. Customs interpret the new immigration laws?); and litigable (Will the courts accept any new theories on the criminality of terrorist acts?).

- Technological issues—direct (How will the genome map affect existing DNA testing?); enabling (Will biochips enable a new cell phone revolution?); and indirect (Will new World Wide Web technologies expand the need for security consultants?).

Next, the analyst isolates the driving forces. Which driving forces are critical to this outcome? Some driving forces affect everyone the same way. Most companies, for instance, are driven by the need to cut costs and incorporate new technologies. But unless one of the target organizations is markedly better or worse than other people at doing these things, the differences will not affect the end result. The important thing is to identify any asymmetric forces that may be present.

Then the analyst should rank the driving forces by importance and uncertainty. Some forces are more important than others. Whether the market will grow may not be as important as whether new players enter the market. And some forces are far more certain than others. Local housing and population patterns usually change fairly slowly. The aging of the U.S. population is fairly predictable over the coming decades and will have a similar effect in any scenario. On the other hand, other questions are highly uncertain. The most critical driving forces will be those that are both very important and highly uncertain.[20]

Identify Possible Solutions. This is probably the most important step. First, the analyst identifies the scenario types to be considered. Three distinct scenario types are typical: The *emergent* scenario (that evolves from an opponent's current strategy); the *unconstrained what-if* scenario (that comes from asking unconstrained questions about completely new strategies); and the *constrained what-if* scenario (that asks what the opponent might do under different environmental conditions or forces).[21]

Next the analyst works with the issues, reshaping and reframing them and drawing out their less obvious elements until a consensus emerges about which two or three underlying questions will make a difference in the decision. This step involves differentiating the scenarios: identifying inconsistencies, finding underlying similarities, and eliminating scenarios that are redundant or implausible.

Now the analyst goes back to all the driving forces and trends that were considered in steps two and three and uses these to flesh out the scenarios. For instance, degree of risk; access to capital; and ability to control costs, raise quality, or extend functionality all might be critical in some scenarios and not so important in others.

There are three commonly used techniques for building scenarios. *Case-based models* are the foundation for a type of analysis called case-based reasoning. This might be called reasoning by analogy or reasoning by history.

Case-based reasoning means using old experiences to understand and solve new problems. An analyst remembers a previous situation similar to the current one and uses that to solve the new problem. This can mean adapting old solutions to meet new demands, using old cases to explain new situations, using old cases to critique new solutions, or reasoning from precedents to interpret a new situation (much like lawyers do) or create an equitable solution to a new problem (much like labor mediators do).[22] The analyst makes inferences based directly on previous cases rather than by the more traditional approach of using general knowledge. He solves a new problem by remembering a previous similar situation (a similar model) and by reusing information and knowledge of that situation (duplicating the model).

We can illustrate case-based reasoning by looking at some typical situations having intelligence implications:

- In 1984 reports indicated that the Soviets were systematically destroying Afghan irrigation systems to drive resistance supporters out of the countryside. This paralleled a Soviet army practice of destroying the irrigation systems in Central Asia during their war against the Basmachi rebels in the 1920s.[23]

- An analyst of the defense industry, monitoring the possible merger of two defense companies, might be reminded of a recent merger between two competing companies in the pharmaceutical industry. She recalls that the merged companies had problems because of dramatically different marketing approaches, similar to the situation in the merger she is monitoring. She commissions a case study of the pharmaceutical merger to obtain details on these potential problems and to determine how they might apply in her own situation.

- A financial consultant, hired by the defense industry analyst to examine financial aspects of the same merger, is reminded of a combination of financial indicators in a previous merger that resulted in serious financial difficulties for the merged companies. He uses this past case to identify likely difficulties in the present one.

- An engineer responsible for the health of a reconnaissance satellite has experienced two past losses of satellite control. He is quickly reminded of these past situations when the combination of critical measurements matches those of the past system breakdowns. He also remembers a mistake he made during both previous failures, and thereby avoids repeating the error.

A second common technique for building scenarios is *contextual mapping*. This technique is used to identify plausible sequences of development in a given field and to relate these sequences to potential developments in a different field. The method is at least as useful for forcing a fresh perspective as it is for predicting actual developments. Its use requires experienced experts familiar both with the method and with the topic of inquiry.

Contextual mapping has been used largely in technological forecasting applications. As an example, one might specify expected future developments in miniaturized chips, combined with a projection of future sensor and wide radio frequency bandwidth transmitter technologies, to define a unique future cheap, small video surveillance device. These future developments are then treated as external forces that alter the likely future state of a system—for example, a crime deterrence system. The output is usually a graphic display, often with timelines, showing the interconnecting paths that lead to the projected development.

The third common technique, *cross-impact analysis*, supports system-change scenarios. It usually shows interactions among events or developments, specifying how one event will influence the likelihood, timing, and mode of impact of another event in a different but associated field.

The essential idea behind a cross-impact model is to examine all of the pairwise connections within a set of forecast developments. Specifically, the analyst might ask how the prior occurrence of one event would affect other events or trends in the set. When these relationships have been specified, the analyst creates a scenario by letting events "happen"—either randomly, in accordance with their estimated probability, or in some prearranged way—and assessing how each development affects others in the sequence. Repeating the process with different event sequences creates contrasting scenarios.

Cross-impact analysis has been used extensively to model the interaction of future events and trends. The Futures Group developed an approach in the 1970s called *trend impact analysis* that became well established and is still in use.[24] Network analysis methodologies, described in Chapter 12, naturally support cross-impact analysis.

Find the Best (Most Likely) Solution(s). Having built a set of potential future scenarios, examine them in light of the original question. Does the idea of paying farmers not to grow coca crops have favorable outcomes in all of the counternarcotics scenarios? Perhaps a common outcome in the scenarios is that new groups of farmers start growing coca crops in order to qualify for the payments, or a bidding war starts between the drug cartels and the government. The customer of intelligence, the operations people who are informed by the scenarios, need to understand these possible outcomes and to prepare their options accordingly.

The final scenarios need to describe relationships among objects or entities (tanks, missiles, airplanes, and units in a military scenario; companies, governments, technologies, and weapons systems in a nonproliferation scenario; governments, farmers, drug cartels, banks, and drug users in a counternarcotics scenario). In a dynamic scenario, the objects must then change in space and time according to known rules (patterns of business competition; military doctrine in military scenarios; past patterns of clandestine trade and of systems development in a nonproliferation scenario). A military scenario, which can be well defined by existing scenario definition tools, is quite different from a nonproliferation or counternarcotics scenario. It is not the same in format, content, event descriptions, or in the types of objects being manipulated. However, the basics remain the same; relationship analysis, for example, is pretty much the same in all scenarios.

Indicators and the Role of Intelligence

The final step in Peter Schwartz's process comes after the scenarios are completed. The job of the intelligence officer becomes one of monitoring. The analyst has to look for the leading indicators that would tell which of the scenarios—or which combination of scenarios—is actually taking place. As Babson College professor Liam Fahey has pointed out, indicators will also give important insights into what scenarios are *not* taking place.[25]

The monitoring job may involve watching trends. An intelligence analyst might monitor demographic and economic trends, spread of infectious diseases, changes in pollution levels, or proliferation of terrorist cells. A political or economic analyst might look at the questions that opponents ask and the positions they take in trade negotiations. A military intelligence analyst might monitor troop movements and radio traffic for signals as to which scenario is developing.

Markers and signals are a specific group of indicators that suggest movement toward a particular scenario.[26] They provide a means to decide which options should be the focus of a customer's decisions. Specifically, markers and signals help identify which outcomes should be prepared for, possibly by use of some of the instruments of national power, and which potential outcomes can be disregarded.

Scenarios, like target models, serve different purposes for different participants. The purpose of scenarios for executives and intelligence customers is to inform decisionmaking. The purpose for intelligence officers is to identify needs, that is, to support intelligence collection.

Intelligence can have one of two roles in scenarios. If an organization has a planning group that develops scenarios, the intelligence officer should participate in the scenario development. Then the role of intelligence is to draw the indicators from the forces and to tell the planner or decisionmaker how the scenarios are playing out based on these indicators. We want to know which forces and indicators need to be monitored to give an early signal of approaching change and point to more likely outcomes. The planning culture in many organizations is still heavily biased toward single-point forecasting. In such cases, the intelligence customer is likely to say, "Tell me what the future will be; then I can make my decision." They are likely to complain that several "forecasts" are more confusing, and less helpful, than a single one. Intelligence can help both the scenario planner and the intelligence unit by providing direction or the most likely scenario. If no scenario planning group exists, then the intelligence officer must develop the scenarios herself to address the questions posed by the decisionmaker. In this case, intelligence synthesis/analysis generally will focus on more narrowly drawn scenarios than planners use and are likely to be more tactical than strategic. For example, an intelligence-generated battlefield scenario might involve looking only at enemy forces and what their actions will be and ignoring the actions that friendly forces might be taking.

Summary

Intelligence analysis, to be useful, must be predictive. Some events or future states of a target are predictable because they are driven by convergent phenomena. Some are not predictable because they are driven by divergent phenomena.

Analysis involves predicting the future state of a target using one of three means—extrapolation (unchanging forces), projection (changing forces), and forecasting (changing and new forces). The task is to assess, from the present state of the intelligence target, the transition process that takes the target to its future state and the forces that shape that transition. Chapter 10 discusses in more detail how extrapolation, projection, and forecasting are done in the intelligence business.

Most predictive analysis results in some form of scenario—a description of the future state of the target. Typically, several alternative scenarios are created based on different assumptions about the forces involved. Two scenarios most used in intelligence are the driving-force scenario, a type of projection, and the system-change, a forecast. Chapters 11–13 describe many of the forces to consider in creating a scenario.

Notes

1. Irving Langmuir, "Science, Common Sense, and Decency," *Science,* 97 (January 1943): 1–7.
2. Jamshid Gharajedaghi, *Systems Thinking: Managing Chaos and Complexity* (Boston: Butterworth-Heinemann, 1999), 52.
3. Paul Carroll, *Big Blues* (New York: Crown Publishers, 1993), 18.
4. George Likourezos, "Prologue to Image Enhanced Estimation Methods," *Proc. IEEE,* 18 (June 1993): 796.
5. Thomas Kempner and B.B. Tregoe, *The New Rational Manager* (Princeton: Princeton Research Press, 1981).
6. M.S. Loescher, C. Schroeder, and C.W. Thomas, *Proteus: Insights from 2020* (Utrecht, Netherlands: The Copernicus Institute Press, 2000), A-iv.
7. Andrew Sleigh, ed., *Project Insight* (Farnborough, U.K.: Centre for Defence Analysis, Defence Evaluation and Research Agency, 1996), 17.
8. Gharajedaghi, *Systems Thinking,* 51.
9. Gharajedaghi, *Systems Thinking,* 122.
10. David Jablonsky, "National Power," *Parameters* (Spring 1997): 34–54.
11. The time frame for most predictions extends over years. On a fast-developing situation, the appropriate time frame for force analysis may be months or even days, not years.
12. T.F. Mandel, "Futures Scenarios and Their Use in Corporate Strategy," in *The Strategic Management Handbook,* ed. K.J. Albert (New York: McGraw-Hill, 1983), 10–21.
13. W.I. Boucher, "Scenario and Scenario Writing," in *Nonextrapolative Methods in Business Forecasting,* ed. J.S. Mendell (Westport, Conn.: Quorum Books, 1985), 47–60.
14. Herman Kahn and Anthony Wiener, *The Year 2000* (New York: Macmillan, 1967).
15. Loescher, Schroeder, and Thomas, *Proteus.*
16. Inertia and countervailing forces are discussed in detail in Chapter 11.
17. Peter Schwartz, *The Art of the Long View* (New York: Currency Doubleday, 1996).
18. Lawrence Wilkinson, "How to Build Scenarios," http://www.wired.com/wired/scenarios/ build.html, February 12, 2002.
19. Ibid.
20. Liam Fahey, *Competitors* (New York: John Wiley and Sons, 1999), 452.
21. Ibid., 453.
22. Janet L. Kolodner, "An Introduction to Case-Based Reasoning," *Artificial Intelligence Review,* 6 (1992): 3–34.
23. Angelo Codevilla, *Informing Statecraft* (New York: Free Press, 1992), 217.
24. T.J. Gordon, "The Nature of Unforeseen Developments" in *The Study of the Future,* ed. W.I. Boucher (Washington, D.C.: U.S. Government Printing Office, 1977), 42–43.
25. Fahey, *Competitors,* 415.
26. Sleigh, *Project Insight,* 13.

10

Predictive Techniques

It's hard to make predictions, especially about the future.

Yogi Berra

An analyst should understand that, no matter how good her methodology and how well it is applied, her predictions are likely to be wrong—at least in the details. The value of a prediction lies in the assessment of the forces that will shape future events and the state of the target model. If the analyst accurately assesses the forces, she has served the intelligence customer well, even if the prediction that she derived from that assessment is wrong. A competent customer will probably make his own predictions anyway, and the force assessments help him to make the prediction or to refine it as new events unfold. And the very best predictions are often wrong, because the customer will act on the intelligence to favorably change the predicted outcome.

Many of the tools used in synthesizing the model fail when applied to prediction. Expert opinion, for example, is often used in creating a target model; but experts' biases, ego, and narrow focus tend to make their subjective predictions wrong. A useful exercise for the skeptic is to look at trade press or technical journal predictions that were made more than ten years ago and that turned out to be way off base—stock market predictions and popular science magazine predictions of automobile designs are particularly entertaining.

This chapter discusses three approaches for predicting the future state of a target—extrapolation, projection, and forecasting. Different terms are used in different books. Babson College professor Liam Fahey uses the term "simple projection" to refer to extrapolation, and "complex projection" to refer to both projection and forecasting.[1] In this book we treat projection and forecasting separately to emphasize the differences in the forces involved. An extrapolation predicts future events by assuming that the current forces influencing the target go unchanged. A projection assumes these forces will change, and a forecast assumes the same, with the addition of new forces along the way.

Extrapolation

An extrapolation is a statement of what is expected to happen based only on past observations. Extrapolation is the most conservative method of prediction. In its simplest form, extrapolation extends a linear curve on a graph based on historical performance. When there is little uncertainty about the present state of a target model, and when an analyst is confident that she knows what forces are acting on the target, the prediction begins from the present and propagates forward along the direction of an unchanged system (straight line extrapolation). In this low-uncertainty, high-confidence situation, new information is given relatively low weight. But when uncertainty about the state of the model is high, then new information is accorded high value in prediction; when uncertainty about the forces acting on the target is high, then prediction uncertainty is high.

Extrapolation is usually accurate in the short run, assuming an accurate starting point and a reasonably accurate understanding of the direction of movement. The assumption is that the forces acting on the target do not change. Inertia (the tendency to stay on course and resist change, discussed in Chapter 11) is what typically causes a straight-line extrapolation to work. Where inertial effects are weak, extrapolation has a shorter "lifetime" of accuracy. Where they are strong, extrapolation can give good results over time.

Extrapolation Techniques

Figure 10-1 shows the simplest type of extrapolation. This example is a trend extrapolation in the aircraft industry from the DC-3 aircraft to the C-17.

Figure 10-1   Trend Extrapolation for Productivity of Civil and Military Transport Aircraft

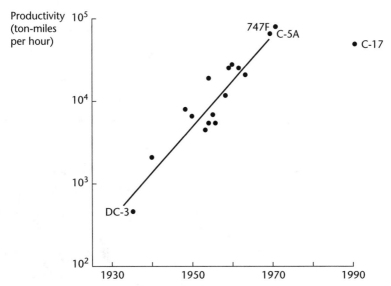

Note: Each dot represents a different type of aircraft. Ton-mile per hour is the cargo load times the distance traveled over time.

The graph shows a remarkably consistent growth in performance of the aircraft (measured as cargo load times distance traveled over time) from the 1930s to 1970, when technology shifted from piston engines to jets and electronic operations took over for manual ones.[2] However, the graph also shows one pitfall of a straight-line trend extrapolation. The straight segment of an "S" curve can look like a straight line. In such a case, the curve will not continue its climb indefinitely, but will level off, as it did in this example; the more recent C-17 did not match the performance of the older C-5A and 747F. Chapter 13 has a section on "S" curves that offers some clues to help select the right type of extrapolation.

Figure 10-2 shows a type of extrapolation that is used to predict periodic (repeating) phenomena. The technique used, called autocorrelation, works well when dealing with a cyclical (sinusoidal) behavior such as wave action. Prediction of sunspot number (the number of "spots" or dark areas observed on the sun, shown in Figure 10-2), economic cycles, and automobile and lawnmower sales are examples.

Adaptive techniques are a more sophisticated method of extrapolating based on new observations. The Box-Jenkins is one such technique and is, in fact, the social sciences equivalent of the Kalman Filter discussed in the previous chapter. Box-Jenkins is useful for quickly spotting changing forces in a target model. It uses a variable's past behavior, such as the sunspot occurrences in Figure 10-2, to select the best forecasting model from a general class of

Figure 10-2   Trend Extrapolation for Repeating Phenomena—
the Sunspot Cycle

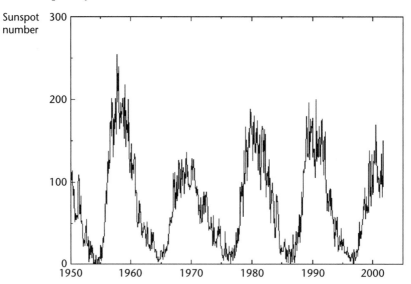

Note: Sunspot number is the number of "spots" or dark areas observed on the sun.

models. Box-Jenkins provides some of the most accurate short-term forecasts. However, it requires a very large amount of data, and it is complex and time consuming to apply.

Limitations of Extrapolation

Extrapolation has two major problems. First, it is inaccurate in the long run because it is narrowly focused and assumes that the static forces that operate on the model will continue unchanged, with no new forces being added. As noted earlier, this method depends on inertia. Second, extrapolation will be inaccurate if the original target model was inaccurate. If the extrapolation starts from the wrong point, it will almost certainly be even farther off as it is extended forward in time.

Projection

Before moving on to projection and forecasting, we need to differentiate them from extrapolation. An extrapolation is an assertion about how some element will materialize in the future. In contrast, a projection or a forecast is a *probabilistic* statement about some element. The underlying form of such statements are, "If A occurs, plus some allowance for unknown or unknowable factors, then we can expect B or something very much like B to occur, or at least B will become more probable."

Projection is more reliable than extrapolation. It predicts a range of likely futures based on the assumption that the forces that have operated in the past will change, whereas extrapolation assumes the forces do not change. This produces a change from the extrapolation line, as shown in Figure 10-1.

Projection (and also forecasting, discussed later) both make use of two major analytical techniques. One technique, force synthesis/analysis, was discussed in Chapter 9. After completing a qualitative force synthesis/analysis, the next step in projection and forecasting is to apply probabilistic reasoning to it. Probabilistic reasoning is a systematic attempt to make subjective estimates of probabilities more explicit and consistent. It can be used at any of several levels of complexity (each successive level of sophistication adding new capability and completeness). But even the simplest level of generating alternatives, discussed next, helps to prevent premature closure and serves to add structure to complicated problems.

Generating Alternatives

The first step to probabilistic reasoning is no more complicated than stating formally that more than one outcome is possible. One can generate alternatives simply by listing all possible outcomes to the problem under consideration. As discussed in Chapter 9, the outcomes can be defined as alternative scenarios.

Ideally the alternatives should be mutually exclusive (only one can occur, not two or more simultaneously) and exhaustive (nothing else can happen; one of the alternates listed must occur).[3] For instance, suppose that an analyst is tracking an opponent's research and development on a revolutionary new technology. The analyst could list two outcomes only:

- The technology is used in producing a product (or weapons system).
- The technology is not used.

This list is mutually exclusive and exhaustive. If a third option called "technology is used within two years" were added, the mutually exclusive principle would have been violated (unless the first outcome had been re-worded to "the technology is used after two years").

This brief list of outcomes may or may not be very useful with just two alternative outcomes. If the analyst is interested in more details, then the outcome can (and should) be decomposed further. A revised list might look like:

- Technology is used:
  —Successfully.
  —But the result is a flawed product.
- Technology is not used:
  —And no new technology is introduced into the process.
  —But a variant or alternative technology is used.

This list illustrates the way that specifying all possible (but relevant) outcomes can expand one's perspective. The expanded possibilities often can generate useful insights to problems. For example, the alternative that a different technology is used in lieu of the technology in question suggests that intelligence analysis focus on whether the target organization has alternative research and development underway.

The key is to list all the outcomes that are meaningful. It is far easier to combine multiple outcomes than it is to think of something new that wasn't listed or to think of separating one combined-event outcome into its subcomponents. The list can serve as both a reminder that multiple outcomes can occur and a checklist to decide how any item of new intelligence might affect an assessment of the relative likelihoods of the diverse outcomes listed. The mere act of generating a complete, detailed list often provides a useful perspective on a problem.

When generating a set of outcomes, beware of using generic terms (such as "other"). As noted in the story of the automobile mechanics in Chapter 5, we do not easily recall the vast number of things that could fall under that seemingly simple label. A catchall outcome label should be included only when a complete list of all alternatives cannot be generated first. In intelligence, it is rare that all possible future states can be included. Also, do not overlook the possibility of nothing happening. For instance, if an analyst is creating a list of all the things that the French government might do regarding a tariff issue, one item on the list should be "nothing at all."

Influence Trees or Diagrams

A list of alternative outcomes is the first step in projection. A simple prediction might not go beyond this level. But for more formal or rigorous analysis, the next step typically is to identify the things that influence the possible outcomes and indicate the interrelationship of these influences. This is frequently done using an influence tree. Influence trees and diagrams represent a systematic approach to the force analysis introduced in Chapter 9.

For instance, let's assume that an analyst wants to assess the outcome of an ongoing African insurgency movement. There are obvious possible outcomes: The insurgency will be crushed, the insurgency will succeed, or there will be a continuing stalemate. Other alternative outcomes may be possible, but we can assume that they are so unlikely as to not be worth including. The three outcomes for the influence diagram are then:

- Regime wins.
- Insurgency wins.
- Stalemate.

The analyst now describes those forces that will influence her assessment of the relative likelihoods of each outcome. For instance, the insurgency's success may depend on whether economic conditions improve, remain the same, or become worse during the next year. It also might depend on the success of a new government poverty relief program. The assumptions about these "driver" events are currently described as *linchpin premises* in U.S. intelligence practice, and these assumptions need to be made explicit.[4]

After listing all of the influencing or driver events, the analyst next focuses on two questions:

- Do any of the influencing events influence each other?
- Is it possible to assess the relative likelihood of the outcomes of the influencing events directly, or do the outcomes of these events depend in turn on other influencing events (and outcomes)?

If the answer to the first question is that the events influence each other, then the analyst must define the direction of influence. In the case at hand, we have two influencing events—economic conditions and the poverty relief program. One can argue that each event influences the other to some extent; but it seems reasonable that the poverty relief program will have more influence on economic conditions than the converse, so we are left with the relationship of:

Poverty relief program influences economic conditions, which influence the outcome of the insurgency.

Figure 10-3   An Influence Tree for Insurgency

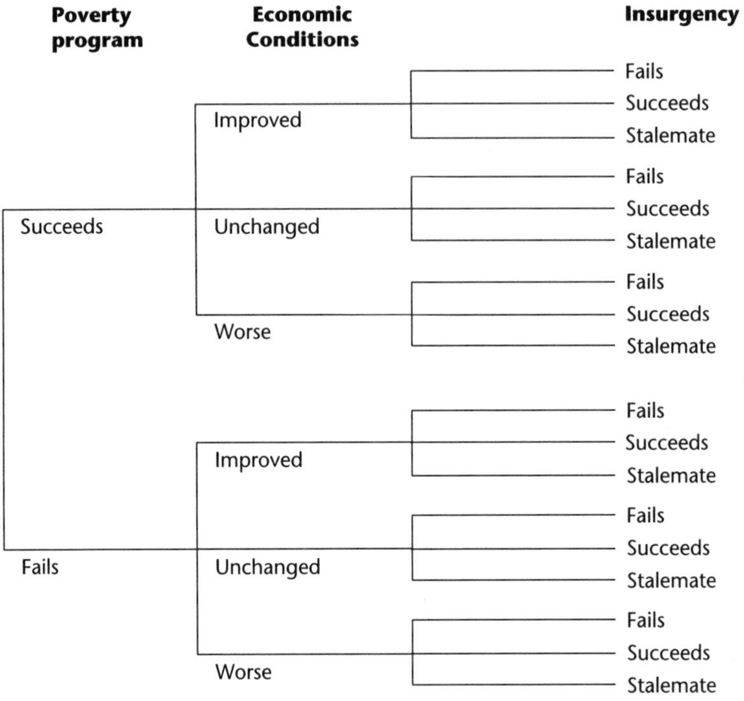

Poverty program	Economic Conditions		Insurgency
			Fails
	Improved		Succeeds
			Stalemate
			Fails
Succeeds	Unchanged		Succeeds
			Stalemate
			Fails
	Worse		Succeeds
			Stalemate
			Fails
	Improved		Succeeds
			Stalemate
			Fails
Fails	Unchanged		Succeeds
			Stalemate
			Fails
	Worse		Succeeds
			Stalemate

Having established the uncertain events that influence the outcome, the analyst proceeds to the first stage of an influence tree, which is shown in Figure 10-3. This tree simply shows all of the different outcomes in the hierarchy of dependency.

The thought process that is invoked when generating the list of influencing events and their outcomes can be useful in several ways. It helps identify and document factors that are relevant to judging whether an alternative outcome is likely to occur. The analyst may need to document the process (create an audit trail) by which she arrived at the influence tree. The audit trail is particularly useful in showing colleagues what the analyst's thinking has been, especially if she desires help in upgrading the diagram with things that she may have overlooked. Software packages for creating influence trees allow the inclusion of notes that create the audit trail.

In the process of generating the alternative lists, the analyst must address the issue of whether the event (or outcome) being listed actually will make a difference in her assessment of the relative likelihood of the outcomes of any of the events being listed. For instance, in the economics example, if she knew that it would make no difference to the success of the insurgency whether economic conditions improved or remained the same, then she has no need to differentiate these as two separate outcomes. She should instead simplify the diagram.

The second question, having to do with additional influences not yet shown on the diagram, allows her to extend this pictorial representation of influences to whatever level of detail she feels necessary. Note, however, that an analyst should avoid adding unneeded layers of detail. Making things more detailed than necessary can degrade, rather than improve, the usefulness of this diagramming technique.

The thought process also should help identify those events that contain no uncertainty. For example, the supply of arms to both government and insurgent forces will also have a strong influence on the outcomes. We assume that, in this problem, these are not uncertain events because intelligence officers have high confidence in their estimates of the future arms supply. They are not linchpins. The analyst will undoubtedly take these influences into account in her analysis. In fact, she would make use of this information when assessing the relative likelihoods of the main event (insurgency) outcome, which will be done next; but she does not need to include it in her diagram of uncertain events.

Probabilistic reasoning is used to evaluate outcome scenarios. The tree of Figure 10-3 must have a relative likelihood assigned for each possible outcome. We do this by starting at the left and estimating the likelihood of the outcome, given that all of the previous outcomes in that branch of the tree have occurred. This is a subjective process done by evaluating the evidence for and against each outcome using the evaluative techniques discussed in Chapter 5. Figure 10-4 shows the result. Note that the sum of the likelihoods for each branch point in the tree equals 1.00, and that the cumulative likelihood of a particular outcome (on the far right) is the product of the probabilities in the branches that reach that point. (For example, the outcome probability of the poverty program succeeding, economic conditions improving, and the insurgency failing is $.224 = 0.7 \times 0.4 \times 0.8$.)

The final step in the evaluation is to sum the probabilities on the right in Figure 10-4 for each outcome—"fails," "succeeds," and "stalemate." When we do this we get the following probabilities:

Insurgency fails	.631
Insurgency succeeds	.144
Stalemate	.225

This influence tree approach to evaluating possible outcomes is more convincing to customers than an unsupported analytic judgment about the prospects for the insurgency. Human beings tend to do poorly at such complex assessments when they are approached in a totally unaided, subjective manner; that is, by the analyst mentally combining the force assessments in an unstructured way. Conversely, though, numerical methods such as the influence tree

Figure 10-4   Influence Tree with Probabilities

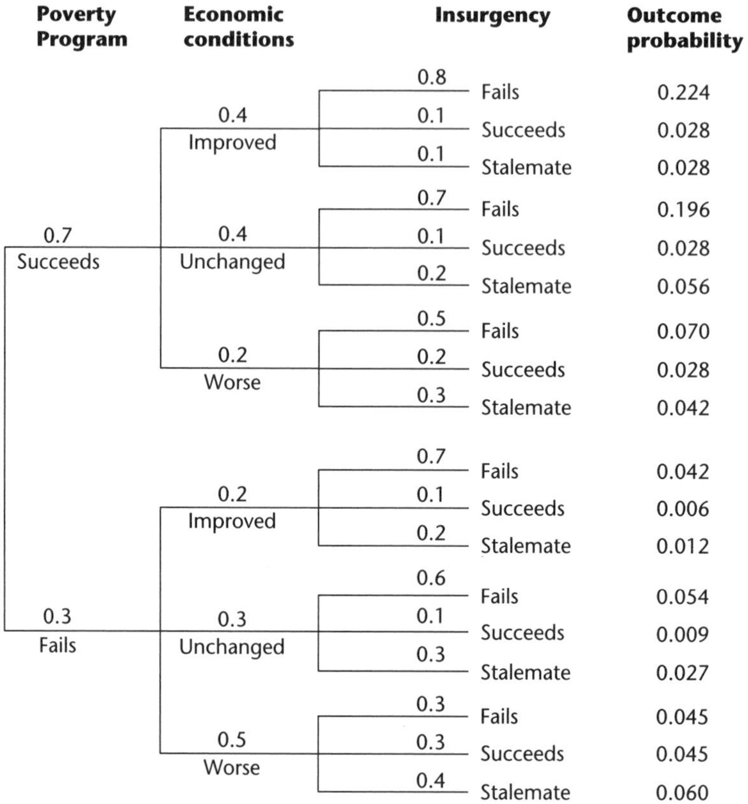

Poverty Program	Economic conditions	Insurgency		Outcome probability
		0.8	Fails	0.224
	0.4 Improved	0.1	Succeeds	0.028
		0.1	Stalemate	0.028
		0.7	Fails	0.196
0.7 Succeeds	0.4 Unchanged	0.1	Succeeds	0.028
		0.2	Stalemate	0.056
		0.5	Fails	0.070
	0.2 Worse	0.2	Succeeds	0.028
		0.3	Stalemate	0.042
		0.7	Fails	0.042
	0.2 Improved	0.1	Succeeds	0.006
		0.2	Stalemate	0.012
		0.6	Fails	0.054
0.3 Fails	0.3 Unchanged	0.1	Succeeds	0.009
		0.3	Stalemate	0.027
		0.3	Fails	0.045
	0.5 Worse	0.3	Succeeds	0.045
		0.4	Stalemate	0.060

have the inherent disadvantage of implying (merely because numbers are used) a false degree of accuracy. The numbers are precise and unambiguous in meaning, but they are no more accurate than the subjective feelings they represent.

The probability calculations and the tree structuring technique demand that feedback loops do not exist, or that the feedback is so small that it can be ignored. A feedback loop would exist if, for example, the economic conditions significantly affect the poverty relief program; or if a continuing insurgency stalemate affects economic conditions. If feedback loops emerge and are needed in influence diagrams, the analyst will need to use techniques designed to handle dynamic feedback situations, such as simulation modeling.

Influence Nets

Influence net modeling is an alternative to the influence tree. It is a powerful tool for projection and forecasting of complex target models where the influence tree would be too cumbersome. Influence net modeling is a combination of two established methods of decision analysis: Bayesian inference net analysis, originally employed by the mathematical community, and influence diagramming techniques, such as the insurgency example, that were originally employed by operations researchers. Influence net modeling is an intuitive, graphical method.

To create an influence net, the analyst defines "influence nodes," which depict events that are part of cause-effect relations within the target model. They also create "influence links" between cause and effect that graphically illustrate the causal relation between the connected pair of events. The influence can be either positive (supporting a given decision) or negative (decreasing the likelihood of the decision), as identified by the link "terminator." The terminator is either an arrowhead (positive influence) or a filled circle (negative influence). The resulting graphical illustration is called the "influence net topology." An example topology, showing some of the influences on Saddam Hussein's decision whether to withdraw from Kuwait in 1990, is pictured in Figure 10-5.[5] The decision is stated as "Hussein decides to withdraw from Kuwait peacefully." The arrows come from boxes that support that decision; the filled circles come from boxes that support the opposite decision, that is, not to withdraw.

Correlation and Regression

Correlation is a measure of the degree of association between two or more sets of data, or a measure of the degree to which two variables are related. Regression is a technique for predicting the value of some unknown variable based only on information about the current values of other variables. Regression makes use of both the degree of association among variables and the mathematical function that is determined to best describe the relationships among variables. If values from only one independent variable are used to predict values for another,

Figure 10-5   An Example Influence Net Model

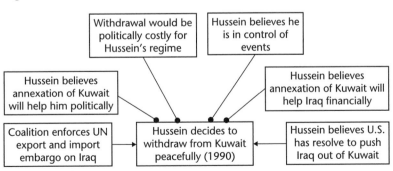

Note: the arrows come from boxes that support the decision for Hussein to withdraw from Kuwait peacefully. The filled dots come from boxes that do not support the decision.

Figure 10-6 Correlation of Number of Telephones with Gross
National Product (GNP), 1998

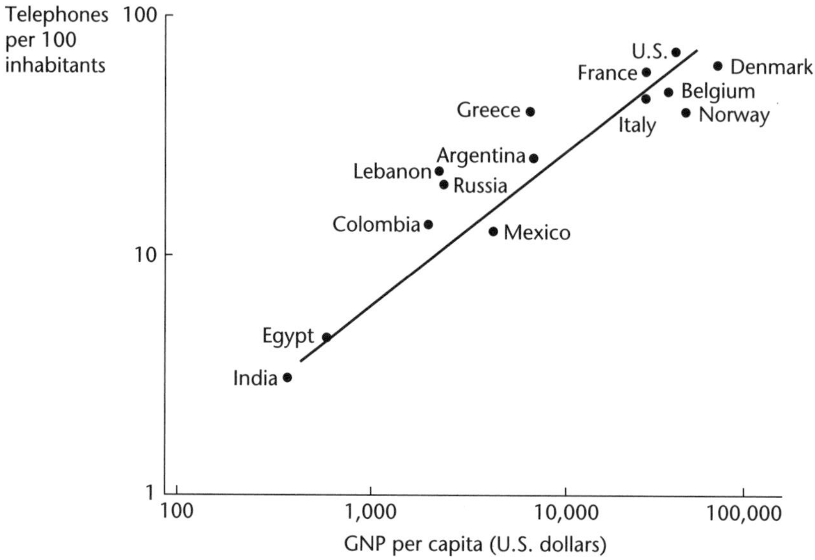

dependent variable, then the process is referred to as bivariate regression. Multivariate regression involves using values from more than one independent variable to predict values for a dependent variable.

Correlation analysis is used in both projection and forecasting to identify the forces involved so that they can be assessed. Figure 10-6 shows an example of such an analysis that was used to project the number of telephones that a country will install. The correlation with gross national product, as the figure shows, is high, so a straight-line extrapolation would allow one to predict the changes in telephone sets as a function of predicted changes in gross national product.

The graph can be used simply for straight-line extrapolation; it bears a striking similarity to the straight-line extrapolation of Figure 10-1, except that time is not a variable. But an extrapolation would probably not account for major technological changes, such as the subsequent proliferation of cellular telephone systems in many of the countries listed. To do that, we have to abandon the correlation graphic and deal with the more sophisticated analytical tools of projection or forecasting.

Making Probability Estimates

Probabilistic projection and probabilistic forecasting are used to predict the probability of future events for some time-dependent random process, such as the health of the Japanese economy. A number of these probabilistic techniques are used in industry for projection and forecasting. Two that we use in intelligence analysis are:

- *Point and interval estimation:* This method attempts to describe the probability of outcomes for a single event. An example would be a country's economic growth rate, and the event of concern might be an economic depression (the point where the growth rate drops below a certain level).

- *Monte Carlo simulation:* This method simulates all or part of a process by running a sequence of events repeatedly, with random combinations of values, until sufficient statistical material is accumulated to determine the probability distribution of the outcome. The probability of intercepting a weak radar signal in ELINT, for example, is often done using a Monte Carlo simulation.

Generally, these techniques and others of their genre require modeling of events and estimations of probability functions.

Most of the predictive problems we deal with in intelligence use subjective probability estimates. Formal probability estimates, such as Monte Carlo simulations, are used infrequently, either because we do not have enough data or because the value of a formal process is not worth the time involved. We routinely use subjective estimates of probabilities both in trivial, snap decisionmaking and in the broad issues for which no objective estimate is feasible. An estimate about the probability of a major terrorist attack occurring somewhere in the United Kingdom next week, for example, would inevitably be subjective; there would not be enough hard data to make a formal quantitative estimate. An estimate of the probability that the Chinese economy will grow by more than 5 percent next year could be made using formal quantitative techniques, because quantitative data are available.

Even if a formal probability estimate is used, it will always have a strong subjective element. A subjective component is incorporated in every estimate of future probability; it is a basis for the weighting of respective outcomes to which no numerical basis can be assigned.

Sensitivity Analysis

When a probability estimate is made in projection or forecasting, it is usually worthwhile to conduct a sensitivity analysis on the result. For example, the occurrence of false alarms in a security system can be evaluated as a probabilistic process. The effect of introducing alarm maintenance procedures can be included in the evaluation by means of sensitivity analysis.

The purpose of sensitivity analysis is to evaluate the relative importance or impact of changes in the values assigned to influencing event outcomes. The inputs to the estimate are varied in a systematic manner to evaluate their

Figure 10-7   Sensitivity Analysis for Biological Warfare Virus
Prediction

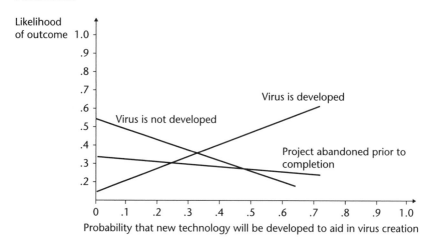

effect on possible outcomes. This process lets an analyst identify variables
whose variation has little or no effect on possible outcomes.

A number of tools and techniques are available for sensitivity analysis.
Most of them are best displayed and examined graphically. Figure 10-7 shows
the results of an analysis of the likelihood of a manufacturer successfully creating a new biological warfare virus. Three possibilities are assumed to exist:
the process will create the new virus; the process will fail; or the manufacturer
will abandon the project before it is conclusive. These three possibilities add
up to a likelihood of 1.0 at any point on Figure 10-7. One of the elements in
the analysis is the probability that a new genetic engineering technology will
be developed to aid the development of the biological warfare virus (the horizontal axis in the figure). The sensitivity analysis indicates that success in producing the virus is relatively sensitive to the genetic engineering technology
(the success line goes up sharply as the probability increases that the technology works). If the probability of success for the new technology is above .55,
then the process is more likely to succeed (likelihood of new virus creation
above .5 on the vertical scale); it is more likely to fail if the probability of success is less than .55. The figure also indicates that the manufacturer's possible
decision not to complete the project is relatively insensitive to the technology's
success, because the project abandonment likelihood does not change much
as the probability of technology success increases; such a decision might be
made for political or economic reasons, for example, rather than technical reasons. The chart is too simplistic, of course; in fact, the straight lines would typically be curves with sharp "knees" at points where the probabilities start
changing at different rates.

Forecasting

Projections usually work out better than extrapolations over the short to medium term. But even the best-prepared projections often seem very conservative when compared to the reality years later. New developments will create results that were not foreseen even by experts in a field. Typically, these new developments are described as disruptive technologies or disruptive organizations. To take these disruptive developments into account, we are forced to go to forecasting techniques.

A major objective of forecasting in intelligence is to define *alternative* futures of the target model, not just the most likely future. These alternative futures are usually scenarios, as discussed in the preceding chapter. The development of alternative futures is essential for effective strategic decision-making. Since there is no single predictable future, customers need to formulate strategy within the context of alternative future states of the target. To this end, it is necessary to develop a model that will make it possible to show systematically the interrelationships of the individually forecast trends and events. A forecast attempts to identify new forces that will affect the target—to consider the possible effects of new developments in distantly related fields, such as new technologies in the realm of plastics, or new constraints posed by the sociological impact of pollution, or new forms of life created through genetic engineering, and to present them all as possibilities to the customer. In forecasting, one also must look at forces such as synergy, feedback, inertia, contamination, and countervailing forces—all discussed in Chapter 11.

Customers generally prefer to have the highest possible level of predictive analysis (forecasting) provided so that they can be confident in it. "Confidence" for some customers might mean that the analysis is conducted according to some sort of accepted (preferably quantitative) methodology. For other customers, it might mean confidence in the person producing the analysis.

A forecast is not a blueprint of the future, and it normally starts from extrapolations or projections. The forecaster then must expand her scope to admit and juggle many additional forces or factors. She must examine key technologies and developments that are far afield but that affect the subject of the forecast.

Although the need for forecasts is widely recognized, as is the need to examine a breadth of disciplines, there is little agreement on the methods and techniques to be used.

The Nonlinear Approach to Forecasting

A forecasting methodology requires analytic tools or principles. It also requires analysts who have significant understanding of many technologies and disciplines and the ability to think about issues in a nonlinear fashion. As with the intelligence process discussed in Chapter 1, an analyst cannot effectively approach forecasting in a linear manner—gathering data, analyzing it, and formulating a solution. This linear and mechanistic view of the universe has never served us well for forecasting, and it is inappropriate for dealing with complex targets. The natural pattern of thinking about the future appears chaotic on the surface, but it is chaos with a purpose. Futuristic thinking examines deeper forces and flows across many disciplines that have their own order and pattern. In predictive analysis, we may seem to wander about, making only halting progress toward the solution. This nonlinear process is not a flaw; rather it is the mark of a natural learning process when dealing with complex and nonlinear issues.

The sort of person who can do such multidisciplinary analysis—analysis of what will happen in the future—has a broad understanding of the principles that cause a physical phenomenon, a chemical reaction, or a social reaction to occur. People who are multidisciplinary can pull together concepts from several technical fields and assess political, economic, and social, as well as technical, factors. This breadth of understanding is a recognition of the similarity of these principles and the underlying forces that make them work. It might also be called "applied common sense," but unfortunately it is not very common.

Techniques and Analytic Tools of Forecasting

Both projection and forecasting use the tools described in this and succeeding chapters. In Chapter 2 we introduced the idea of a conceptual model. The conceptual model on which projection and forecasting are based is the assessment of the dynamic forces acting on the entity being studied. Forecasting is based on a number of assumptions, among them the following:

- The future cannot be predicted, but it can be forecast probabilistically taking explicit account of uncertainty.

- Forecasts will be misleading if they do not sweep widely across possible future developments in such areas as demography, values and lifestyles, technology, economics, law and regulation, and institutional change.

- Alternative futures, including the "most likely" future, are defined primarily by human judgment, creativity, and imagination.[6]

For executives and policymakers, the aim of defining alternative futures is to try to determine how to create a better future than the one that would materialize if we merely kept doing what we're doing. In intelligence, the aim is to predict an opponent's actions so that a response can be formulated.

Forecasting starts from our experiences or through examination of the changing political, military, economic, and social environments. We identify issues or concerns that may require attention. These issues/concerns are then defined in terms of their component forces. Forecasts of changes to these forces (mostly in the form of trends and events) are generated and subsequently interrelated through techniques such as cross-impact analysis. A "most likely" forecast future is written in a scenario format from the trend and event forecasts; outlines of alternative scenarios to that future are generated by synthesis/analysis or by cross-impact modeling—pairwise connection of forecast developments, as discussed in Chapter 9.

If the forecast is done well, these scenarios stimulate the customer of intelligence—the executive—to make decisions that are appropriate for each scenario. These decisions are analyzed for their robustness across scenarios. The purpose is to arrive at a set of decisions that effectively address the issues and concerns identified in the initial stage of the process. These decisions are then implemented in action plans.[7]

Evaluating Forecasts

Forecasts are judged on the following criteria:

- *Clarity.* Are the objects of the forecast and the forecast itself intelligible? Is it clear enough for practical purposes? Users may, for example, be incapable of rigorously defining "gross national product" or "the strategic nuclear balance," but they may still have a very good ability to deal with forecasts of these subjects. On the other hand, they may not have the least familiarity with the difference between households and families, and thus be puzzled by forecasts in this area. Most users have difficulty interpreting the statistics used in forecasting (for example, medians and interquartile ranges).
- *Intrinsic credibility.* To what extent do the results make sense to the customer? Do the results appear valid based on common sense?
- *Plausibility.* To what extent are the results consistent with what the customer knows about the world outside of the scenario and how this world *really* works or may work in the future?
- *Relevance.* If the forecasts are believed to be plausible, to what extent will they affect the successful achievement of the customer's mission or assignment?
- *Urgency.* To what extent do the forecasts indicate that, if action is required, time is of the essence in developing and implementing the necessary changes?
- *Comparative advantage.* To what extent do the results provide a better foundation now for investigating decision options than other sources available to the customer *today*? To what extent do they provide a better foundation now for future efforts in forecasting and policy planning?
- *Technical quality.* Was the process that produced the forecasts technically sound? To what extent are the basic forecasts mutually consistent?[8]

These criteria should be viewed as filters. To reject a forecast requires making an argument that shows that the scenario cannot pass through all or most of these filters. A "good" forecast is one that survives such an assault; a "bad" forecast is one that does not. It is important to communicate to customers that forecasts are transitory and need constant adjustment to be helpful in guiding thought and action. It is not uncommon for customers to criticize forecasts. Common complaints are that the forecast is obvious; it states nothing new; it is too optimistic, pessimistic, or naive; or it is not credible because obvious trends, events, causes, or consequences were overlooked. Such objections, far from undercutting the results, facilitate strategic thinking. The response to these objections is simple: If something important is missing, add it. If something unimportant is included, strike it. If something important is included but the forecast seems obvious, or the forecast seems highly counterintuitive, probe the underlying logic. If the results survive, use them. If not, reject or revise them.

Summary

Predictions seldom come true. But a good prediction—one that accurately describes the forces acting on a target model and the assumptions about those forces—has lasting value for the intelligence customer. As a situation develops, the customer can revise the prediction if the intelligence analyst gets the forces right. Three predictive techniques are used in intelligence.

Extrapolation is the easiest of the three, because it simply assumes that the existing forces will not change. Over the short term, extrapolation is usually reliable, but it seldom gives an accurate picture over the medium to long term, because the forces do change.

Projection assumes a probability that the forces will change, and it uses several techniques to evaluate the probabilities and the effects of such changes. This probabilistic reasoning relies on techniques such as influence trees and influence nets.

Forecasting is the most difficult predictive technique. It must include the probabilities of changing forces, as for projection. It must also identify possible new forces from across the political, economic, social, and technical arenas and assess their likely impact. Because of the resulting complexity of the problem, most forecasting relies on the use of scenarios. Forecasting, like projection, also takes into account the effects of shaping forces that are discussed in the next chapter.

Notes

1. Liam Fahey, *Competitors* (New York: John Wiley and Sons, 1999), 448.
2. Joseph P. Martino, "Trend Extrapolation," in *A Practical Guide to Technological Forecasting*, ed. James R. Bright and Milton E. F. Schoeman (Englewood Cliffs, N.J.: Prentice-Hall, 1973), 108.
3. This will permit later extension to more sophisticated analyses, such as Bayesian analysis.
4. Jack Davis, *Intelligence Changes in Analytic Tradecraft in CIA's Directorate of Intelligence* (Washington, D.C.: CIA, 1995), 8.

5. Julie A. Rosen and Wayne L. Smith, "Influencing Global Situations: A Collaborative Approach," *Air Chronicles,* Summer 1966.

6. James L. Morrison and Thomas V. Mecca, "Managing Uncertainty: Environmental Analysis/Forecasting in Academic Planning," http://horizon.unc.edu/courses/papers/Mang.asp, January 12, 2003.

7. Ibid.

8. W. I. Boucher, *Technical Advisors' Final Report: Chapters Prepared by Benton International, Inc.,* prepared for the Futures Team of the Professional Development of Officers Study (PDOS), Office of U.S. Army Chief of Staff (Torrance, Calif.: Benton International, 1984).

11

Shaping Forces

I think there is a world market for maybe five computers.
Thomas Watson, chairman of IBM, 1943

We have reached the limits of what is possible with computers.
John van Neuman, University of Illinois, 1949

Six hundred and forty thousand bytes of memory ought to be enough for anybody.
Bill Gates, chairman of Microsoft Corp., 1981

The Internet will catastrophically collapse in 1996.
Robert Metcalfe, inventor of the Internet, 1995

We introduced the idea of force synthesis/analysis in Chapter 9. The forces that have to be considered—economic, political, social, environmental, military—vary from one intelligence problem to another. This book does not attempt to catalog them—there are too many. However, some broad-based forces apply to most types of predictive analysis in technology, economic, and political issues. They tend to shape or temper other forces. These forces are mostly social or environmental. An analyst should start a predictive effort by asking which of these forces are relevant.

Inertia

One force that has broad implications is inertia, the tendency to stay on course and resist change. Newton's first law (see Box 11-1) says that bodies at rest tend to stay at rest, and that bodies in motion tend to remain in motion.

Opposition to change is a common reason for organizations coming to rest. Opposition to technology in general is an inertial matter; it results from a desire of both workers and managers to preserve society as it is, including its institutions and traditions. The price of inertia is illustrated in the history of the Bessemer steelmaking process in America.

The Bessemer process was invented at about the same time (1856) by two men, each working independently—Henry Bessemer, an Englishman, and

Analysis Principle ●──────────────────────────────────────

Box 11-1   Newton's First Law

Newton's first law (liberally translated) says that:

1. Bodies at rest tend to remain at rest.
2. Bodies in motion tend to remain in motion.

Unless you place them in the real world, where friction applies; then:

3. Bodies in motion tend to come to rest; and then you go back to part 1.

William Kelly, an American. The process involved blowing air under pressure into the bottom of a crucible of molten iron. Within a few years the Bessemer process almost completely replaced the conventional crucible method of steel-making. It lowered the price of producing steel and was the basis for the modern steel industries. It was one of the major factors in the industrial revolution.

From 1864 to 1871, ten U.S. companies began making steel using the Bessemer process. All but one imported English workmen familiar with the process. By 1871 that one, the Cambria Company, dominated the industry. Although Cambria had an initial disadvantage, its workers were able to adapt to changes and improvements in the process that took place between 1864 and 1871. The British steel workers at the other companies, secure in the tradition of their craft, resented and resisted all change, and their companies did not adapt.

The most common manifestation of the law of inertia is the "not-invented-here" or "NIH" factor, where the organization opposes pressures for change from the outside. It was powerful in the old Soviet technical bureaucracies and in the U.S. defense industry. The Soviet system developed a high level of stability as a result of central economic planning. But all societies resist change to a certain extent. The societies that succeed seem able to adapt by preserving that part of their heritage that is useful or relevant.

A textbook example of resistance to innovation is the story of the U.S. Navy vs. Lt. William Sims. One century ago the standard gunnery method used a highly trained gun crew to manipulate the heavy set of gears that aimed naval guns at opposing ships. Because both ships would be moving, and the gun platform would also move with the pitch and roll of the ship, naval gunnery became an art, and accuracy depended on professionalism and teamwork.

In the early 1900s a young naval officer, Lt. William Sims, developed a new method that made use of the inertial movement of the ship. He was able to simplify the aiming gear set and remove the gunnery sight from the gun's recoil so that the operator could keep his eye on the gunsight and move the gears at the same time. His tests demonstrated that the new method would markedly improve the accuracy of naval gunnery.

Sims then attempted to attract the attention of U.S. Navy headquarters, and was told that the navy was not interested. Sims persisted, however, and the navy finally consented to a test with some conditions: Sims' aiming device had to be strapped to a solid block in the Washington Naval Yard. Deprived of the ship's inertial movement, the aiming device failed, proving to the navy that continuous-aim firing was impractical.

Sims, however, was as persistent and bold as the person he next contacted with his idea—President Theodore Roosevelt. Roosevelt forced the navy to take the device and give it a fair test. Sims' device was subsequently adopted and significantly improved naval gunnery accuracy.[1]

The organizational resistance to change that Sims encountered is common. The structure of the U.S. Navy is a highly organized society, and Sims's innovation directly threatened that society by making some skills less essential. The navy resisted his innovation, and it took someone outside the society—the president of the United States—to force the change. A company is a society just as a U.S. Navy ship's crew is a society. Any change that threatens it will be opposed.

All organizations possess this basic antipathy to changes that threaten their structure. Most research and development groups restrict their members' freedom to innovate: Ideas that don't fit the mold of the group are unwelcome. Inertia was a powerful restraining force on attempts to modernize the Soviet telecommunications system during the 1970s and 1980s, as discussed in the Appendix. The established ministries, (the Ministry of Communications and the Ministry of Communications Equipment Industry) were resistant to introducing new technologies.

Countervailing Forces

All forces are likely to have countervailing or resistive forces that must be considered. Countervailing forces are similar to inertial forces. The principle is summarized well by another of Newton's laws of physics: For every action there is an equal and opposite reaction (see Box 11-2).[2]

When applied to organizations, Newton's third law can be stated in a form all bureaucrats understand: for a given amount of effort, one can effect a small change in a large system, or a large change in a small system; but one cannot make a large change in a large system.

Applications of Newton's third law are found in all organizations and groups, commercial, national, and civilizational. As Samuel P. Huntington notes, "we know who we are ... often only when we know who we are against."[3] The rallying cry of Japan's Komatsu Corporation, and the definition of its being, was summed up in its slogan, "Beat Caterpillar." Caterpillar, Inc., is Komatsu's chief competitor worldwide.

In Isaac Asimov's brilliant short story *The Last Trump,* the Archangel Gabriel sounds the last trump and judgment day arrives (on January 1, 1957, to be precise). Earth's residents (and former residents, who are coming back to

Analysis Principle ●────────────────────────────────

Box 11-2   Newton's Third Law (the Dialectic)

Newton's third law of physics states that whenever one body exerts a force on another, the second always exerts on the first a force that is equal in magnitude but oppositely directed. In the social sciences, Hegel's dialectic is the philosophical equivalent of Newton's third law. Hegel described a process of thesis-antithesis-synthesis by which views of one type lead, by their internal contradictions, to views of the opposite type and eventually to a synthesis of the two views.

The extension of Hegel's dialectic is that no entity (country, organization, or project) can expand unopposed. Opponents will always arise. Every action creates an equal and opposite reaction. If the force reaction is not equal, then a change in momentum (in physics) or in the situation (in the social sciences) takes place until the reactions are equal. An analysis will always be incomplete until the analyst has identified and assessed opposing forces.

life in their last corporeal form) slowly realize that boredom, not the fire and ice of Dante's *Inferno,* is the ultimate hell. Etheriel, Earth's guardian angel, meanwhile is appealing to a higher court—the Almighty—for an *ex post facto* reversal of the judgment day order. Finally Etheriel, realizing who has actually won the final battle for the souls of mankind, asks, "Is then the Adversary your servant also?" God invokes Newton's third law in his reply: "Without him I can have no other ... for what is Good but the eternal fight against Evil?"[4]

All forces eventually meet counterforces. An effort to expand free trade inevitably arouses protectionist counterefforts. If sexual Web sites proliferate, the forces of parental concern and moralistic outrage will grow stronger. If laws bar access to obscenity online, then you can count on offshore evasion of restrictions and growing pressures for free speech.

Counterforces need not be of the same nature as the force they are countering. A wise organization is not likely to play to its opponent's strengths. Today's threats to U.S. national security are asymmetric; that is, there is little threat of a conventional force-on-force engagement by an opposing military, but there is a threat of an unconventional yet highly lethal attack by a loosely organized terrorist group, as the events of September 11, 2001, demonstrated.[5] Asymmetric counterforces are common in industry as well. Industrial organizations try to achieve cost asymmetry using defensive tactics that have a large favorable cost differential between one's own organization and that of an opponent.[6] Any intelligence assessment of the consequences of a policymaker's or field commander's decision should take countervailing forces into account, because the opponents will react and are likely to react asymmetrically.

Contamination

Contamination is the degradation of any political, social, economic, or technical entity due to an infection-like process (see Box 11-3).

Analysis Principle ●───────────────────────────

Box 11-3   Gresham's Law of Currency

Sir Thomas Gresham was Queen Elizabeth I's financial agent. Although he did not formulate the law that bears his name, he was its proponent in England. Gresham's Law of Currency is based on the observation that, when currencies of different metallic content but the same face value are in circulation at the same time, people will hoard the more valuable currency or use it for foreign purchases, leaving only the "bad" money in domestic circulation. The law explains a major disadvantage of a bimetallic currency system. Gresham's Law is generally summarized as "the bad drives out the good."

Nobel Laureate Irving Langmuir best described the contamination phenomenon in this story about a glycerin refinery:

Glycerin is commonly known as a viscous liquid, even at low temperatures. Yet if crystals are once formed, they melt only at 64 degrees Fahrenheit. If a minute crystal of this kind is introduced into pure glycerin at temperatures below 64 degrees Fahrenheit, the entire liquid gradually solidifies.

A glycerin refinery in Canada had operated for many years without having any experience with crystalline glycerin. But suddenly one winter, without exceptionally low temperatures, the pipe carrying the glycerin from one piece of apparatus to another froze up. The whole plant and even the dust on the ground became contaminated with nuclei, and although any part of the plant could be temporarily freed from crystals by heating above 64 degrees, it was found that whenever the temperature anywhere fell below 64 degrees crystals would begin forming. The whole plant had to be shut down for months until outdoor temperatures rose above 64 degrees.[7]

Contamination phenomena can be found throughout organizations as well as in the science and technical disciplines. Once such an infection starts, it is almost impossible to eradicate. It keeps poisoning its host, and there are too many little bits to stamp out entirely—like the solid glycerin or a cancer. For example, in the U.S. electronics industry, a company's microwave tube production line suddenly went bad. With no observable change in the process, the tubes no longer met specifications. Attempts to find or correct the problems failed, and the only solution was to close down the production line and rebuild it completely.

Contamination phenomena have analogies in the social sciences, organization theory, and folklore. Folklore tells us that "One bad apple spoils the barrel." At some point in organizations, contamination can become so thorough that only drastic measures will help—such as shutting down the glycerin plant or rebuilding the microwave tube plant. Predictive intelligence has to consider the extent of such social contamination in organizations, because contamination is a strong restraining force on an organization's ability to deal with change.

Effects of this social contamination are hard to measure, but they are often highly visible. Large sectors of industry in Russia reached a level of hopeless contamination some time ago, and recovery is proving to be very difficult. It can be seen in the production results, but it also has visible symptoms. For example, most Japanese plants are clean and neat, with grass and flowers even in unlikely areas, like underneath drying kilns. A Russian factory is likely to have a dirty, cluttered environment, buildings with a staggering energy loss, employees with chronic alcohol problems and absenteeism. The environment in the Japanese plant reinforces the positive image. The environment in the Russian plant reinforces and prolongs the contamination. Such contamination can be reversed—the cleanup of New York City in the 1990s is an example—but the reversal normally requires a massive effort.

The contamination phenomenon has an interesting analogy in the use of euphemisms in language. It is well known that if a word has or develops negative associations, it will be replaced by a succession of euphemisms. Such words have a half-life, or decay rate, that is shorter as the word association becomes more negative. In older English, the word *stink* meant "to smell." The problem is that most of the strong impressions we get from scents are unpleasant ones, so each word for olfactory senses becomes contaminated over time, and must be replaced. *Smell* has a generally unpleasant connotation now, and words such as *scent, aroma,* and *bouquet* are replacing it, to fall in their turn. Similarly, words that denote any racially, mentally, or physically disadvantaged group seem to become contaminated over time; words such as *deaf, blind,* and *retarded* were replaced by *handicapped,* and then by *mentally/physically challenged,* reflecting the negative associations and opprobrium that attach to the words as contamination sets in.

Synergy

Predictive intelligence analysis almost always requires multidisciplinary understanding. Therefore it is essential that the analysis organization's professional development program produce a professional staff that can understand a broad range of concepts and can function in a multidisciplinary environment. One of the most basic concepts is that of synergy: The whole can be more than the sum of its parts due to interactions among the parts. Synergy is therefore, in some respects, the opposite of the countervailing forces discussed earlier.

Synergy is not really a force or factor so much as a way of thinking about how forces or factors interact. Synergy can result from cooperative efforts and alliances among organizations (synergy on a large scale). It can also result from interactions within a physical system, as the following example shows.

When the U.S. Nike-Hercules surface-to-air missile system was deployed in the 1950s, its target tracking radar proved very difficult for attacking aircraft to defeat in combat training exercises. The three standard techniques for defeating such radars at the time were rapid maneuvers, radar decoys, and noise jamming. None of the three techniques worked very well against the Nike-Hercules radar:

- Maneuvers had no effect.
- The radar could not be pulled off target by releasing the radar decoy material known as chaff (thin strips of aluminum foil that cause a radar signal resembling an aircraft), because the radar range rate tracking system could discriminate between slow-moving chaff and a fast-moving aircraft.
- The radar's antijam circuits eliminated conventional noise jamming.

The U.S. Air Force's Strategic Air Command (SAC) put its electronic warfare planners on the problem, because the Nike-Hercules capabilities could be expected to appear in future radars that SAC's B-52s would face. SAC's planners found that a combination of the three techniques—noise jamming with an "S" maneuver in which chaff was dropped when the aircraft track was perpendicular to the radar bearing—consistently defeated the tracking radar. The secret to the success of what became called the "side-step" maneuver was synergy.

In electronics warfare, it is now well known that a weapons system may be unaffected by a single countermeasure; however, it may be degraded by a combination of countermeasures, each of which fail individually to defeat it. The same principle applies in a wide range of systems and technology developments: The combination may be much greater than the sum of the components taken individually.

An example of synergy on a large scale is in the fields of computers and communications. These two distinct technical areas have been merging over three decades as we expand our ability to use one to enhance performance of the other. Managing the merger of these two required technical knowledge in both, plus an understanding of political issues (regulation in communications) and economic issues (cost-performance tradeoffs of central vs. distributed computing). It also required a keen market sense that can determine the willingness of large numbers of people to take advantage of the merger, as people have done in using networks such as the Internet.

Synergy is the foundation of the "swarm" approach that military forces have applied for centuries—the coordinated application of overwhelming force. The massed English longbows at the battle of Crecy in 1346 were more lethal than the sum of many single longbows might indicate. In planning a business strategy against a competitive threat, a company will often put in place several actions that, each taken alone, would not succeed. But the combination can be very effective. As a simple example, a company might use several tactics to cut sales of a competitor's new product: start rumors of their own improved product release, circulate reports on the defects or expected obsolescence of the competitor's product, raise buyers' costs of switching from their own to the competitor's product, and tie up suppliers via exclusive contracts. Each action, taken separately, might have little impact, but the synergy—the "swarm" effect of the actions taken in combination—might shatter the competitor's market.

In intelligence support to policy, the same rule holds. A combination of policy actions may be much more effective than any single action. The policymaker or executive usually identifies the possible combinations and, in the end, selects one combination. The usual job of the intelligence analyst is to evaluate the likely effects of a given combination, though in some cases he may also formulate likely combinations for the executive.

Most of the major innovations and changes that make straight-line extrapolation obsolete occur because of some form of synergy. Synergy was a major factor in the spread of television, CB radio, and personal computing. It should be constantly on the analyst's mind as she evaluates the factors going into a forecast.

Feedback

Forces change over time due to evaluation and decision processes. These processes are *adaptive,* and the adaptation is called feedback. Feedback is the mechanism whereby the system learns and changes itself. Feedback was introduced as a third class of force (along with internal and external forces) in Chapter 9; the following discussion provides more detail about how feedback works to change a system.

Many of the techniques for prediction depend on the assumption that the process being analyzed can be described, using systems theory, as a closed-loop system. Under the mathematical theory of such systems, feedback is a controlling force in which the output is compared with the objective or standard, and the input or process corrected as necessary to bring the output toward a desired state, as shown in Figure 11-1. The results (the output) are evaluated and the result of the evaluation fed back as an input to the system at the point shown in the figure. The feedback function therefore determines the behavior of the total system with time. Only one feedback loop is shown in the figure, but many feedback loops can exist, and usually do in a complex system.

The model shown in Figure 11-1 is a generalized one and is used extensively in electrical engineering to describe the operation of mechanical and electrical control systems. It also has been found to represent many social processes, especially how organizations adapt. It appears to be valid in describing the process of invention, information transfer, and the application of new technology. Although its general validity has not been tested, the model is accepted here as having some validity in describing the process by which forces that change the future vary over time.

Figure 11-1   The Feedback Process

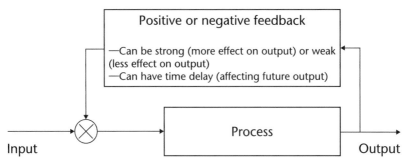

Note: The encircled X shows where the input and the feedback combine before they feed into the process.

An analyst should not consider a prediction complete until she has assessed the potential effects of feedback. This assessment requires that she predict the nature and extent of feedback. Feedback can be positive and encourage more output, or it can be negative and encourage less output. Feedback can also be strong and have a greater effect on output, or be weak and have less of an effect. Finally, feedback can be immediate and reflected immediately in the output, or it can have a time delay that changes the output at some future time.

In most processes being predicted, the evaluative tool that creates feedback is benefit-cost analysis. In the context of the feedback loop, perceived benefits constitute positive feedback; perceived costs constitute negative feedback. The total output of the system will tend to grow with time if net feedback is positive (benefits outweigh costs) and to shrink with time if net feedback is negative (costs outweigh benefits).

Strength

Most systems are adaptive. Feedback causes changes in the input and should also cause the management assessment and innovation parts of a process to change. The measure of this adaptivity is the strength of feedback. In most systems, a change in the output (type, quantity, and so on) changes the input due to an evaluatory process. In positive feedback systems, where benefits outweigh costs, the output causes a reinforcement of the input, and the output therefore tends to grow at a rate determined in part by the amount of positive feedback. In negative feedback systems, where costs outweigh benefits, output is fed back in such a manner as to decrease input, and the output tends to stabilize or decrease.

The rate of change in forces due to feedback is a result of weighing observed benefits of a development (positive feedback) against costs (negative feedback). This is the evaluation or decisionmaking step.

Organizations tend to act to reduce the strength of feedback in two ways. First, all organizations try to hold things constant so they can deal with them, and this is a powerful constraint on feedback.[8] Few organizations can readily cope with the uncertainty that comes from adaptivity; Sims's problem with introducing his gunnery innovation is one of many examples of the problem.

Second, feedback must reach decisionmakers or action-takers to be effective. Only in this way can it shape future actions. But the organization itself—its administrative layers and staff—diffuses, weakens, misdirects, and delays feedback, effectively reducing its strength. A large bureaucratic organization or a centralized economy, with its relative inflexibility and numerous layers of administrators, keeps feedback at a feeble level. Funding is set through political processes that have only an indirect relation to previous industrial successes and failures. The market provides poor feedback in such an economy.

In contrast, one of the big advantages of a small, uncluttered organization can be that it allows feedback to reach decisionmakers undiluted, that is, at full strength. The consensus decisionmaking approach traditionally used in Japanese companies gets information through the system to key individuals, albeit slowly.

Time Delay

All feedback loops, whether in technological or social systems, have inherent time delays. In electronic systems, such delays pose no problem when they are slight compared with the overall system response time. However, when the delays become a significant fraction of system response time, they can have catastrophic results. When feedback is slow the system must operate as an open loop in which output is controlled solely by input and not by feedback. The primary reason for the U.S. military's elaborate and expensive command and control systems is to reduce the time delay involved in feedback.

Feedback delays could cause the system to receive positive feedback at a time when costs of the output are far exceeding the benefits, or vice versa. And the evaluation process does introduce inherent delays. Often, feedback of positive benefits comes more slowly than feedback of negative benefits. The benefits of deregulation or free trade agreements, for example, may be much more difficult to identify and take longer to observe than the costs.

It is fairly common, however, that benefits are more quickly perceived than costs. The drug industry has provided us with examples of this phenomenon, one of the most dramatic of which was thalidomide. First introduced in Europe in 1956 as a sedative, thalidomide was withdrawn from the market in 1961, but only after it was found to have caused severe birth defects in thousands of infants.[9]

The delayed effects of environmental pollution have provided other examples of such "false positive" feedback. The nuclear power industry, however, probably provided the most spectacular examples. This industry benefited from extensive government-supported efforts to advance technology for some years. The resulting pace of nuclear power technology development was described, years ago, by then Atomic Energy Commission chair James Schlesinger as being "similar to the entire history of commercial aviation from Kitty Hawk to the Boeing 747 being compressed into less than a score of years."[10] As a result the United States suffered from the Three Mile Island reactor incident that released radioactive material into the air creating widespread panic, and Russia had its Chernobyl disaster—a reactor meltdown that contaminated a wide area in the Ukraine and caused several deaths.

As these examples suggest, delays in negative feedback are a continuing problem in areas of rapid technological advance. The rapid advances depend on technology diffusion mechanisms that work extremely well in the United States, with its information gatekeepers and high mobility of workers. Multinational corporations provide a powerful technological diffusion mechanism. This fast advance of technology, compared to the technology evaluation process, leads to examples of "technology-driven" systems, where the constraining effects of regulatory, human resources, organizational, and management factors is too slow to have much effect. The pharmaceutical, communications, and computer industries have been examples of this technology drive in action for several decades. Genetic engineering is one example of a current technology-driven field that may result in serious problems worldwide in coming decades.

Regulation

Any analysis of an industry or organization must take into account the role of government regulatory forces. Some such forces are positive, but more government support does not necessarily mean success. An analysis of protected industries provides some examples.

Governmental ownership of and participation in European businesses increased in the 1970s. One driving force was the need to rescue European businesses from failure or foreign takeover, especially in the aftermath of the 1973 oil problem. When the computer merger of Honeywell-Bull was being negotiated in France in the 1970s, the French government agreed to the merger on the conditions that no employees would lose their jobs and no plants would be closed. Since there were an estimated 15,000 surplus employees as a result of the merger, these conditions placed a heavy burden on the new firm. The result was low plant utilization, and Honeywell-Bull was not competitive in France in spite of its guaranteed market in French government-controlled firms.

Over the past century, government regulatory powers have increased their influence over industrial decisions worldwide. In some countries, this intervention has predominantly been for the purpose of worker safety and health, environmental protection, and so forth. In others it has primarily been to protect jobs and to promote the economy. In some, the intent has been to financially benefit the government leadership.

Analysis Principle ●————————————————————————

Box 11-4   The Law of Unintended Consequences

In England before 1535, real property passed by descent to the oldest son upon his father's death. At that transfer, a tax was owed to the king. Over the years feudal lawyers created a device called the "Use" that allowed trustees to hold legal title to land in trust for the true owner so that, unless all of the trustees died at once, the land could be repeatedly passed from father to son without the requirement for a tax.

The story goes that King Henry VIII, as his financial needs increased, "contemplated the state of his exchequer with great dismay."[1] A survey of the kingdom's assets revealed to Henry how England's landowners were avoiding his taxes through the device of the Use. In 1535 Henry prevailed upon a reluctant parliament to pass the Statute of Uses[2]. The statute was simple and direct: it vested legal title in the land's true owner, not in the trustee, so that taxes would be due upon the death of the true owner.

The law is remarkable for two reasons:

- First, it totally failed in its revenue-raising purpose. Within a few years the British lawyers, who were no less clever than tax lawyers are today, had found enough loopholes in the law to thwart it.
- Second, the *unintended* consequences of this tax-raising statute were vast, so that it has been called the most important single piece of legislation in the Anglo-American law of property. Specifically, the law gave rise both to the modern law of trusts and to the modern methods of transferring real estate. The British Parliament's reaction to the Statute of Uses also led to the law of wills as we know it.

The law of unintended consequences, simply stated, says that:

- Any deliberate change to a complex (social or technical) system will have unintended (and usually unforeseen) consequences.
- The consequences are normally undesirable. (The Statute of Uses itself is one of the few known exceptions—it had highly beneficial results for succeeding generations, though not for Henry VIII.)

[1] John E. Cribbet, *Principles of the Law of Property* (New York: Foundation Press, 1975).
[2] Ibid.

Governments have a disadvantage in this intervention: they seem to look at things one facet at a time in a relatively simplistic manner. In part because of slower feedback processes and a more cumbersome structure, governments are not as quick on their feet as the corporations they deal with. And in the intervention, governments continually encounter the law of unintended consequences: Actions taken to change a complex system will have unintended, and usually adverse, consequences (see Box 11-4).

The law has an analogy in the world of data processing. In a modern distributed processing network, or in a very complex software package, one cannot predict all the effects of changes. But it is predictable that most of the unintended consequences—system crashes, lockouts, and so forth—will be undesirable outcomes.

The law of unintended consequences may be merely an elegant expression of Murphy's law (which states that anything that can go wrong, will) or simply an expression of human inability to foretell the outcome of a complex social process. One facet of the law has been described as "counterintuitiveness." One generic model of a welfare system demonstrated that expanding a welfare system to reduce the number of poor families in a community actually (and counterintuitively) increases their numbers.[11] Another model indicated that making drugs illegal—an act intended to curb drug abuse and reduce other societal problems—had the opposite effect.[12] As another example, during the cold war, Soviet secrecy forced U.S. defense planners to assume the worst-case scenario and provoked a military buildup that the Soviets did not want.

The impact of regulation is difficult to measure—not only are the consequences unexpected, but they are often difficult to trace back to the regulations that spawned them. One measure of these consequences occurs when an industry is deregulated, as when the United States deregulated the telecommunications industry. The effect in telecommunications was dramatic: new industries sprang up. Spurred by the competitive threat, AT&T became more innovative and market oriented than it had been in the past. The application of new technologies, such as packet switching for data communications, got a boost.

Just as government support does not mean automatic success, so government opposition does not mean automatic failure. Worldwide, the narcotics industry marches on in spite of strong opposition from many governments. During the Prohibition era in the United States, the liquor industry thrived.

Summary

Predictive analysis relies on assessing the impact of forces that shape organizations, lead to new developments, and motivate people.

- *Inertia,* or resistance to change, is common in established organizations. Organizations naturally seek to establish and maintain a stable state.

- *Countervailing forces* will always appear to oppose any significant force, and the countervailing force may be of an asymmetric type.

- *Contamination* phenomena can dilute the effectiveness of national or organizational instruments of power (political, economic, social, or technical).

- *Synergy*—the combination of forces to achieve unexpected results—is behind many social and technical advances. Synergy determines the effectiveness of the "swarm" attack that organizations increasingly use to win conflicts.

- *Feedback* is an adaptive force that can be beneficial or detrimental, depending on the strength and time delay. Rapid advances in technology, along with the significant time delays in restraining feedback on the technology, can cause problems.

- Government *regulatory forces* often constrain technical or social evolution, and often result in unintended consequences.

These shaping forces should be a "first stop" in any predictive analysis about a target model. The following two chapters give some examples of their application in organizational and technology analysis.

Notes

1. Elting Morrison, *Men, Machines, and Modern Times* (Cambridge: MIT Press, 1966).
2. Sir Isaac Newton, Philo. Naturalis Principia mathematica
3. Samuel P. Huntington, *The Clash of Civilizations and the Remaking of World Order* (New York: Simon and Schuster, 1996), 21.
4. Isaac Asimov, "The Last Trump," in *Isaac Asimov: The Complete Stories,* vol. 1 (New York: Doubleday, 1990), 106–119.
5. Another thoughtful perspective on the use of asymmetric attack against the United States is presented in the book *Unrestricted Warfare* by Chinese People's Liberation Army colonels Qiao Liang and Wang Xiangsui.
6. Michael E. Porter, *Competitive Advantage* (New York: Free Press, 1985), 500.
7. Irving Langmuir, "Science, Common Sense, and Decency," Science 97 (January 1943): 1–7.
8. Donald A. Schon, *Organizational Learning* (Boston: Addison-Wesley, 1978).
9. Crohn's and Colitis Foundation of America, "Thalidomide and IBD," March 10, 2003, www.ccfa.org/weekly/wkly828.htm.
10. Ibid.
11. Jamshid Gharajedaghi, *Systems Thinking: Managing Chaos and Complexity* (Boston: Butterworth-Heinemann, 1999), 49.
12. Ibid, 48.

12

Organizational Analysis

The first duty of government ... is to preserve order within the realm; the first duty of management is to prevent baronial warfare.

Antony Jay, author of *Management and Machiavelli*

This chapter and the next two chapters discuss analytical techniques focused on some of the major forces that shape most entities (companies, industries, military forces, and so on). The techniques should be applied in answering questions about force impact, as discussed in Chapter 9, and in constructing influence trees. Most forces can be analysis targets as well as forces in another analysis. A country's information technology, for example, might be the target of a technology assessment. The results of the assessment would be a force to be considered in an analysis of the country's information warfare capability. The results would also be a force to consider in an organizational assessment, such as that of an industrial concern located in that country. An organizational assessment of the country's software development firms would be a significant input into an analysis of the country's information technology. Organizational and technology forces are important in predictive analyses of many targets, and that is why they are the subjects of this chapter and the next.

The typical organization is a system that, as noted in Chapter 1, can be viewed (and analyzed) from three perspectives: structure, function, and process. Structure refers to the components of the organization, especially people and their relationships. Function refers to the outcome or results produced, and tends to focus on decisionmaking. Process describes the sequences of activities and the expertise needed to produce the results or outcome. Babson College professor Liam Fahey, in his assessment of organizational infrastructure, describes four perspectives: structure, systems, people, and decisionmaking processes.[1] Whatever their names, all three (or four, following Fahey's example) perspectives need to be considered.

For the analyst, one goal of organizational analysis is to understand the strengths and weaknesses of the target organization. Another goal is predictive: to forewarn of change in the target organization's structure, function, or process due to changing forces. Policy-oriented customers can use the analysis in planning strategy; operations units can use it to adversely affect the target, possibly with information warfare. Depending on the goal, an analyst may need to assess the organization's mission, its power distribution, its human resources, and its decisionmaking processes. The analyst might ask questions like: Where is control exercised? Which elements provide support services? Are their roles changing? Hierarchical analysis tools and network analysis tools, discussed later in this chapter, are valuable for this sort of organizational analysis.

An analyst identifies vulnerability points in the target organization so that her customers—the decisionmakers—can select the appropriate target to act on; that is, to identify where perception management or coercive techniques would be most effective. For example, her customers may want to know when and how to convey to the opponent that it can expect strong retaliatory actions if it behaves in a certain way.

Structure

There are many ways to analyze an organization's structure, but three approaches are more common than others. The first is to examine the size and capabilities of the organization along with its mission. Do size and capabilities fit well with the mission? The second way is to assess the effectiveness of the structure itself. A structure that works for one group may be disastrous if applied to another. The third approach is to analyze the relationships among groups in the organizational hierarchy. These three approaches can complement each other to give a more complete structural picture.

Organizational Size and Capabilities

The usual way to measure whether an organization's size and capabilities facilitate its mission is to compare the organization to other organizations with a similar mission—a technique called benchmarking. If size and capability hinder the mission rather than promote it, the organization will have problems, as illustrated by a variant of the bathtub curve (see Chapter 4), popularized in economic circles as the Laffer curve.[2] The Laffer curve is the bathtub curve upside down, as seen in Figure 12-1. It illustrates an observation that

Figure 12-1   The Laffer Curve for Tax Rates

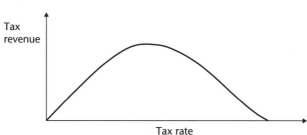

many governments have made about tax policies. At low rates of taxation, increasing the rate increases the total revenue generated. At some point, diminishing returns set in, and each tax increment generates less new revenue than the previous increment did. As rates rise even higher, revenue actually begins to drop as taxation drives people away from the activity being taxed.

This upside-down bathtub curve has a similar application for organizations. Here the vertical axis would be mission effectiveness, and the horizontal axis would describe how well the organizational structure is matched to its mission and environment. The organization must have a mission that it can accomplish but which is not too narrowly defined. If the organization's size and capabilities are inadequate for the mission and environment (the left side of the graph in Figure 12-1) the result is frustration and loss of focus. A mission that is too narrowly defined for organizational size and capabilities can result in stagnation and loss of opportunities, or worse.

Type of Structure

One of the most challenging areas of organizational analysis is that of assessing structural effectiveness. Some questions to ask include: Where does the power lie? Does the organizational structure encourage reaching and executing good decisions? Does it fit with the culture?

But the first question is this: Does the target organization make sense in its environment? Any form of government or economic structure can work—socialism, capitalism, dictatorship, democracy, theocracy—if it suits the people affected by it. Democracy, a preferred structure in Japan, Western Europe, and English-speaking countries, has not fared well in Africa or the Middle East because of this cultural mismatch. In business, the structure that works for an Internet start-up culture, a traditional bricks-and-mortar company, a research and development firm, a microelectronics device company, a food products company, or a natural gas pipeline company are not interchangeable. In fact, these different types of groups may have dramatically different structures.

One way to analyze organizational structure is to look at the trends in an organization and its management toward decentralization (devolving authority and responsibility to the lowest possible level) or centralization (keeping authority at the top level). Decentralization is not necessarily better as an organizational approach; it may be a great thing in a U.S. or European company, but it probably will fail in an Arab country because it does not fit the culture. Historical examples of successes and failures help such an analysis. Decentralization historically has worked if done according to the "colony" principle: Give maximum autonomy to the "colony" chief, but insure that he is a company loyalist in training, belief, and tradition.[3] Both the Roman Empire and the Roman Catholic Church successfully applied the colony principle to decentralize.

Network Analysis

Network analysis, sometimes referred to as relationship analysis, is a well-developed discipline for analyzing organizational structure. The traditional hierarchical description of an organizational structure doesn't sufficiently distinguish entities and their relationships. Social network analysis, where all of the network nodes are persons, is widely used in the social sciences, especially in studies of organizational behavior. In intelligence we more frequently use generalized network analysis, in which the nodes can be persons, organizations, places, or things. The Abacha funds laundering network of Figure 3-10 illustrates the need to include entities such as banks, airlines, and bank accounts as nodes. However, the basic techniques of social network analysis, discussed in the following section, apply to generalized network analysis as well.

Network analysis has been used for years in the U.S. intelligence community for targets such as terrorist groups and narcotics traffickers and is becoming increasingly important in business intelligence. As Liam Fahey notes, competition in many industries is now as much between networked enterprises (companies such as Cisco and Wal-Mart that have created collaborative business networks) as it is between individual stand-alone firms.[4] The Netwar model of multidimensional conflict of opposing networks is more and more applicable to all intelligence, and network analysis is our tool for examining the opposing network.

Social Network Analysis. A social network is a set of individuals referred to as *actors* (shown graphically as nodes on Figure 12-2) that are connected by some form of relationship (shown as lines on Figure 12-2). Such networks can

Figure 12-2   Social Network Analysis Diagram

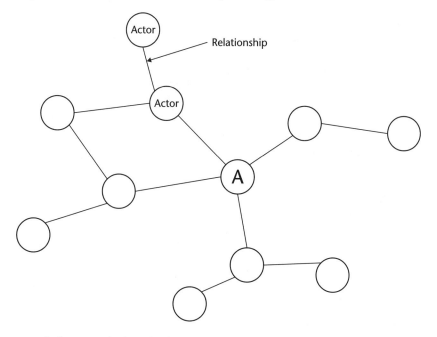

Note: The letter A marks the node whose removal will have the greatest effect on the network.

have few or many actors and many kinds of relations between pairs of actors. To build a useful understanding of a social network, a complete and rigorous description of a pattern of social relationships is a necessary starting point for analysis. Ideally, we would know about all of the relationships between each pair of actors in the population.

We prefer to use mathematical and graphical techniques in social network analysis to represent the descriptions of networks compactly and systematically. This also enables us to use computers to store and manipulate the information quickly and more accurately than we could by hand. Suppose we had information about trade flows of fifty different commodities (coffee, sugar, tea, copper, bauxite, and so on) among 170 or so nations in a given year. Here, the 170 nations can be thought of as nodes, and the amount of each commodity exported from each nation to each of the other 169 can be thought of as the strength of a directed tie from the focal nation to the other. An intelligence analyst might be interested in how the networks of trade in mineral products differ from networks of trade in vegetable products. To answer this fairly simple (but also important) question, a huge amount of data manipulation is necessary. It could take years to do by hand; a computer can do it in a few minutes.

Another reason for using "formal" methods (mathematics and graphs) for representing social network data is that the techniques of graphing and the rules of mathematics themselves suggest things that we might look for in our data—things that might not have occurred to us if we presented our data using descriptions in words. It is fairly easy to see, in Figure 12-2, that taking out node A will have the most impact on the network. It might not be so obvious if all the relationships were described textually.

Several analytic concepts come along with social network analysis, and they also apply to generalized network analysis. The most useful concepts are *centrality* and *equivalence*. These are used today in the analysis of intelligence problems related to terrorism, arms networks, and illegal narcotics organizations.

Centrality refers to the sources and distribution of power in a social structure. The network perspective suggests that the power of individual actors arises from their relations with others. Whole social structures may be seen as displaying high levels or low levels of power as a result of variations in the patterns of ties among actors. Furthermore, the degree of inequality or concentration of power in an organization and among organizations may be estimated.

Power arises from occupying advantageous positions in social networks. An actor's position in the network tells us much about the extent to which an actor may be constrained by, or constrain, others. The extent to which an actor can reach others in the network may be useful in describing the actor's opportunity structure. Three basic sources of advantage are *high degree, high closeness,* and *high betweenness.*

The more ties an actor has to other actors, the more power (higher degree) that actor has. In Figure 12-3, actor A has degree five (ties to five other actors);

Figure 12-3 Social Network Analysis—
A Star Network

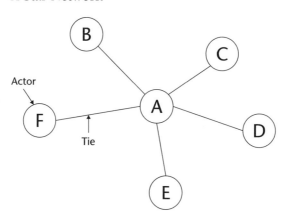

all other actors have degree one (ties to just one other actor). Actor A's high degree gives him more opportunities and alternatives than other actors in the
network. If actor D elects to not provide A with a resource, A has other places
to go to get it; however, if D elects to not exchange with A, then D will not be
able to exchange at all. Actors who have more ties have greater opportunities
because they have choices. This autonomy makes them less dependent and
hence more powerful.

The second reason why actor A is more powerful than the other actors in
the star network is that actor A is closer (high closeness) to more actors than
any other actor. Power can be exerted by direct bargaining and exchange, but
power also comes from being a center of attention whose views are heard by
larger numbers of actors. Actors who are able to reach other actors by shorter
paths or who are more reachable by other actors by shorter paths have favored
positions. This structural advantage can be translated into power.

The third reason that actor A is advantaged is that he lies between all other
pairs of actors (high betweenness), and no other actors lie between A and other
actors. If A wants to contact F, A may do so directly. If F wants to contact B,
she must do so by way of A. This gives actor A the capacity to broker contacts
among other actors—to extract "service charges" and to isolate actors or prevent contacts.

In simple structures such as the star, these advantages tend to all accrue
to one actor. In more complex and larger networks, an actor may be located in
a position that is advantageous in some ways and disadvantageous in others.

Let's look at a terrorist network to illustrate the concept of centrality. In
seeking to disrupt terrorists, one obvious approach is to identify the central
players and then target them for assessment, removal, or surveillance. The network centrality of the individuals removed will determine the extent to which

the removal impedes continued operation of the activity. Thus centrality is an important ingredient (but by no means the only one) in considering the identification of network vulnerabilities.

The second analytic concept that accompanies social network analysis is equivalence. The disruptive effectiveness of removing one individual or a set of individuals from a network (such as by making an arrest or hiring a key executive away from a business competitor) depends not only on their centrality, but also upon some notion of their uniqueness, that is, on whether or not they have *equivalents*. The notion of equivalence is useful for strategic targeting and is closely tied to the concept of centrality. If nodes in the social network have a unique role (no equivalents), they will be harder to replace. The most valuable targets will be both central and without equivalents.

The network analysis literature offers a variety of concepts of equivalence. Three in particular are quite distinct and, between them, seem to capture most of the important ideas on the subject. The three concepts are *substitutability, stochastic equivalence,* and *role equivalence.* Each can be important in specific analysis and targeting applications.

Substitutability is easiest to understand; it could best be described as interchangeability. Two objects or persons in a category are substitutable if they have identical relationships with every other object in the category. If a target individual has no substitute, then his removal will cause more damage to the operation of the network than if a substitute exists. If another individual can take over the same role and already has the same connections, then to damage the network one would need to remove or incapacitate not only the target individual but all other substitutable individuals as well. Individuals who have no available network substitutes make more worthwhile targets.

Substitutability also has relevance to detecting the use of aliases. The use of an alias by a criminal might also show up in a network analysis as the presence of two or more substitutable individuals (who are in reality the same person with an alias). The interchangeability of the nodes indicates the interchangeability of the names.

Stochastic equivalence is a slightly more sophisticated idea. Two network nodes are stochastically equivalent if the probabilities of their being linked to any other particular node are the same. Narcotics dealers working for one distribution organization could be seen as stochastically equivalent if they, as a group, all knew roughly 70 percent of the group, did not mix with dealers from any other organizations, and all received their narcotics from one source.

Role equivalence means that two individuals play the same role in different organizations, even if they have no common acquaintances at all. Substitutability implies role equivalence, but not the converse. As an example, the chief financial officer (CFO) of company A can be mapped onto the CFO of company B if companies A and B are similar enough (the two CFOs have similar roles and responsibilities). Or, an explosives expert in terrorist group A can be mapped onto a biological weapons expert in terrorist group B if group A specializes in use of explosives against its target and group B specializes in use of biological terrorism. Stochastic equivalence and role equivalence are useful in creating generic models of target organizations and in targeting by analogy—for example, the explosives expert is analogous to the biological expert in planning collection, analyzing terrorist groups, or attacking them.

Generalized Network Analysis. In intelligence work we usually apply an extension of social network analysis that retains its basic concepts. But whereas all of the entities in social network analysis are people, in generalized network analysis they can be anything—organizations, places, and objects, for example. In charting out a generalized network diagram for a terrorist organization, it will be important to include associated organizations, weapons, locations, and means of conducting terrorist activities (vehicles, types of explosives). The purpose of such generalized network displays is usually to reveal such things as the patterns of operations, likely future targets, and weaponry. Generalized network analysis thereby includes some aspects of functional analysis and process analysis.

In intelligence, generalized relationship analysis tends to focus on networks where the nodes are organizations or people within organizations. Liam Fahey has described several such networks and defined five principal types:

- *Vertical:* organized across the value chain, for example 3M Corporation goes from mining raw materials to delivering finished products.
- *Technology:* alliances with technology sources that allow a firm to maintain technological superiority, such as the CISCO Systems network.
- *Development:* an alliance focused on developing new products or processes, such as the multimedia entertainment venture Dreamworks SKG.
- *Ownership:* a dominant firm owns part or all of its suppliers, as do the Japanese keiretsu.
- *Political:* focused on political or regulatory gains for its members, for example the National Association of Manufacturers.[5]

Hybrids of the five are possible, and in some cultures such as the Middle East and Far East, family can be the basis for a type of hybrid business network.

Generalized relationship analysis may become one of the principal tools for dealing with complex systems, thanks to the intense investigation of new computer-based analytical methods that currently is underway. Future prospects include systems that can learn from the analysts and create models from data. But any system that purports to organize massive amounts of data will have massive false alarms. The analyst still will have to do cognitive correlation and evaluate sources. Much of the current work is being funded by the U.S. Defense Advanced Research Projects Agency.[6]

As implemented in software, generalized relationship analysis tools need to convey dynamic information to be of the most value to intelligence analysts. That is, links should appear and disappear, expand or contract in size, change intensity, change color, all to convey additional information to the user. Nodes should move up or down, closer or farther away (or have size changes) on the display to indicate importance. Such tools don't exist today, but they will.

Function

Functional analysis of an organization tends to focus on behavioral analysis, specifically on predicting decisions. The purpose of behavioral analysis is always predictive: how will the target react to a given situation? In all behavioral analysis, but especially in decision prediction, three aspects of the decision process have to be considered—rational, cultural, and emotional.[7] Too often we try to predict decisions based on the rational aspect alone.

Rational Aspect

Russell Ackoff, in his entertaining book *The Art of Problem Solving: Ackoff's Fables,* tells the story of a household appliance manager who claimed that consumers are often irrational. The manager cited examples of an improved dishwasher that had been poorly received, whereas new cooktops and ovens had been very successful even though they offered no new features and were more expensive. Ackoff and the manager agreed to an experiment—putting the failed products on one side of the room, the successes on the other, and the two would tour the room together with a fresh eye. Within a minute after entering the room, the manager retracted his assertion about consumer irrationality. All of the successful appliances could be used without bending or climbing, and all of the failed products required bending or climbing.[8] The opponent is seldom irrational, and consumers are almost never irrational, but both are often misunderstood. Rational decisionmaking is broadly defined as a logical and normally quantitative procedure for thinking about difficult problems. Stated formally, rational decisionmaking requires the systematic evaluation of costs or benefits accruing to courses of action that might be taken. It entails identifying the choices involved, assigning values (costs/benefits) for possible outcomes, and expressing the probability of those outcomes being realized.

Predictive intelligence analysis often attempts to identify the most likely option that a decisionmaker will select in a given situation. This approach is based on the assumption that decisions are made on an explicit or implicit cost/benefit analysis, also known as expected utility theory. The theory's origins are in the study of economic decisionmaking and behavior, notably in the work of John von Neumann and Oskar Morgenstern.[9] The theory views decisionmaking as behavior that maximizes utility. An individual faced with a decision will, consciously or subconsciously, identify the available options, the possible outcomes associated with each option, the utility of each option/outcome combination, and the probability that each option/outcome combination will occur. The decisionmaker will then choose an option that is likely to yield, in his own terms, the highest overall utility.

Rational decision prediction, based on expected utility theory, is the place to start any predictive analysis, but it is not the end point. In Chapter 5 we introduced R. V. Jones's "principles of impotence"—the false assumption that a problem has limits. Principles of impotence have been applied in intelligence to unnecessarily constrain thinking; but fundamental limits do exist, and one applies both in physics and in an analogous field of behavioral analysis. In physics, we know it as Heisenberg's Uncertainty Principle, which states that it is impossible to measure accurately both the velocity and position of any single elementary particle. It is therefore impossible to predict with certainty the movement of a single particle. The limitation occurs because the act of measurement affects the object being measured.

This principle applies to a wide range of phenomena in both the physical and social sciences. Although physicists can predict the average behavior of large groups of particles, the behavior of any one particle, as Heisenberg said, cannot be predicted with certainty. The analogy in predicting human behavior is that it is possible to predict the behavior of groups of people (as political pollsters know well) but not the behavior of an individual.

A second fundamental principle from Heisenberg has to do with feedback. In Chapter 11 we discussed feedback as a basic shaping force. It is also a significant factor in decision prediction. Heisenberg's Uncertainty Principle says that the process of measurement alters the quantity being measured. In other words, the more precisely you try to measure a phenomenon, the more you affect the result. When pollsters take a sample of public opinion, the questions they ask tend to alter the opinion of the group polled. A thermometer, measuring the temperature of an object, alters that temperature slightly.[10] Attempts to measure an employee's performance skew her behavior. The problem is one of unintentional feedback. In management theory, the principle was perhaps first documented in the Hawthorne Experiment.

In 1927 the Western Electric Company began an investigation into the effectiveness of lighting on the productivity of factory workers. Western Electric chose its Hawthorne Works for the experiment. The test involved varying the illumination levels within the plant and observing the effect on production. The researchers were surprised to observe that production increased whether the lights were made brighter, dimmed, or left constant. Only by reducing the lighting to levels approaching darkness could the researchers cause production to drop.

The researchers followed up with a more carefully designed study of the effects of rest periods and length of the work day. The study lasted five years from 1927 to 1932. Again, the work teams whose performance was being measured steadily increased their production independent of changes in rest period timing and work day length. Furthermore, major increases in worker morale and health, along with decreases in absenteeism, were observed throughout the test period.[11]

The Hawthorne Experiment became a management science classic because of the insights it gave on motivating workers. For our purposes, the important point was that the workers knew they were being measured and thus changed their behavior to affect the measurement. In short, the attempt to measure changed the behavior being measured.

The Uncertainty Principle has several applications in intelligence analysis. In any analysis, the result tends to affect the entity being measured. The publication of economic trend predictions affects those trends. A broker's "strong buy" rating on a stock causes people to buy the stock and the price to rise, making it a self-fulfilling prediction.

In summary, the utility theory (rational) approach is useful in decision prediction, but has to be used with caution for two reasons. First, people will seldom make the effort to find the optimum action in a decision problem. The complexity of any realistic decision problem dissuades them. Instead, they select a number of possible outcomes that would be "good enough." They then choose a strategy or an action that is likely to achieve one of the good-enough outcomes.[12] Second, the social sciences version of the Uncertainty Principle places limits on how well we can predict decisions based on rationality. To improve the decision prediction, we have to include cultural and emotional factors that are discussed in the following sections. These are the factors that often cause an opponent's decision to be labeled "irrational."

Cultural Aspect

A critical component of decision modeling is the prediction of a single human's behavior, within the limitations of the Uncertainty Principle. And behavior cannot be predicted with any confidence without putting it in the actor's social and cultural context. An analyst needs to understand such elements of a culture as how it trains its youth for adult roles and how it defines what is important in life. In behavioral analysis, culture defines the ethical norms of the collective that a decisionmaker belongs to. It dictates values and constrains decisions.[13] In general, culture is a constraining social or environmental force. Different cultures have different habits of thought, different values, and different motivations. Straight modeling of a decision-making process, without this understanding, can lead the analyst into the "irrational behavior" trap, which is what happened to U.S. and Japanese planners in 1941.

Before Japan attacked Pearl Harbor, both the United States and Japan made exceptionally poor predictions about the other's decisions. Both sides indulged in "mirror imaging"—that is, they acted as though the opponent would use a "rational" decisionmaking process as *they* defined rationality.

U.S. planners reasoned that the superior military, economic, and industrial strength of the United States would deter attack; Japan could not win a war against the United States, so a Japanese decision to attack would be irrational.[14]

The Japanese, on the other hand, knew that a long-term war with the United States was not winnable because of the countries' disparity in industrial capacity. But Japan predicted that a knockout blow at Pearl Harbor would encourage the United States to seek a negotiated settlement in the Pacific and East Asia.[15] To validate this assumption, the Japanese drew on their past experience—a similar surprise attack on the Russian fleet at Port Arthur in 1904 had eventually resulted in the Japanese obtaining a favorable negotiated settlement. The Japanese did not mirror image the United States with themselves, however, but with the Russians of 1904 and 1905. Japan believed that the U.S. government would behave much as the Tsarist government had.

Such errors in predicting an opponent's decisionmaking process are common when the analyst does not take cultural factors into account. Cultural differences cause competitors to not take the "obvious" decision. The intelligence analyst has to understand these different motivations or be caught in the sort of surprise that U.S. television manufacturers encountered during the 1960s. At that time, all TV manufacturers could foresee a glut of TV sets on the market. U.S. manufacturers responded by cutting back production, assuming that other manufacturers would follow suit. Japanese manufacturers, working different assumptions (giving priority to capturing market share instead of maintaining short-term profit) kept production up. As U.S. manufacturers' market share dropped, they found that their per-unit costs were rising, while the Japanese per-unit costs were dropping due to economies of scale. The U.S. TV industry never recovered.

Culture is too often ignored or downplayed in both organizational and behavioral analysis. But history tells us that national declines are preceded by cultural declines.[16] Of immediate concern to intelligence analysis, *organizational* declines follow cultural declines. Culture has been described as representing the heartbeat and lifeblood of an organization.[17] Therefore, cultural analysis should always be a part of both organizational analysis and behavioral analysis.

For most countries and ethnic groups, a considerable volume of material is available to aid in cultural analysis, thanks to the work of many cultural anthropologists worldwide. Liam Fahey, in his book *Competitors,* has described a methodology for cultural analysis that highlights four elements of an organizational culture: values, beliefs, norms, and behaviors. He provides an example of the contrast in these four elements between a culture that is product or technology oriented and one that is customer or marketplace oriented.[18] But suppose that an analyst knows nothing about a country's culture and needs a quick lesson. How would she start?

One of the more effective ways to quickly grasp some elements of a culture is to look at the culture's proverbs or "old wives' tales" The analyst should examine the similarities and differences from her own culture. To illustrate, let's try a guessing game. The following are some selected proverbs from different cultures. Try to guess the culture or country of origin. The answers are in accompanying endnotes.

Culture 1
Without bread and wine even love will pine.
Better a good dinner than a fine coat.
When the hostess is handsome the wine is good.[19]

Culture 2
Study others' advantages and they will become your own.
We learn little from victory, much from defeat.
It is not wise to stay long when the husband is not at home.
Proclaim by your deeds who your ancestors are.
Women should associate with women.
A single arrow is easily broken, but not ten in a bundle.
Two birds of prey do not keep each other company.
It is the nail that sticks out that is struck.[20]

Culture 3
The weapon of a woman is her tears.
My brother and I against my cousin, my cousin and I against a stranger.
Be contrary and be known.
He who reproduces does not die.
We say, "it's a bull"; he says, "milk it."[21]

Culture 4
In war there can never be too much deception.
Sit atop the mountain and watch the tigers fight.
Life and shame are never equal to death and glory.
Kill the chicken to frighten the monkey.
Fight only when you can win; move away when you cannot.[22]

Culture 5
If you are sitting on his cart you must sing his song.
To live is either to beat or to be beaten.[23]

Organizations also have their own cultures, distinct from the national culture; but only long-established companies are likely to have standard sayings that are the equivalent of proverbs, and many of these no longer define the culture—if they ever did. Finding the information needed to assess an organizational culture can be difficult. Clues are sometimes available from unofficial (that is, not sponsored by the company) Web sites that feature comments from ex-employees. These sites have to be used with caution, though; they rarely present the positive side of the organization's culture.

Part of assessing the culture of an organization is assessing the people in it—their attitudes or motivation, their educational background, and their commitment to the organization. It is in these features that countries and organizations vary markedly from their peers.

Some guidelines for assessing motivation of the people in an organization were defined years ago by professor A. H. Maslow and are widely known as the Maslow hierarchy of needs. Humans, according to this theory, have a basic set of prioritized needs; and as each need in turn is satisfied, the next need becomes predominant. The needs, in hierarchical order, are:

- Physiological—food, shelter, the essentials of survival.
- Safety—freedom from physical danger.
- Belongingness—friends and affection.
- Esteem—self-respect and the esteem of others.
- Self-actualization—to "be all that you can be."[24]

The effectiveness of organizations in developed countries depends on their ability to meet the higher-order needs in the hierarchy. In less developed countries, food, shelter, and safety may be the upper limit of employee expectations. Innovation, in particular, depends on satisfying the need for self-actualization of the innovators.

Finally, all organizations have what is called a "psychological contract" with their members—an unwritten agreement on the rules each side is expected to follow.[25] People form bonds with organizations and develop expectations of how organizations should behave toward them. The strength of the employees' commitment, and the strength of the organizational culture, depend on how well the organization lives up to its half of the contract.

Educational background as a part of culture involves more than simply counting the number and levels of university degrees in the organization. Particularly in comparing organizations in different countries, one important educational tradeoff is that of breadth of knowledge versus depth of specialization. Each has its advantages. Universities in countries such as Japan and Russia tend to develop specialists that are highly trained in a field that is currently needed by industry. For example, each year Russia graduates large numbers of "engineers," but a breakdown of specialties shows that many of these are welding engineers or have some similar narrow specialty. In fact, most Russian engineers have no particular interests outside their specialty and are remarkably inflexible. But they tend to be very good within that narrow specialty. U.S. universities, in contrast, have tended to develop generalists—people who have a broad area of expertise, who tend to be more flexible and to draw on disciplines outside their primary fields.

The U.S. employment pattern tends to reinforce this flexibility; white-collar workers have high mobility and will change companies and fields easily. Japanese and Russian white-collar workers traditionally have tended to stay with one company for a long time, though this pattern in both countries may be changing.

Emotional Aspect

The final aspect of the decision process to consider when analyzing behavior is the emotional. We do many things because they are exciting or challenging. Wharton business school professor Russell Ackoff tells the story of a hand tool manufacturer whose executive team was eager to get into the business of manufacturing the (then) newly discovered transistor—not because they knew what a transistor was, but because they were bored with their existing business and wanted a new challenge.[26] Pride and revenge are also motivators. Business leaders, generals, and even presidents of the United States make some decisions simply because they want to get even with someone. The emotional aspect of behavioral prediction cannot be ignored, and personality profiling is one way to grasp it.

Business intelligence analysts have developed a methodology for personality profiling of competitors based on the lesson that personal idiosyncrasies and predisposition will have a greater bearing on an executive's decisions than will a calculated assessment of resources and capabilities.[27] The resulting profile is a model that can be used to assess likely decisions.[28]

In evaluating the likely decision of an executive, it may help to apply the Myers-Briggs model discussed in Chapter 3. A decision by one Myers-Briggs type will predictably be different from a decision made by another Myers-Briggs type. An executive who was the linebacker of his college football team will have a completely different decisionmaking style than an executive who was president of her chess club.[29]

Collective Decisionmaking

Very often a decision will be made by a group instead of by one person. In such cases, a collective decision prediction approach must be used. In such decision modeling, one must identify the decisionmakers—often the most difficult step of the process—and then determine the likely decisions. The organization and management structures that make collective decisions vary from company to company and from country to country.

Some analytical tools and techniques can predict the likely outcome of group decisionmaking. These tools and techniques are based on the theories of social choice expounded by the Marquis de Condorcet, an eighteenth-century mathematician. He suggested that the prevailing alternative should be the one that is preferred by a majority over each of the other choices in an exhaustive series of pairwise comparisons. Another technique is to start by drawing an influence diagram that shows the persons involved in the collective decision.

Collective decisions tend to have more of the rational and less of the emotional elements. But unless the decision participants come from different cultures, the end decision will be no less cultural in nature.

The collective decisions of an organization are usually formalized in its plans, especially its strategic plans. The best way to assess a strategic plan is to identify and then attempt to duplicate the target organization's strategic planning process. If the analyst comes from the same culture as the target, this may be relatively easy to do. If not, it may be necessary to hire some executives from that culture and have them attempt the duplication. The analyst also can order a collection operation to determine which strategic planning books the target's planners read or which approach they favor.

Process

The functions of the organizations discussed in the previous section are carried out by means of a process. A new system—whether a banking system, a weapons system, or computer software—develops and evolves through a process commonly known as the program cycle or system life cycle. Beginning with the system requirement and progressing to production, deployment, and operations, each phase bears unique indicators and opportunities for collection and synthesis/analysis.

Each country, industry, or company has its own version of the program cycle. Figure 12-4 illustrates the major components. Different types of systems

Figure 12-4 The Program Cycle

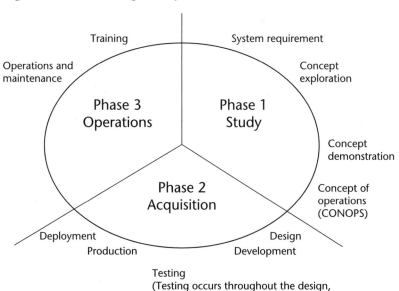

may evolve through different versions of the cycle, and product development differs somewhat from systems development. It is therefore important for the analyst to first determine the specific names and functions of the cycle phases for the target country, industry, or company and then determine exactly where the target program is in that cycle. From this information, analytic techniques can be used to predict when the program might become operational or begin producing output.

A general rule of thumb is that the more phases in the program cycle, the longer the process will take, all other things being equal. Countries and organizations with large stable bureaucracies typically have many phases, and the process takes that much longer.

Project Loading

Fred Brooks, one of the premier figures in computer systems development, defined four types of projects in his well-known book, *The Mythical Man-Month*.[30] Each type of project has a unique relationship between the number of workers needed (the project loading) and the time it takes to complete the project.

The upper left of Figure 12-5 shows the time-labor profile for a perfectly partitionable task—that is, one that can be completed in half the time by doubling the number of workers. It is referred to as the cotton-picking curve; twice as many workers can pick a cotton field in half the time. Few projects fit this mold, but the common misperception of management is that people and time are interchangeable on any given project, such that a project done

Figure 12-5   Brooks Curves for Projects

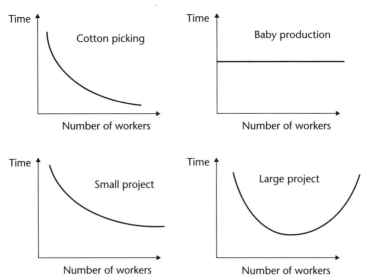

in ten months by one person could be completed in one month by ten. As Brooks noted, this is the dangerous and deceptive myth that gives his book its title.

A second type of project involves the unpartitionable task, and its profile is shown in the upper right of Figure 12-5. The profile is referred to here as the baby production curve, because no matter how many women are assigned to the task, it takes nine months to produce a baby.

Most small projects fit the curve shown in the lower left, which is a combination of the first two curves. In this case a project can be partitioned into subtasks, but the time it takes for people working on different subtasks to communicate with one another will eventually balance out the time saved by adding workers, and the curve levels off.

Large projects tend to be dominated by communication. At some point, shown as the bottom point of the lower right curve, adding additional workers begins to slow the project because all workers have to spend more time in communication. The result is simply another form of the familiar bathtub curve. Failure to recognize this pattern, or to understand where a project is on the curve, has been the ruin of many large projects. As Brooks observed, adding workers to a late project makes it later.[31]

The large or complex project curve has appeared in other forms and with other applications. It applies to the operation of large systems that involve a mix of people and equipment, and is typically shown in inverted form: The vertical axis represents the net benefit of the system, and the horizontal axis represents system size. The peak of the curve, in inverted form, is caused by the same limitation—communication costs begin to dominate the system, and benefit decreases with increasing cost.[32]

Risk Analysis

Analysts too often assume that the programs and projects that they are evaluating will be completed on time and that the target system will work perfectly. They would seldom be so foolish in evaluating their own projects or the performance of their own organizations. Risk analysis needs to be done in any assessment of a target project. It is typically difficult to do and, once done, difficult to get the customer to accept. But the customer's decisionmaking may hinge on the likelihood that the competitor's project will not succeed.

One fairly simple but often overlooked approach to evaluating the probability of success is to examine the success rate of similar ventures. In planning the 1980 Iranian hostage rescue attempt, the Carter administration could have referenced the Vietnam prisoner of war rescue attempts, only 21 percent of which succeeded. The Carter team did not study those cases, however, deeming them irrelevant, though the Iranian mission was more complex.[33] Similar miscalculations are made every day in the world of information technology. Most software projects fail. The failure rate is higher for large projects, though the failures typically are covered up.

Risk analysis, along with a project-loading review as discussed previously, are common tools for predicting the likely success of programs. Risk analysis is an iterative process in which an analyst identifies and prioritizes risks associated with the program, assesses the effects of the risks, and then identifies alternative actions to reduce the risks. Known risk areas can be readily identified from past experience and from discussions with technical experts who have been through similar projects. The risks fall into four major categories for a program—programmatic, technical, production, and engineering. Analyzing potential problems requires identifying specific potential risks from each category. Some of these include:

- Programmatic: funding, schedule, contract relationships, political issues.
- Technical: feasibility, survivability, system performance.
- Production: manufacturability, lead times, packaging, equipment.
- Engineering: reliability, maintainability, training, operations.

Risk assessment is a quantitative assessment of the risk and ranking of items to establish those of most concern. A typical ranking is based on the risk factor, which is a mathematical combination of the probability of failure and the consequence of failure. This assessment requires a combination of expertise and software tools in a structured and consistent approach to ensure that all risk categories are considered and ranked.

Risk management is the definition of alternative paths to minimize risk and criteria on which to initiate or terminate these activities. This includes identifying alternatives, options, and mitigation approaches. Examples are initiation of parallel developments (for example, funding two manufacturers to build a satellite, where only one satellite is needed), extensive development testing, addition of simulations to check performance predictions, design reviews by consultants, or focused management attention on specific elements of the program. A number of decision analysis tools are useful for risk management assessment. The most widely used tool is the Program Evaluation and Review Technique (PERT) chart, which shows the interrelationships and dependencies among tasks in a program on a time line.

Risk management is of less concern to the intelligence analyst than risk assessment; but one factor in evaluating the likelihood of a program failure is how well the target organization can assess and manage its program risks.

Comparative Analysis

Benchmarking is widely used in industry for measuring and comparing the work processes of one organization to those of another. It brings an external focus to internal activities, functions, or operations. The common approach is to compare an organization's performance against "best-in-class" organizations and determine how they achieved their performance levels. The goal is to identify, understand, and adapt outstanding practices to help an organization improve.

Three types of benchmarking are of interest in intelligence. *Competitive (peer) benchmarking* measures performance against peer or competitor organizations. *Functional benchmarking* is similar to competitive benchmarking, but the group of organizations included is larger and more broad, possibly including organizations in other industries. *Generic (best-in-class) benchmarking* compares work processes to those of organizations with truly innovative and exemplary performance: Who does this activity best?

Comparative performance analysis has a different focus than benchmarking. It includes analysis of one group's system or product performance versus an opponent's. It has a number of pitfalls, however; the opponent's system or product (such as an airplane, missile, tank, supercomputer) may be designed to do different things or serve a different market than the one to which it is being compared. The risk in comparative performance analysis is therefore one of mirror imaging, which is much the same as the mirror imaging problem in decisionmaking that was discussed earlier. Recall that U.S. analysts of Soviet military developments made a number of bad calls over the cold war years as a result of mirror imaging. It is useful to review some of the major differences we observed in the Soviet case.

- *Technological asymmetry.* Technology does not necessarily function in the same way everywhere. An analyst in a technologically advanced country, such as the United States, tends to take for granted that certain equipment—test equipment, for example—will be readily available and of a certain quality. This is a bad assumption in the typical state-run economy.

  U.S. intelligence frequently overestimated the capability of Soviet military research and development institutes based on the large number of engineers that they employed. It took some time to recognize how low the productivity of these engineers could be, but the reasons had nothing to do with their capability. They often had to build their own oscilloscopes and voltmeters—items available in the United States at a nearby Radio Shack. Sometimes plant engineers would be idle for weeks waiting for a resistor so that they could finish the oscilloscope needed to test the microwave tube for the radar they were supposed to build.

- *Unexpected simplicity.* In effect, the Soviets applied a version of Occam's razor (choose the simplest explanation that fits the facts at hand) in their industrial practice. Because they were cautious in adopting new technology, they tended to keep everything as simple as possible. They liked straightforward, proven designs. When they copied a design, they simplified it in obvious ways and got rid of the frills that the United States tends to put on its weapons systems. The Soviets made maintenance as simple as possible, because the hardware was going to be maintained by people who did not have extensive training.

In a comparison of Soviet and U.S. small jet engine technology, the U.S. model engine was found to have 2.5 times as much materials cost per pound of weight. It was smaller and lighter than the Soviet engine, of course, but it had 12 times as many maintenance hours per flight hour as the Soviet model, and overall the Soviet engine had a life cycle cost half that of the U.S. engine.[34] The ability to keep things simple was the Soviets' primary advantage over the United States in technology, especially military technology.

- *A narrowly defined mission.* The Soviets built their systems to perform specific, relatively narrow (by U.S. standards) functions. The MIG-25 is an example of an aircraft built this way—overweight and inefficient by U.S. standards but simple and effective for its intended mission. The United States tends to optimize its weapons systems for a broad range of missions.

- *The advantage of being number two.* A country or organization that is not a leader in technology development has the advantage of learning from the leader's mistakes, an advantage that entails being able to keep research and development costs low and avoid wrong paths. It took much less time for the Soviets to develop atomic and hydrogen bombs than U.S. intelligence had predicted. The Soviets had no principles of impotence or doubts to slow them down. They knew that the bombs would work. The Japanese have long enjoyed this advantage in commercial areas.

- *Quantity may replace quality.* U.S. analysts often underestimated the number of units that the Soviets would produce. The United States needed fewer units of a given system to perform a mission, since each unit had more flexibility, quality, and performance ability than its Soviet counterpart. The United States forgot a lesson that it had learned in World War II—U.S. Sherman tanks were inferior to the German Tiger tanks in combat, but the United States deployed a lot of Shermans and overwhelmed the Tigers with numbers.

Summary

To analyze an organization, examine its structure, function, and process. The result should be a series of models, usually in scenario form, that describe likely future states of the structure, function, and process in order to track the indicators of organizational change.

Within the organizational structure, relationship analysis usually is of most intelligence interest. Structural position confers power. We have reviewed three basic measures of "centrality" of an individual's positions and some elaboration on each of the three main ideas of degree, closeness, and betweenness.

Functional analysis tends to focus on behavior, specifically the decision-making process. Decisionmaking has three aspects—rational, emotional, and cultural, with cultural being probably the dominant aspect.

Process analysis centers on the programs that the organization undertakes. Intelligence is commonly interested in measuring the probabilities of success of programs. Comparative analysis and risk analysis are frequently used to measure these probabilities.

Organizational analysis is almost always a significant force to consider in predicting the development or use of a technology, as discussed in the next chapter.

Notes

1. Liam Fahey, *Competitors* (New York: John Wiley and Sons, 1999), 403.
2. The curve is named after professor Art Laffer, an adviser to President Reagan in the 1980s.
3. Ibid., 67.
4. Fahey, *Competitors,* 237.
5. Ibid., 238.
6. See Defense Advanced Research Projects Agency, "DARPA Evidence Extraction and Link Discovery pamphlet," www.darpa.mil/iso2/EELD/BAA01-27PIP.htm, November 22, 2002.
7. Jamshid Gharajedaghi, *Systems Thinking: Managing Chaos and Complexity* (Boston: Butterworth-Heinemann, 1999), 34.
8. Russell Ackoff, *The Art of Problem Solving* (New York: John Wiley and Sons, 1978), 62.
9. Oskar Morgenstern and John von Neumann, *Theory of Games and Economic Behavior* (Princeton: Princeton University Press, 1980).
10. M.R. Wehr and J.A. Richards, *Physics of the Atom* (Boston: Addison-Wesley, 1960), 199.
11. Ralph M. Barnes, *Motion and Time Study: Design and Measurement of Work* (New York: Wiley, 1968), 662–663.
12. David W. Miller and Marin K. Starr, *Executive Decisions and Operations Research* (Englewood Cliffs, N.J.: Prentice-Hall, 1961), 45–47.
13. Gharajedaghi, *Systems Thinking,* 35.
14. Harold P. Ford, *Estimative Intelligence* (Lanham, Md.: University Press of America, 1993), 17.
15. Ibid., 29.
16. Gharajedaghi, *Systems Thinking,* 174.
17. Fahey, *Competitors,* 444.
18. Fahey, *Competitors,* 419.
19. The proverbs are French. Wolfgang Mieder, *Illuminating Wit, Inspiring Wisdom* (Englewood Cliffs, N.J.: Prentice Hall, 1998).
20. The proverbs are Japanese. Guy A. Zona, *Even Withered Trees Give Prosperity to the Mountain* (New York: Touchstone, 1996).
21. The proverbs are Arabic. The last one, "We say, 'it's a bull'; he says, 'milk it,'" is another way of saying, "don't confuse me with the facts." Primrose Arnander and Ashkhain Skipwith, *The Son of a Duck is a Floater* (London: Stacey International, 1985).
22. The proverbs are Chinese. The second one, "Sit atop the mountain and watch the tigers fight," means, "Watch two opponents contend and hope that they will eliminate each other." The fourth one, "Kill the chicken to frighten the monkey," means "Punish the less important to warn the real culprit." Theodora Lau, *Best Loved Chinese Proverbs* (New York: HarperCollins, 1995).

23. The proverbs are Russian. Wolfgang Mieder, *Illuminating Wit,* 32, 135

24. A.H. Maslow, "A Theory of Human Motivation," in *Psychological Review* 50 (1943): 370–396.

25. Harry Levinson, *Psychological Man* (Cambridge, Mass.: The Levinson Institute, 1976), 90.

26. Ackoff, *The Art of Problem Solving,* 22.

27. Walter D. Barndt Jr., *User-Directed Competitive Intelligence* (Westport, Conn.: Quorum Books, 1984), 78.

28. Ibid., 93.

29. Comment by Michael Pitcher, vice president of i2Go.com, in *Competitive Intelligence Magazine,* 3 (July–September 2000): 9.

30. Ibid., 16–19.

31. Frederick P. Brooks Jr., *The Mythical Man-Month* (Reading, Mass.: Addison-Wesley, 1975), 16–25.

32. Martin K. Starr, *Management: A Modern Approach* (San Diego, Calif.: Harcourt Brace Jovanovich, 1971), 675.

33. Hossein Askari, "It's Time to Make Peace with Iran," *Harvard Business Review* (September––October 1993): 13.

34. Arthur J. Alexander, "The Process of Soviet Weapons Design," Technology Trends Colloquium, U.S. Naval Academy, Annapolis, Md., March 29–April 1, 1978.

13

Technology Analysis

If we increase our engineers' efficiency, we reduce our corporate income. Engineering time is what we sell.
Wendell Anderson, RCA Government Systems Division, 1983 (in response to a query why RCA engineers were not provided with personal computers).

Technology helps shape intelligence predictions and is the object of predictions. There are three types of technology predictions:

- Future performance of the technology.
- The usage, transfer, or dissemination of the technology.
- A forecast of the likelihood of innovation or breakthroughs in a technology.

We in the intelligence business look closely at organizations and at technology because of their importance in aiding prediction. Identifying an opponent's plans is insufficient. We need to understand whether the opponent has the resources—organizational and technological—to execute that plan.

In following a technology's development, it is easy to become entranced with its performance and promise. Technology doesn't exist in a vacuum; it is a resource like any other, and it can be well applied or poorly applied. What an organization does with a technology matters, not just the technology itself.

As an introduction to this chapter, it is worth examining two independent assessments of Soviet science and technology that were published in the late 1970s. Both assessments considered the same forces, but they came to strikingly different conclusions. In 1976 the U.S. Defense Intelligence Agency published an unclassified report entitled "Soviet Science Policy of the Seventies." The report concluded, in part:

- The Soviet Union in the Seventies continues its high commitment to scientific and technical development. In contrast to growing Western uncertainty about the social utility or costs of technological development, Soviet leadership is unwavering in its identification of science as the linchpin of all its domestic and international goals and policies.

- In the Soviet Union there is no question that science and technology will continue to receive growing allocations of resources.[1]
- Soviet science policy of the Seventies provides a guide to action for the creation of a strong science-technology-production triad. It calls for continued dramatic growth in science investment.
- At present, there is a perceptible strong willingness to continue organizational change in order to increase science's efficiency. Also, steps are being taken to improve the motivation and productivity of R&D performers by providing new forms of material incentives.
- Finally, Soviet science policy in the Seventies is marked by its vigor and the high resolve of Soviet leadership to achieve national goals through continued growth of national R&D capability and achievement.[2]

Less than three years later, Robert Wesson, a senior research fellow at the Hoover Institution, published a short article entitled "Why Soviet Technology is Lagging." His main conclusions were:

- The Soviet economy is going through a natural and predictable change. All dictatorships lose dynamism and decay in time because they lack the means of renewal and renovation. The marvel of the Soviet system is that it has held up so well for so long.
- There are many reasons for the decay, including loss of inspiration, atrophy of the ideology, replacement of vigorous men tempered in revolution and war by apparatus-men and timeservers, physical aging of the once-youthful leaders, development of a new self-serving elite, stagnation of an immobile system, concentration of authority, and the effort of the political powers to control more than they can effectively manage.
- The Soviet is no longer a revolutionary system, but an inordinately bureaucratic one, fearfully overcentralized because of fears of autonomy, lacking the controls and feedback that keep the governing apparatus in bounds in the U.S. and other democratic countries. The technological gap seems sure to continue and grow unless or until the Soviet state can recover its inspiration or cast off the encumbrances frustrating its people. This would probably mean a new revolution.[3]

What is remarkable is that both articles drew their conclusions from considerations of the same forces and from equally accurate descriptions of the evidence. But the writer of the Defense Intelligence Agency article, a scientist, ignored the organizational and cultural forces that were dominant in Soviet science and technology. Wesson, a political scientist by training, correctly assessed the impact of these forces and made a clear and unequivocal prediction that turned out to be uncannily accurate.[4] The important lesson from this example is that a technology prediction should not be made without considering the surrounding environment.

Performance

A technology assessment methodology must correctly characterize the performance of the technology; that is, it must use the correct measures of performance. For example, one useful measure of high-power microwave tube technology is average power as a function of frequency. Second, the methodology must identify the critical supporting technologies (forces) that can make a difference in the performance of the target technology. Third, the methodology must allow comparison of like developments; it is misleading, for example, to compare the performance of a one-of-a-kind laboratory device with the performance of a production-line component or system. Finally, the methodology must take time into account—the time frame for development in the country or organization of interest, not another country's or organization's time—since the methodology requires a projection into the future.

A five-stage category system has been used for describing the development of a technology or product. Transitions between stages are difficult to establish, because there is a natural overlap and blending between stages. This scheme provides for development milestones that can be measured based on how much or how little has been published on the research involved in the technology. The categories, or stages, are shown in Table 13-1.

These five stages of technology growth are often represented on the "S" curve introduced in Chapter 3. The technology has a slow start, followed by rapid growth and, ultimately, maturity, where additional performance improvements are slight.[5] The vertical axis of the curve can represent many things, including the performance of the technology according to some standard or the popularity or usage of the technology.

In the "S" curve that shows the progress of a technology through the five stages of its lifetime, the vertical axis represents the number of patents or publications about the technology. Another type of "S" curve measures the performance improvement of the technology at some stage of its development, generally at the fourth (production) stage, though it can be drawn for all stages simultaneously. The horizontal axis for both curves is time. A technology is available for industrial use when it reaches the steepest slope on the "S" curve, as Figure 13-1 illustrates. In this region, the technology is a "hot" item and is being widely publicized.

When the "S" curve for technology use flattens, the technology is mature; only incremental performance improvements are possible. Generally, at this point, the technology has reached some fundamental limit defined by physical laws. The incremental improvements flow from clever design techniques, increases in scale size, or improvements in materials, but these changes translate into only modest improvements in the technology's performance.

Table 13-1   Stages of Technology Development

Stage	Description
1. Basic research	Observation of a phenomenon and development of a theoretical understanding. *Publication indicators:* Publication of research begins near the end of this stage.
2. Item fabrication	Recognition that items can be built using the phenomenon followed by the development of a simplified theory and experimental confirmation for each item. *Publication indicators:* Publications focus on the basic theory of the item and how it works. Most technology predictions rely on open literature, and publications pattern analysis can reveal where a technology is on the "S" curve and identify emerging innovations in the technology. Technology predictions also tend to rely on quantitative techniques, the subject of the next chapter.
3. Production prototype	Demonstration of production feasibility. Prototype items are produced. Development of computer modeling techniques or of experimental evidence showing that the item is practical. *Publication indicators:* Publication of theoretical results on performance and design and of initial experimental results on the prototypes. If the item is being developed for military use or in proprietary commercial channels, open publication typically stops.
4. Full production	Production begins, and items are offered to customers, designers, or systems developers. Intense development including investigations of minor variations, improvements, and anomalous behavior on both the experimental and theoretical levels accompanied by increasing production and use. *Publication indicators:* Items are offered online, in stores, or in catalogs. A surge of applied publications occurs at the beginning of this level, as large numbers of people are able to examine the item and explore minor variations.
5. Maturity	Stable production and general use accompanied by only minor changes. Performance stabilizes near the top of the "S" curve. *Publication indicators:* Drop off in publication. Focus is on improving technology's lifetime or applying more economical fabrication techniques.

Figure 13-1   The "S" Curve for Technology Development

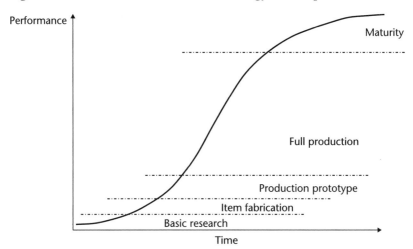

Predicting Innovation

Innovation is a divergent, not a convergent, phenomenon; no body of evidence builds up to point to an inevitable innovation in a technical field. Predicting innovation is an art, not a science. As noted earlier, the U.S. intelligence community long ago gave up trying to predict a divergent act such as a coup, for good reasons.[6] When we attempt to predict innovation, we are trying to predict a breakthrough, which is of the same nature as a coup. A breakthrough is a discontinuity in the "S" curve of technology development. Therefore, we cannot predict when an innovation will happen, but we can determine when conditions are right for it, and we can recognize when it starts to develop.

Because technology development does follow the "S" curve, we have some prospects for success. Guidelines based on past experiences with innovation can sometimes help predict who will produce an innovation. We say *sometimes* because innovation often comes from a completely unexpected source, as noted below. Finally, standard evidence gathering and synthesis/analysis techniques can help determine what the innovation will be, but only very late in the process.

Predicting the Timing of Innovation

Predicting when the timing is right for innovation in a technology is a matter of drawing the "S" curve of performance versus time for the technology. When the curve reaches the saturation level and flattens out, the timing is right. The replacement technology normally will start to take over sometime after that point, and will eventually reach a higher level of performance. It will

Figure 13-2   "S" Curves for Related Electronic Devices

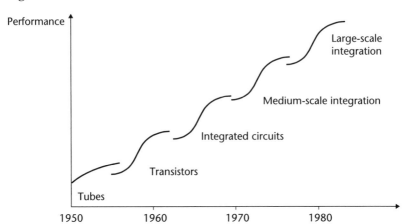

not necessarily start at a higher level. Over time in a given field, we obtain a series of "S" curves on one graph, as shown in Figure 13-2 for the evolution of electronic devices. This figure shows a series of "S" curves that do not represent a single technology but the cumulative effects of a series of technologies. By the 1950s tubes had come near the top of their performance curve for low-power applications. They began to be replaced by a succession of solid-state technologies: transistors, and then groups of transistors and electronic devices on a single chip. In each case the replacement technology began at a lower performance level but quickly surpassed its predecessor technology.

Predicting Sources

Innovation generally comes from an individual or small organization that is driven by an incentive force and not held back by restraining forces. Let us consider Dupont's innovation record. Table 13-2 shows Dupont's major technology introductions from 1920 to 1950. Of these major innovations, only five—neoprene, nylon, teflon, orlon, and polymeric color film—originated within Dupont. The rest came from small companies or individual inventors and were acquired by Dupont. Many came from a U.K. chemical company under a technology exchange agreement. For comparison we'll look at Dupont's major product and process improvements over the same period, shown on the right-hand side of the table. Of the seven improvements, five originated within Dupont, and two came from outside. The Dupont case is one of many examples that suggest that innovation does not typically take place in a large organization, but product and process improvements do.

It is worth asking why Dupont chose to acquire those outside innovations. In the time frame of this study, Dupont maintained one of the best business intelligence operations in the world. Their business intelligence group, which

Table 13-2   Dupont's Major Product Innovations and
Improvements, 1920–1950

Product innovations	Year	Product or process improvements	Year
Viscose rayon	1920	*Duco lacquers*	*1923*
Tetraethyl lead (bromide process)	1923	Tetraethyl lead (chloride process)	1924
Cellophane	1924	*Moistureproof cellophane*	*1927*
Synthetic ammonia	1926	Dulux finishes	1928
Synthetic methanol	1927	*Cordura high-tenacity rayon*	*1934*
Acetate rayon	1929	*Rutile titanium oxide*	*1941*
Freon	1931	*Fermate fungicides*	*1942*
Neoprene	*1931*		
Titanium pigments	1931		
Lucite	1936		
Nylon	*1939*		
Polyvinyl acetate	1940		
Teflon	*1943*		
Alathon polyethylene	1944		
Orlon	*1948*		
Titanium metal	1948		
Polymeric color film	*1949*		
Dacron	1949		

Note: Italics indicate innovations or improvements that originated within Dupont.

remains largely unpublicized, achieved success by a combination of solid collection (open literature search, human intelligence, and materials acquisition and testing) with good technical analysis to identify promising targets and acquire needed technology effectively and cheaply.

The same generalization held true in the planned economy of the former USSR: Most innovations came from outside the country, and those that came from within were developed by individual scientists or very small groups in academy of sciences laboratories. Soviet defense and industrial laboratories did very well on engineering improvements, but almost never innovated. And like Dupont, Soviet commercial espionage was reasonably effective at acquiring the technology. The Soviets, however, were considerably less effective in analyzing, evaluating, and adopting the technology than was Dupont.

These examples, along with others discussed later in this chapter, have a common theme: a revolutionary project has a much higher chance of success if it is placed under a completely separate management structure from that used for evolutionary developments. In evaluating an organization that is pursuing a potential breakthrough technology, the analyst therefore should assess the organizational structure, as discussed in the preceding chapter, and note how the organization has handled new technologies in the past. Does the organization welcome and aggressively pursue new technologies like Dupont, 3M, and most Internet companies do? Or does it more closely resemble the former Soviet industrial ministries, which saw new technologies as a hindrance?

Innovation Climate and Pressure

The following example sets the stage for a discussion of two forces—freedom and demand-driven incentive—that foster innovation and that need to be considered in any force analysis.

Back in 1891 an American named Almon B. Strowger developed one of the most significant innovations in telecommunications history—the step-by-step electromechanical switch. The Strowger switch made possible the dial telephone. Strowger's innovation is remarkable because he was not an engineer, he was an undertaker. But Strowger had two things going for him that are at the core of all innovation: freedom and incentive. He had freedom, because no one required him to be an electrical engineer in order to develop communications equipment. He did not even have to work for Bell Telephone Company, which at that time had an entrenched monopoly. And he had a special kind of incentive. Strowger was one of two morticians in Kansas City. The other mortician's wife was one of the city's telephone switchboard operators. Strowger was convinced that she was directing all telephone calls for mortician services to his competitor. Strowger had a powerful economic incentive to replace her with an objective telephone call director.

The elements of freedom and incentive, which we see in Strowger's case, appear in most significant innovations throughout history. The incentive does not have to be economic; in fact, we can use the nature of the incentive to define the difference between scientists and engineers or technologists: Science is driven primarily by noneconomic incentives, and engineering or technology is driven primarily by economic incentives. The difference is an important one, because it explains why the Soviet Union produced so many competent scientists and scientific discoveries, yet failed so miserably in technological innovation. Soviet scientists, like their U.S. counterparts, had as incentives knowledge, recognition, and prestige. In contrast, the engineer tends to depend on economic incentives, and these are notably absent in planned economies such as the Soviet one. The Soviet patent system was almost confiscatory, and provided no more financial return to an innovative engineer than the typical U.S. company's patent-rights agreement does. Patents aside, the Soviet engineer who developed something new would likely see his manager take credit for the innovation.

Freedom and incentive may foster innovation, but alone they do not make for commercial success. Throughout the 1970s and 1980s, Xerox Corporation funded a think tank called the Palo Alto Research Center (PARC). PARC's staff was perhaps the greatest gathering of computer talent ever assembled. It developed the concept of the desktop computer long before IBM launched its PC. It created a prototype graphical user interface of icons and layered screens that evolved into Microsoft Windows. It developed much of the technology underlying the Internet. But despite PARC's many industry-altering breakthroughs, Xerox repeatedly failed to exploit the financial potential of such achievements (though the return on investment to Xerox on laser printers alone more than paid for PARC). PARC's culture was well suited to developing new technologies, but not so well suited to exploiting them for financial gain.

Freedom is a more subtle factor in the innovation equation, but it is just as important as an incentive. In the 1920s the USSR and the United States were world leaders in genetics. At that time, Russian geneticist Trofim D. Lysenko proposed the theory that environmentally acquired characteristics of an organism were inheritable. Lysenko rejected the chromosome theory of heredity and denied the existence of genes. Lysenko was dismissed as a charlatan by Russia's leading geneticists, including N. I. Vavilov. But he had one powerful argument in his favor: Josef Stalin liked his theories. They were compatible with Stalin's view of the world. If a person could pass on to descendants the behavior patterns they acquired in Soviet society, then the type of state that Stalin sought to establish could become a permanent one. So, with the backing of the Communist Party, the environmental theory became the only acceptable theory of genetics in the USSR. In August 1940 Vavilov was arrested and subsequently died in prison. At least six of Russia's other top geneticists disappeared. In later years, the Soviets would admit that "Lysenkoism" set back their effort in genetics by about twelve years.

Intelligence analysts sometimes looked on the Lysenko affair as an aberration. It was in fact a fairly accurate picture of the research environment of the USSR. Although there were no more cases as dramatic as Lysenko's, the contamination of Lysenkoism spread to many other scientific fields in the USSR during the 1930s and 1940s. Restrictions on freedom to innovate contributed substantially to the USSR's economic decline. Most of them stem from two phenomena—the risk aversion that is common to most large established organizations, and the constraints of central economic planning that are unique to state-run economies such as that of the USSR.

The Soviet Union was organized for central economic planning, and meeting the plan had first priority. This gave Soviet industries a powerful incentive to continue their established lines. Inertial forces, discussed in Chapter 11, dominated. If current production declined, a plant manager would strip his research and development organization to maintain production. Furthermore, central planning seems inevitably to imply short supplies. These supplies become even shorter if a plan manager attempted to innovate, and new types of supplies needed for innovation wouldn't be available at all. The Soviet plant that needed something out of the ordinary—a special type of test instrument, for example—had to build the device itself at a high cost in resources.

Also, Soviet management subscribed, at least in principle, to Marx's labor theory of value. This means that if one device takes twice as much labor to produce as another, it should command twice the price. Such theories provide a powerful deterrent to both innovation and automation. Many contractors supporting the U.S. government work on much the same principle, as the epigraph that begins this chapter (from a U.S. defense contractor) suggests.

In sum, the Soviet industrial structure provided severe penalties for risk taking if a project failed. It provided little in rewards if the project succeeded. And it provided no special penalty for doing nothing. This set of pressures often led the Soviet or East European plant manager into an interesting response when he was forced to start a new project. Since there were no rewards for success, and severe penalties for failure, he would choose an expendable worker—usually someone who was due to retire shortly—and place him in charge of the project. When the project failed—and the cards were always stacked against it—the plant manager could blame his carefully prepared scapegoat and fire or retire him.

The lesson of this example for the analyst is: In evaluating the ability of an organization or a country to develop or use a technology, look at the culture. Is it a risk-accepting or risk-averse culture? Does it place a high priority on protecting its current product line? What political, economic, organizational or social constraints does the organization place on development or use of technology?

Inertia's Effect on Innovation

Resistance to change is a constraint on innovation and on technology diffusion. Everyone knows about it, but intelligence analysts often ignore it, blithely assuming that instant diffusion exists and forgetting about inertial forces and the "not-invented-here" factor (see Chapter 11). Analysts assume that a preeminent laboratory in a given country will grab any available technology in that country.

It may be obvious, but it should be stressed that technology includes only *available* technology—that which the engineer can get her hands on. The actual range of usable technology is probably narrowed still further to that of familiar technology, that which the engineer feels comfortable with. The distinction is an important one, because it points out the significance of feedback in making technology available.

General Electric (GE), in its race with Bell Laboratories to invent the transistor, paid dearly for the inertial constraint of dependence on familiar technology. As described in Lester Thurow's article, "Brainpower and the Future of Capitalism," Bell Laboratories developed the transistor exactly one day prior to GE. The reason that Bell was able to trump GE in spite of GE's large technological edge in the field was that GE gave the job of testing the transistor to its vacuum tube engineers. The vacuum tube engineers spent three years trying to prove that the transistor would not work. Bell Laboratories, on the other hand, spent its time trying to prove that the transistor would work. As Thurow so clearly puts it, "There were five companies in America that made vacuum tubes and not a single one of them ever successfully made transistors or semiconductor chips. They could not adjust to the new realities." If GE had spun off a new company based solely on the viability of the transistor, then GE might now have all the patents and Nobel prizes and revenues from the transistor that Bell enjoyed. More importantly, GE would also have been in a better position to benefit from the revolution in miniaturization that marked the introduction of the transistor. Instead, GE ended up having to buy transistors and semiconductors from suppliers.[7]

External Factors

A technology may carry with it risks of liability or action by government regulatory agencies. Pollution control regulations increasingly shape technology decisions. Possible tort liability or patent infringement suits are risks that might cause a technology to be rejected.

The assessment of regulatory forces (discussed in Chapter 11) has become a key decision point for new innovation in recent years. Analysts need to ask: Can the product be produced within environmental restrictions on air and water pollution? Does it meet government safety standards? Does it face import barriers in other countries? Can the innovation be protected, either by patents or trade secrets, long enough to obtain a payoff of production costs?

Within the framework of the questions outlined above, large and small companies have strikingly different approaches to the acquisition of new technology. Within large companies, the rejection rate of new technology is high. Less than one idea in a hundred is taken up, and when commercialized, two of three new products fail. Institutional resistance to change is endemic and new technologies face enormous hurdles—even though a large company's access to new technologies is typically much greater than that of small companies.

In large companies, a "champion" of a major new technology typically must emerge before the company will accept the new technology. Such champions, also described as "change agents," are innovators who are willing to risk their personal and professional future for a development of doubtful success. The unpopularity of such champions in large companies is understandable because of two factors: the vulnerability of established product lines to the new technology, and the high costs of converting the established production line. These factors are particularly important in a large and complex industry such as the automotive industry, where new technology is welcome only if it is incremental and evolutionary.

As a consequence, revolutionary technologies often are brought into the market by outsiders after being rejected by leaders in the relevant industry—witness Kodak's rejection of Dr. Edwin H. Land's instant photography process, and its subsequent development by Polaroid; or the refusal of several large corporations to accept the challenge of commercializing the photocopying process that led to the creation of Xerox.

Publications Pattern Analysis

Pattern analysis is used extensively in making technology estimates based on open literature. Articles published by a research group will identify the people working on a particular technology. Patents are an especially fruitful source of information about technology trends. Tracking patent trends over time can reveal whether enthusiasm for a technology is growing or diminishing, what companies are entering or leaving a field, and whether a technology is dominated by a small number of companies.[8] Patent counting by field is used in technology indicators; technology policy assessments; and corporate, industry, or national technological activity assessments. Corporate technology profiles, based on patents, are used for strategic targeting, competitor analysis, and investment decisions. They are used to create citation network diagrams (that show the patterns of citations to prior relevant research) for identifying markets and forecasting technology.

Another publications pattern analysis tool, citation analysis, involves counting the number of citations to a particular report. A high number of citations is a proven indicator of the impact, or quality, of the cited report.[9] Citation analysis indicates relationships and interdependencies of reports, organizations, and researchers. It can indicate whether a country's research is internally or externally centered, and show relationships between basic and applied research. Productivity in research and development has been shown to be highly concentrated in a few key people.[10] Citations identify those people. Commercial publications now routinely track citation counts and publish citation analysis results.

Summary

Technology analysis is used in business intelligence, where it can provide a competitive advantage to companies, and in military intelligence for assessing the performance of current and future weapons systems. It can be used to assess the future performance of a technology, the usage or transfer of the technology, or in forecasts of technology breakthroughs. In all such assessments, the most difficult task is to assess how the technology will be used; it is the usage, not the technology itself, that matters.

The natural starting point for technology performance analysis is to project how the technology will evolve assuming no major breakthroughs. It must identify the supporting or ancillary technologies that drive such evolution. All technologies evolve through an "S" curve of performance improvement, eventually reaching the top of the "S" and becoming mature. When a given technology is mature, the analyst should be alert for the advent of a replacement technology.

The next step is identifying innovative developments that represent a break in the "S" curve. This step is an art, not a science. The technique is to identify new forces or technologies, or synergies among existing technologies, and to look outside the established companies or organizations within an industry. Evolutionary technologies and improvements come from within establishment organizations; innovation seldom does. The shaping forces discussed in Chapter 11—inertia, contamination, synergy, and feedback—all promote or constrain innovation. Organizational forces, especially culture and the decisionmaking process, are often critical in determining whether a technology will be developed or used when it has been developed.

Most technology predictions rely on open literature, and publications pattern analysis is used both to tell where a technology is on the "S" curve and to identify emerging innovations in the technology. Technology predictions also tend to rely on quantitative techniques, the subject of the next chapter.

Notes

1. This is a bald assertion with no evidence in the report to support it.
2. Note that the author of the report shows a bias against the Western approach to technology evaluation. From his conclusions we can see that he approves of the Soviet's "high commitment to scientific and technical development," and that this opinion shapes his assessment. Such a bias has no place in intelligence analysis. Defense Intelligence Agency, "Soviet Science Policy of the Seventies," DST-1830S-160-76, May 10, 1976.
3. In this last paragraph, Wesson may show a bias against bureaucracy and central economic planning. However, as a researcher, Wesson is not held to the same standards of objectivity as intelligence analysts (such as the author of the Defense Intelligence Agency report) are held to. Robert Wesson, "Why Soviet Technology Is Lagging," *Business Week,* February 26, 1979, 11.
4. In all fairness to the author of the Defense Intelligence Agency article, which originated in the air force's Foreign Technology Division, the conclusions were politically correct and in line with official air force policy at the time.
5. Joseph P. Martino, "Trend Extrapolation," in *A Practical Guide to Technological Forecasting,* ed. James R. Bright and Milton E. F. Schoeman (Englewood Cliffs, N.J.: Prentice-Hall, 1973), 106.
6. John Prados, *The Soviet Estimate* (Princeton: Princeton University Press, 1987), 324.
7. Lester Thurow, "Brainpower and the Future of Capitalism" in *The Knowledge Advantage: 14 Visionaries Define Marketplace Success in the New Economy,* ed. Rudy Ruggles and Dan Holtshouse (New York: John Wiley/Capstone, 1999).
8. Francis Narin, Mark P. Carpenter, and Patricia Woolf, "Technological Performance Assessments Based on Patents and Patent Citations," *IEEE Transactions on Engineering Management* 4 (November 1984): 172.
9. Ibid.
10. Ibid.

14

Quantitative Techniques

When you hear "calculated risk," don't ask to see the calculations.
Dr. Gus Weiss
former assistant secretary of defense for space policy

Many intelligence fields rely heavily on quantitative methods. Intelligence analysts in the scientific and technical field are particularly comfortable using quantitative methods, because the techniques are logical extensions of the general principles of scientific research. Although the basic principles of scientific and technical intelligence have been set out clearly and simply since the 1950s (in the many writings of Dr. R.V. Jones, for example), the nature of intelligence and the complexity of intelligence problems have changed significantly.[1] These changes correspond to the changes in basic science, applied science, the social sciences, and all fields of engineering since that time. In the early 1940s Jones could do much of his analysis in concepts and calculations that another physicist could understand; as a result, one person's analytic work could be checked by another similarly trained person.

Increasingly, managers cannot check the results of quantitative analysts, especially where extensive data processing is involved; in fact, no one except the analyst herself can check the work in many cases. Such quantitative analysis increasingly uses very complex models; it is very hard to determine whether complex models represent the real world that they purport to model, and their poor validation and poor or nonexistent documentation makes decisionmakers mistrust them.

The quantitative analysis problem can be looked at as one of the following types, though most quantitative analysis is a combination of them.

- A physical problem (such as solving an equation).
- A systems analysis problem.
- A modeling and simulation problem.
- An operations research problem.

Quantitative data analysis may take the form of curve fitting; that is, an analyst fits a curve to the data, obtaining an analytical function such as an equation that can be used in other analysis. It may take the form of comparison, where analysts compare different events graphically to determine time coincidence or relationship. Several sophisticated tools have been developed for each type of analysis, and some of them are discussed in the following sections.

Quantitative techniques have advantages, but they offer a potentially fatal attraction for analysts; perfecting the technique can become more important than accomplishing the mission. It is a waste of time to measure or analyze a problem to a greater precision than necessary to satisfy your customer.

Out of the rich set of quantitative techniques used in intelligence analysis, this chapter will deal with only five of the most widely used: statistical analysis, systems performance analysis, cost/utility analysis, simulation, and operations research.

Statistical Analysis

Most statistical analysis in intelligence probably is done using one of the popular spreadsheet programs, and the best of these have a rich set of statistical analysis functions. Furthermore, powerful statistical packages combined with data mining software offer intelligence analysts tools that enable them to leverage stored information and raw data.

Statistical analysis tools empower intelligence analysts to go beyond simple summaries and basic row-and-column math to get more insight into their data. Spreadsheets are good at telling the analyst what is occurring, but not why it is happening. Statistics, on the other hand, are effective for looking at patterns and associations, enabling the analyst to draw conclusions and make predictions. They reveal hidden patterns when analysts group data and compare the different groups. And relative to simpler data analysis, statistics allow analysts to be more productive by quickly and easily running reports and graphs for different groups.

Statistical analysis is used in a wide range of intelligence applications. A few examples are:

- Terrorism and crime incident analysis—establishing patterns of terrorist activity, understanding which type of crimes are committed and where they occur.

- Econometric forecasting and analysis—assessing industrywide and global economic patterns and predicting future economic conditions.

- Cost/utility analysis—understanding which programs are the most cost effective.

- Fraud analysis—profiling those persons with the greatest propensity to commit fraud.

- Epidemiology—identifying the causes, the distribution, and the control of diseases regionally or globally.

Statistics play an important role in data warehousing and data mining because they enable intelligence analysts to use massive amounts of data to explore, discover interesting relationships, and formulate hypotheses to test further. Good statistical tools make it easy to manipulate intelligence data beyond the facilities contained in most data warehouses.

Systems Performance Analysis

Any entity having the attributes of structure, function, and process can be described and analyzed as a system, as noted in previous chapters. Air defense systems, transportation networks, welfare systems—all of these and many others have been the object of systems analysis. Many of the formal applications of systems analysis took place in the U.S. Department of Defense during the 1960s.

Analysis of any complex system is, of necessity, multidisciplinary. Specifically, it typically requires analysis of the system's:

- Technical capabilities and performance.
- Cost.
- Suitability in the system's environment, or in performing the mission it was designed for.
- Environmental considerations.

Much systems analysis is parametric, sensitivity, or "what if" type of analysis; that is, the analyst needs to try a relationship between two variables (parameters), run a computer analysis and examine the results, change the input constants, and run the analysis again. Most decision support involves an analysis of this type. A systems analysis package must be interactive; the analyst has to see what the results look like and make changes as new ideas surface.

Systems performance analyses are done on two different types of systems—one simple and one complex. Determining the performance of a narrowly defined system, such as a surface-to-air missile system, is straightforward. More challenging is assessing the performance of a complex system such as an air defense system or a narcotics distribution system. Because of the complexity of the systems performance problem, most such analysis is now done using simulation, as discussed later in this chapter.

Cost/Utility Analysis

Cost/utility analysis is an important part of decision prediction, as discussed in Chapter 12. Many decisionmaking processes, especially those that require resource allocation, make use of cost/utility analysis. In assessing a foreign military's decision whether to produce a new weapons system, such an analysis is a useful place to start, and the analyst must be sure to take "rationality" into account. As noted in Chapter 12, rationality differs across cultures and from one individual to the next. It is important for the analyst to understand the logic of the decisionmaker, that is, how the opposing decisionmaker thinks about topics such as cost and utility. A French decision to develop a new antiship cruise missile would be amenable to cost/utility analysis. Hardware costs could be estimated fairly well. Utility is measurable to some extent. Export sales figures could be estimated. The benefits in prestige and advancements in French missile technology would have to be quantified subjectively.

Determining Utility

Utility must be measured using a specific type of scale. Four types of measurement scales are in use: nominal scales, ordinal scales, interval scales, and ratio scales.

Nominal Scales. Nominal scales use numbers to name, identify, or classify. The only arithmetical procedures that this scale permits are counting and statistical techniques based on counting. An example of a nominal scale number is a telephone number; it can be identified with a specific person, for example, but adding two telephone numbers together has no meaning. Nominal scales cannot be used to rank alternatives.

Ordinal Scales. In ordinal scales, numbers indicate rank or order. Ranking methods and other statistical techniques based on interpretations of "greater than" and "less than" are permissible. But ordinal scales make no statement about the interval between adjacent numbers; thus, no standard mathematical operations (addition, subtraction, division, multiplication) can be accomplished. If an intelligence analyst ranks three Iraqi communications sites as 1, 2, 3 in order of importance to the Iraqi leadership, the ranking does not mean that site 1 is twice as important as site 2; it only says that site 1 is more important.

Interval Scales. In this scale the intervals between numbers are equal, but it is not known how far any of them is from zero. The existence of equal intervals allows addition and subtraction. However, the lack of an origin still prohibits multiplication and division. Examples of interval scale data are the Fahrenheit and Centigrade scales for temperature measurement, both of which use rather arbitrary points as the zero point (the Centigrade scale defines zero as the temperature where water freezes). In both cases it makes sense to say that 50 degrees plus 20 degrees equals 70 degrees (addition), but on neither scale is it correct to say that 50 degrees is twice the temperature of 25 degrees (multiplication).

Ratio Scales. In ratio scales the intervals between numbers are equal and each number can be thought of as a distance measured from zero or some other origin. Addition, subtraction, multiplication, and division are all permitted. An example of a ratio scale is the Kelvin scale for the measurement of temperature (0 degrees Kelvin equal −273.15 Centigrade), where 0 K is "absolute zero." Here it does make sense, by definition, to say that 50 degrees is twice as hot as 25 degrees.

Customers often require translations of utility judgments (excellent, good, poor) or subjective analysis judgments (probable, possible, unlikely) to number scales, but these calculations must be handled carefully. A scale by which "probable" = 3, "possible" = 2, and "unlikely" = 1, states that the interval between "probable" and "possible" is equal to the interval between "possible" and "unlikely." It is more likely that the distance between "possible" and "unlikely" is greater than the distance between "probable" and "possible." If so, perhaps the scale should be, "probable" = 7, "possible" = 5, "unlikely" = 1. In making translations from subjective judgments to numbers, it is best to write the judgments down and then discuss, with fellow members of your collaborative team, what numbers should be assigned to the verbal judgments. Where utility judgments are to be aggregated or multiplied, as sometimes happens in decision analyses that use intelligence judgments, it is critical that utility be defined using ratio scales. If not, then the resulting numbers will be misleading.

Determining Cost

This section discusses the estimation of monetary costs in assessing a target's decision process. The analyst must match cost figures to the same time horizon over which utility is being assessed. This will be a difficult task if the horizon reaches past a few years away. Life cycle cost should be considered for new systems, and most new systems have life cycles in the tens of years.

The analyst must think carefully about how to combine cost and utility. One common way is to view alternatives as "bang per buck." This view necessitates some type of ratio of benefit to cost. The previous section discussed the need for ratio scale data for creating ratios of any kind.

Whereas utility must be measured on a ratio scale, it is generally believed that all costs are already on a ratio scale; they have an origin ($0) and it makes sense to say that $50 is twice as expensive as $25. However, the analyst must think carefully about whether the "origin" for the dollars under consideration is truly zero. It makes little sense to use zero as origin if none of the alternatives can be fielded for zero. Also, the marginal worth of dollars in decisions is not always equal. For instance, alternative 1, costing X dollars may be executable; alternative 2, at 2X dollars, may be so expensive that it is viewed as affordable only if it has three times the benefit of alternative 1. Finally, alternative 3, costing 3X dollars, may simply be unaffordable regardless of benefit.

Combining Cost and Utility

Perhaps the most widely used approach to cost/utility analysis is to simply create a graph where cost and utility are the two axes. An example of such a graph is shown in Figure 14-1. The "x"s in the graph represent the alternatives being considered. Each alternative has a utility and a cost, which determine its

Figure 14-1 A Cost/Utility Plot

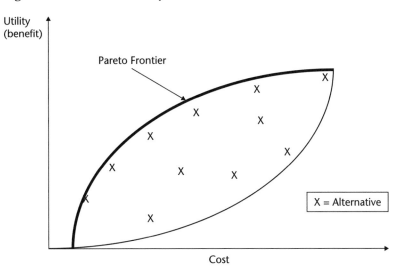

place on the graph. The alternatives that lie high and to the left (low cost, high utility) generally form a curve known as the Pareto Frontier. The optimal choices lie along this frontier, although as the curve levels out utility increases only at higher and higher costs.

The total set of options usually group into a roughly oval shape, as shown in Figure 14-1. This oval is often referred to as the "football" in cost/utility analyses. All of the options lying on the interior of the "football" are suboptimum choices compared with those lying on the Pareto Frontier.

Simulation

A conceptual model that is to be used in a simulation (usually referred to as a "simulation model" to distinguish it from other model types) describes all the pertinent systems to be simulated as well as the interrelationship or interactions of the systems. In many ways, this simulation model is similar to a software specification. The modeler must specify these systems and interactions in sufficient detail to allow the selection of analytical tools and methodologies or the development of new tools.

Simulation models used in the intelligence business are often very complex because they describe complex systems. Often, only their developer can run them because too many shortcuts were taken in development, and user documentation is inadequate or nonexistent.

Most models comprise programs that solve individual equations or systems of equations and graphically portray the results. These models should be interactive; the analyst has to see what the result looks like and change it as new ideas occur. In creating (synthesizing) a simulation model, the analyst must define the time frame of the problem, which could be one year for the narcotics problem or a few minutes for a tactical missile test or a stock market sales decision. For trend analysis, the problem often must be analyzed or simulations run over several years.

One of the most difficult steps of synthesis is to define the desired analytic measures of the solution. In most assessments of foreign capabilities, or of "us versus them" (known in the analysis trade as net technical assessments or net assessments), it is essential to define measures of effectiveness. The measures establish, quantitatively, how good "we" are against "them," or vice versa. Analytic questions are often posed in terms of benefit, impact, effectiveness, or affordability. These analytic measures, or metrics, are used to quantify the subsequent analysis results. They translate to the analytic measures of requirements satisfaction, cost, or performance measures (specific or aggregate).

Measures of effectiveness, also known as figures of merit, can be used to quantify how well a system meets its objectives. In commercial ventures, return on investment is such a measure. In aircraft performance, top speed is a measure of effectiveness. In an air defense system, probability of kill (P_k) is a measure. Measures of effectiveness are used extensively in systems performance analysis. They address characteristics like flexibility, reliability, accessibility of collected data, and compatibility.

Measures of effectiveness, or similar quantitative measures, are needed so that a numerical model can be created. It can be as simple as a decision-support model on a desktop computer (which takes only a few hours for a novice to create and use). Even without a computer model, measures of effectiveness offer a structured approach to the problem.

They can be defined in three categories:

- Performance measures look at, for example, the number of successful actions, timeliness or speed of response, or how well data is merged from different sources (fusion). Performance measures must measure output, not input.

- Flexibility measures look at the ability of systems or programs to react to changing situations or new targets.

- Architectural measures evaluate risk, impact on other programs, security, and similar features.

Once synthesis is complete, the analyst executes the simulation model with the defined inputs. The results are displayed in terms of the analysis measures of effectiveness. If the problem requires comparison of alternatives, trend analysis, or sensitivity analysis, then the system, the requirements, or the problem are changed and the simulation is rerun for each distinct case.

Analysis includes not only the graphical and statistical analysis of the final simulation model output, but also the selected in-depth review or investigation of requirements, system definitions, system interactions, other inputs, and intermediate results to explain the final output.

The analysis approach must provide the capability to store and access all data in a manner to facilitate a "drill-down" or "onion-peeling" approach to analysis (for example, start with high-level data and progressively analyze sublevel data until satisfactory conclusions can be drawn about the high-level data).

A general set of displays supports the analysis processes. These include numerical data and relationship displays, geographic displays as appropriate, and a number of chart displays for timeline analysis and statistical or pattern analysis.

Analyzing the results of any modeling effort requires that one do a "sanity check" on the model results. Sophisticated models are very complex. Independent checks are difficult to run on such models, so examining the results to see if they "feel" right may be the best possible check. It is well known, for example, that combat models tend to overrate an opponent's defense. One of the better known examples of this problem is modeling that was done of the offense and defense prior to the B-52 strikes on Hanoi during the Vietnam War. The prestrike model predictions were that enemy fire would inflict significant losses on U.S. forces. In the initial raids, no losses were suffered. A similar disparity existed in models of allied force losses in the Desert Storm operation.

As these examples suggest, models tend to be overbalanced in favor of the defense in the initial stage of any conflict. The reason is that most such models assume a steady state; that is, that both offense and defense have some awareness of what is going to happen. But in the initial stages of an engagement, the offense has a big advantage: it can dictate the rules of engagement, knows what it has to do, and has the advantage of surprise. The defense must prepare for the estimated threat and react. Furthermore, the defense must make every link in the chain strong; the offense need only find the weak link in a system, then attack it. Al Qaeda operatives demonstrated the very large advantage that a determined offense has in their September 11, 2001, attacks on the World Trade Center and the Pentagon. Most models do not take this initial offensive advantage, and defensive disadvantage, into account.

Operations Research

Operations research involves objectively comparing alternative means of achieving a goal, or alternative means of solving a problem, and selecting an optimum choice. The techniques grew out of the military sciences in World War II. One of the first applications was in antisubmarine warfare against German U-Boats in the North Atlantic.[2] Operations research also was used to predict bombing effectiveness, to compare weapons mixes, and to assess military strategies.[3] In the communications arena, operations research techniques have helped planners and decisionmakers select transmitter locations and satellite orbits, providing competitive services that stay within goals for efficiency and costs, and increasing overall system reliability.

Three of the most widely used operations research techniques are linear programming, network analysis, and queuing theory. These three are used in fields such as network planning, reliability analysis, capacity planning, expansion capability determination, and quality control.

Linear Programming

Linear programs are simply systems of linear equations or inequalities that are solved in a manner that yields as its solution an optimum value—the best way to allocate limited resources, for example.[4] The optimum value is determined based on some single goal statement (provided to the program in the form of what is called a linear objective function). Linear programming is often used in intelligence for estimating production rates, though it has applicability in a wide range of disciplines.

Suppose that an analyst is trying to establish the maximum number of tanks per day that can be produced by a tank assembly plant. Intelligence indicates that the primary limits on tank production are the availability of skilled welders and the amount of electricity that can be supplied to the plant. These two limits are called "constraints" in linear programming.

The plant produces two types of tanks:

- The T-76 requires 30 hours of welder time and 20 kilowatt-hours of electricity per tank.

- The T-81 requires 40 hours of welder time and 5 kilowatt-hours of electricity per tank.

The plant has 100 kilowatt-hours of electricity and 410 hours of welder time available per day. The goal statement, or objective function, is to determine the maximum possible number of tanks produced per day, where:

$$\text{Tanks per day} = (\text{\# of T-76s}) + (\text{\# of T-81s})$$

subject to two constraints, represented by inequalities. It takes four times as much power to produce a T-76 than a T-81, so one inequality is:

$$20(\text{\# of T-76s}) + 5(\text{\# of T-81s}) \leq 100 \text{ kilowatt-hours.}$$

And a T-76 takes only three-quarters as many welder hours to produce as does a T-81, so the second inequality is:

$$30(\text{\# of T-76s}) + 40(\text{\# of T-81s}) \leq 410 \text{ welder hours.}$$

The solution to the linear program is most easily observed in a graph, as shown in Figure 14-2. The two constraints are shown as solid lines. Both are inequalities that define a limit; an acceptable solution must lie below and to the left of both lines to satisfy both inequalities. According to the lines, the

Figure 14-2   Linear Programming Solution for Tank Production

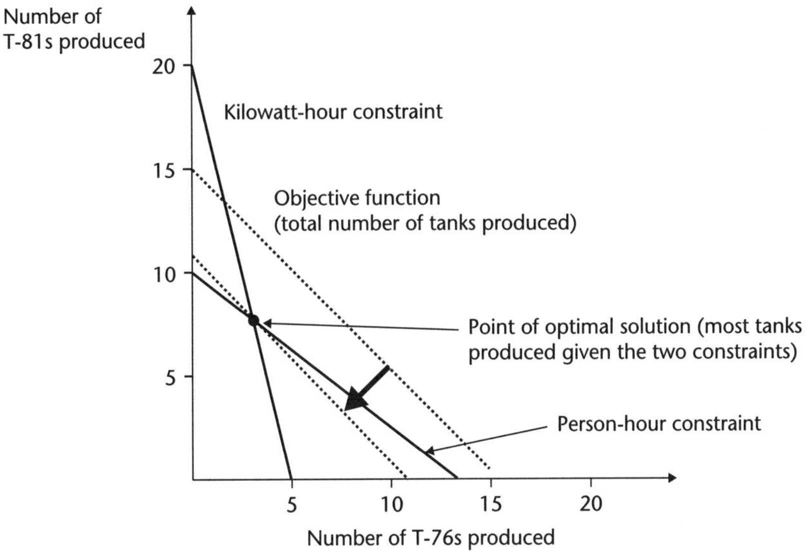

Note: The large arrow between the two dotted lines shows how the objective function was moved down and to the left to a point where it intersected the two constraints and created a point of optimal solution.

plant could produce ten T-81s and no T-76s or five T-76s and no T-81s. The objective function or goal statement is shown as a dotted line representing the total number of tanks produced. Anywhere on this dotted line, the total number of tanks produced is a constant, which changes as the line is moved up and to the right, or down and to the left; we start the line at a total of fifteen tanks produced, and move it down and left, as indicated by the large arrow, until it touches a point that meets both constraints. This point—approximately eight T-81s and three T-76s, for a total of eleven tanks—represents the optimal solution to the problem.

Goal programming is a variant of linear programming that provides a methodology for dealing with multiple goals. Linear programming yields an optimum value in terms of one goal. In reality, it is very difficult to reduce a problem down to a single objective or goal. Most problems are very complex and often include not only multiple goals but also conflicting multiple goals. Goal programming is a technique developed in response to this multiple-goal problem.

Network Analysis

We previously introduced a concept of network analysis as applied to analysis of relationships among entities. Network analysis in an operations research sense is not the same. Here, networks are interconnected paths over which things move. The things can be automobiles (in which case we are deal-ing with a network of roads), oil (with a pipeline system), electricity (with wiring diagrams or circuits), information signals (with communication sys-tems), or people (with elevators or hallways).

In intelligence against such networks, we frequently are concerned with such things as maximum throughput of the system, the shortest (or cheapest) route between two or more locations, or with bottlenecks in the system. Net-work analysis is frequently used to identify vulnerable points for attack.

Queuing Theory

Queuing theory deals with waiting-line situations (predicting the speed of service and the number of customers served in a given time when a queue forms). If we know something about the way a given service system performs, we can estimate many items of interest about both the system and the units that it serves:

- The percent of time or probability that the service facilities are idle.
- The probability of a specific number of units in the system.
- The average number of units in the system.
- The average time each unit spends in the system (service time plus time spent waiting).
- The average number of units waiting for service.
- The probability that an arriving unit will have to wait.

In general, to develop a mathematical description of a service system (such as a telephone switching network or a railroad switching yard) we need to know:

- The arrival distribution (the histogram describing the relative like-lihood of specific time intervals between consecutive arrivals).
- The service time distribution (the probability density function de-scribing the relative likelihood of specific service times).
- The waiting-line discipline (the rules governing which unit gets served next—first come, first served or some sort of priority sys-tem, like women and children first).

Summary

Quantitative analysis techniques are widely used for in-depth intelligence analysis. They allow the analyst to draw more profound conclusions and in-ferences about the target. Many significant conclusions or patterns become vis-ible only through quantitative techniques.

Statistical analysis is widely used, especially in economic intelligence. Spreadsheets are most commonly used for statistical analysis, but a wide range of more advanced tools are available for in-depth data investigation. Pattern analysis commonly relies on statistical techniques.

Systems performance analysis has been long used to assess the capabilities of an opponent's military hardware such as aircraft, tanks, and naval vessels. It is increasingly being used to assess the performance of larger systems—air defense systems, narcotics distribution systems, or economies, for example.

Cost/utility analysis is often used to support predictions about an opponent's decisions. Most leaders go through some form of cost/utility analysis in making major decisions; the trick is to apply the proper cultural and individual "biases" to both cost and utility. What appears to be a high cost in the analyst's culture can appear to be very modest in the target's culture.

Complex targets—for example, large systems—usually are analyzed using simulation models. Econometric models are examples of large simulation models. Most simulation models are systems of equations that must be solved for different input assumptions. The critical issues in dealing with simulation models are to validate the model (ensure that it approximates reality), to establish realistic input assumptions, and to select appropriate measures of effectiveness for the output.

Operations research techniques are useful for many types of process analysis. Linear programming is used to establish optimum values for a process. Network analysis is used to define flows and vulnerable points within a physical network such as a communications or transportation network. Queuing theory is used to examine waiting-line situations.

Notes

1. See, for example, R. V. Jones, "Scientific Intelligence," *Research,* 9 (September 1956): 347–352.
2. Brian McCue, *U-Boats in the Bay of Biscay* (Washington, D.C.: National Defense University Press, 1990).
3. Theodore J. Gordon and M.J. Raffensperger, "The Relevance Tree Method for Planning Basic Research," in *A Practical Guide to Technological Forecasting,* ed. James R. Bright and Milton E.F. Schoeman (Englewood Cliffs, N.J.: Prentice-Hall, 1973), 129.
4. The two sides of an equation are connected by an "equals" or "=" sign. The two sides of an inequality are connected by an inequality sign, such as "is less than ($<$)" or "is equal to or less than ($\leq$)."

Appendix

Case Study on Force Analysis

What follows is the unclassified executive summary of a report that was prepared in 1988 and published in 1989. While the conclusions are dated because of dramatic changes in the former USSR, the summary will be useful to analysts in training because:

- The report makes extensive use of prediction techniques.
- The results of a force analysis—especially organizational (inertia) forces, culture, process (programs), and technology—show clearly in the summary.
- The report provides a good comparison of straight-line extrapolation (shown as "Soviet expected trends" in Table A-1) and projection techniques (shown as "probable actual trends" in the table).
- Its predictions ran counter to accepted U.S. intelligence estimates of the time (which were based on mirror imaging and did not use force analysis), but the predictions turned out to be reasonably accurate.
- It is the result of a synthesis/analysis effort. The analysis team created a model template for the "expected trends" shown in Table A-1 and attempted to fit the evidence about Soviet communications technology, infrastructure, finances, culture, and so on into the model. The evidence didn't fit, and the team had to develop an "actual trends" model.

The summary is also useful to analysts as an illustration of how to write a summary on a complex technical topic that policymakers can understand.

Executive Summary

The Soviet telecommunications system is not developing as they had anticipated.

Table A-1 Trends in Soviet Telecommunications

Soviet expected trends	Probable actual trends
Increased use of stored program control electronic and reed relay telephone exchanges.	New exchanges at the local level only; continued dependence on older crossbar exchanges for critical long-haul trunks.
Digital transmission systems.	Further development and deployment of analog multiplexing devices to handle traffic demand; continued support to analog transmission systems.
Fiber optic transmission media.	The aging conventional metal cable system will undergo additional construction and possible replacement.
New radio relay technology, including digital radio.	Continued problems with new generation radio relay systems and reliance on older generation systems; digital radio at the local level only.
Integrated digital communications networks, followed by Integrated Services Digital Networks (ISDN).	An increase in the number of incompatible local and special purpose networks that do not integrate well with the long-planned central system.

The primary reasons for this adverse trend are:

- Overly optimistic Soviet forecasts of their technical capabilities;
- An outdated infrastructure that does not adequately support indigenous development and production technology; and
- The need to support an obsolete and outdated telecommunications system.

The Soviets see their future telecommunications being dominated by the trends shown on the left in Table A-1. While the Soviets will continue to make some progress in all of these areas, technical and budget limitations will force them to continue maintaining and expanding their antiquated, largely analog, system. The actual trends expected are as shown on the right.

In summary, the Soviets will be forced to compromise their long-range plans because of short-term pressures to meet existing demand and support the existing system. The result is likely to be a series of delays and adjustments to the long-range plan.

The centrally planned system is in trouble.

The Soviets have a clearly stated need for a unified, standardized digital telecommunications system. Their long-range plans since the mid-1960s envision such a system, which they call the Unified Automated Communications System. However, progress toward this system has been slow and is likely to be even slower in the future. The centrally planned system has a number of problems associated with equipment unavailability, poor quality control, and poor network planning. As a result, many localities are solving locally the problems created by the central system, and the impact of resulting variations from standards is to make future system integration even more difficult than it is today.

Local systems are leading the way in modernization.

The Soviets are installing digital communications and fiber optic lines in their local networks. Rural local systems are being digitized first, because the smaller digital switches for rural use are available, while the larger (intrazonal) switches are not available. Urban local networks are receiving fiber optics first, because they do not require long cable runs of intrazonal communications and they can best take advantage of the high data rates available on fiber optic lines.

The central system problems will adversely impact on ISDN.

A unified and standardized system as envisioned for [Unified Automated Communications System] is an essential prerequisite for an Integrated Services Digital Network (ISDN). The continued use of analog systems and proliferation of different local systems will hinder the Soviet move toward a standardized system.

As the Soviets are able to move toward an ISDN, they will probably pursue a gradual implementation, moving data onto the system first but providing for concurrent usage by telephones so that the network will be used while the data usage builds up. This approach is intended to minimize implementation costs and system disruption.

Soviet manufacturing capability is a major problem area.

Soviet telecommunications manufacturing capability is oriented toward improvements on existing analog technology, not to adoption of new digital technology. It has serious problems in several key technology areas such as microelectronics and multilayer circuit board production. Where they try to build systems employing several of these new technologies simultaneously, as with third generation radio relay systems, even more serious problems are likely to develop. The Soviets cannot produce large capacity switches or fiber optic cable having the quality needed for operational use. Shortages of test equipment appear to be a root cause of widespread quality control problems.

Bureaucratic and organizational problems make the manufacturing problem a difficult one to solve. The Ministry of Communications (MOC) does not control its production facilities. It designs equipment that must be produced by the Ministry of Communications Equipment Industry (MPSS), and the poor communications between the two ministries during equipment design make a difficult problem worse. The MPSS also must support a higher priority customer—the Ministry of Defense—so that MOC requirements are often unheeded. Local organizations, frustrated with the bureaucratic inertia, sometimes bypass both ministries in developing or acquiring communications equipment.

Software problems are worsening

Software has been a major problem in the Soviet development of advanced communications systems. All indications are that the problem will become more severe as the Soviets attempt to move to more complex systems. Software problems currently impede the introduction of stored program control exchanges, and they are expected to slow Soviet development of an ISDN.

In the near term, an increased volume of traffic will be carried on coaxial cables.

The Soviets have an enormous capital investment in their current conventional coaxial cable system. They repeatedly emphasize concerns about the enormous costs of constructing or replacing cable communications lines. Their concerns are about the depletion of nonferrous metal resources (primarily copper and lead). Their solutions have been threefold: first, to increase the capacity of existing cable lines by introducing newer analog multiplexers with greater channel capacity; second, to use other transmission means, primarily microwave radio relay (terrestrial line-of-sight—TLOS) systems, but also troposcatter and satellite systems; and third, by the eventual use of fiber optic cable.

Some of these solutions have been successful in the past, but they are not sufficient to solve their current and short-term problems. It will not be cost effective to increase the number of channels by means of greater capacity analog multiplexers since they require an increased number of repeaters (regenerators). Radio relay systems are operating at near capacity, and new radio relay systems are expensive.

Fiber optic cable will not solve Soviet capacity problems during the next decade.

There are indications that the Soviets regard fiber optic cable as a solution to their transmission capacity problems. However, due to production and quality control problems, the Soviets have yet to introduce fiber optic cable into their mainline (long distance) network and probably will not do so, except for showcase and test projects, in the next decade. The slow pace the Soviets have demonstrated in installing fiber optic cable for local and intrazonal networks, the requirement to use unavailable digital multiplexers, and the enormous amount of conventional cable in the telecommunications network, all together rule out fiber optic cable relieving much of the burden from the radio relay and metal cable networks during the next ten years.

Index